Voice-Enabling the Data Network: H.323, MGCP, SIP, QoS, SLAs, and Security

James F. Durkin

Cisco Press

Cisco Press
201 West 103rd Street
Indianapolis, IN 46290 USA

Voice-Enabling the Data Network: H.323, MGCP, SIP, QoS, SLAs, and Security

James F. Durkin

Copyright © 2003 Cisco Systems, Inc.

Published by:
Cisco Press
201 West 103rd Street
Indianapolis, IN 46290 USA

Printed in the United States of America 1 2 3 4 5 6 7 8 9 0

First Printing September 2002

Library of Congress Cataloging-in-Publication Number: 00-105225

ISBN: 1-58705-014-5

Warning and Disclaimer

This book provides information about designing a VoIP network. Every effort has been made to make this book as complete and as accurate as possible, but no warranty or fitness is implied.

The information is provided on an "as is" basis. The authors, Cisco Press, and Cisco Systems, Inc. shall have neither liability nor responsibility to any person or entity with respect to any loss or damages arising from the information contained in this book or from the use of the discs or programs that may accompany it.

The opinions expressed in this book belong to the author and are not necessarily those of Cisco Systems, Inc.

Trademark Acknowledgments

All terms mentioned in this book that are known to be trademarks or service marks have been appropriately capitalized. Cisco Press or Cisco systems, Inc. cannot attest to the accuracy of this information. Use of a term in this book should not be regarded as affecting the validity of any trademark or service mark.

Feedback Information

At Cisco Press, our goal is to create in-depth technical books of the highest quality and value. Each book is crafted with care and precision, undergoing rigorous development that involves the unique expertise of members from the professional technical community.

Readers' feedback is a natural continuation of this process. If you have any comments regarding how we could improve the quality of this book, or otherwise alter it to better suit your needs, you can contact us through e-mail at feedback@ciscopress.com. Please make sure to include the book title and ISBN in your message.

We greatly appreciate your assistance.

Publisher	John Wait
Editor-In-Chief	John Kane
Cisco Systems Management	Michael Hakkert
	Tom Geitner
Acquisitions Editor	Karen Gettman
Editorial Assistant	Emily Frey
Production Manager	Patrick Kanouse
Project Editor	San Dee Phillips
Copy Editor	Christopher Mattison
Technical Editors	Roy Emery Hanzel, Christina Hattingh, Peter Macaulay, Bob Dye, Martin Taylor, Ravi Prakash, Gregory Hersh, Kevin Tracy
Team Coordinator	Tammi Ross
Book Designer	Gina Rexrode
Cover Designer	Louisa Adair
Composition	Octal Publishing, Inc.
Indexer	Tim Wright

CISCO SYSTEMS

Corporate Headquarters
Cisco Systems, Inc.
170 West Tasman Drive
San Jose, CA 95134-1706
USA
http://www.cisco.com
Tel: 408 526-4000
        800 553-NETS (6387)
Fax: 408 526-4100

European Headquarters
Cisco Systems Europe
11 Rue Camille Desmoulins
92782 Issy-les-Moulineaux
Cedex 9
France
http://www-europe.cisco.com
Tel: 33 1 58 04 60 00
Fax: 33 1 58 04 61 00

Americas Headquarters
Cisco Systems, Inc.
170 West Tasman Drive
San Jose, CA 95134-1706
USA
http://www.cisco.com
Tel: 408 526-7660
Fax: 408 527-0883

Asia Pacific Headquarters
Cisco Systems Australia,
Pty., Ltd
Level 17, 99 Walker Street
North Sydney
NSW 2059 Australia
http://www.cisco.com
Tel: +61 2 8448 7100
Fax: +61 2 9957 4350

Cisco Systems has more than 200 offices in the following countries. Addresses, phone numbers, and fax numbers are listed on the Cisco Web site at www.cisco.com/go/offices

Argentina • Australia • Austria • Belgium • Brazil • Bulgaria • Canada • Chile • China • Colombia • Costa Rica • Croatia • Czech Republic • Denmark • Dubai, UAE • Finland • France • Germany • Greece • Hong Kong Hungary • India • Indonesia • Ireland • Israel • Italy • Japan • Korea • Luxembourg • Malaysia • Mexico The Netherlands • New Zealand • Norway • Peru • Philippines • Poland • Portugal • Puerto Rico • Romania Russia • Saudi Arabia • Scotland • Singapore • Slovakia • Slovenia • South Africa • Spain • Sweden Switzerland • Taiwan • Thailand • Turkey • Ukraine • United Kingdom • United States • Venezuela • Vietnam Zimbabwe

About the Author

James F. Durkin has been working in the industry with voice and data technologies for over 13 years. Jim graduated from Georgia Institute of Technology with bachelor's and master's degrees in electrical engineering. Jim worked for Hitachi Telecom and for Scientific Research Corporation as a systems engineer, designing and supporting multiservice networks and network management systems. He was a principal representative for the following standards organizations: ANSI T1S1, Network Management Forum, and ATM Forum. Jim also worked for Rapid Link as a lead network engineer designing and implementing an international VoIP network that provided wholesale and retail VoIP services. Currently, Jim works as a systems engineer for Cisco Systems responsible for selling and supporting optical network solutions. Jim has a wife and two children.

Dedications

This book is dedicated to Jimmy and Kristina who arrived in this world during the course of writing this book. Thanks to my wife, Susan, for patience, understanding, and support during the many hours of writing. Thanks to my mother, Janet Durkin, and my uncle, John Richards, who have always provided encouragement to achieve beyond what is expected. Also, thanks to my father who is no longer in this world for demonstrating that great achievements can be attained in life.

Acknowledgments

I'd like to give thanks to a number of key people in my career who have helped me gain knowledge and understanding about voice and data networking. In particular, David Foote and Mike Medin are two people early in my telecom career who taught me my first "real-world" lessons about the various technologies surrounding PBXs—those impromptu white-board sessions were invaluable. Thanks for giving me the opportunity to participate in worldwide standards meetings and to exchange ideas with leading voice and data experts. I learned a great deal on my trips to Nice, London, and Tokyo. Thanks to my colleagues—Scott, Jerry, David, Shamim, and Bill—for being part of this learning process.

Thanks to Tony and Bill and the rest of the Rapid Link crew for letting me take an active role in the VoIP network designs and implementations. I had many good times in Prague and Frankfurt while turning-up those VoIP gateways!

This book would never have come to fruition without the enormous resources readily available to an SE at Cisco Systems. Many thanks to the VoIP TMEs and other VoIP experts in Cisco—I've learned a great deal from the many application notes and countless other resources you have made available. Thanks to the many volunteers who reviewed chapters of this book and provided great feedback. Specifically, I would like to thank the following VoIP experts at Cisco that have reviewed specific chapters in this book:

Bruce Davie, Emery Hanzel, Christina Hattingh, Dan Wing, Leo Nieuwesteeg, Amrit Hanspal, Darryl Sladden, Graeme Allen, Michael Sonnier, Flemming Andreasen, Shahin Razavi, Evan Zeng, Mark Rankin, Basudeb Dash, Bryan Deaver, David Lewis, Michael Hammer, Carl Lindner, Mark Eastman, Christian Coridas, Eric Osborne, Mahesh Bommareddy, Jay Kumarasamy, Syed Zaidi, Todd Baker, Ralf Wolter, Jon Heaton, Kui Zhang, Kenneth Ross, Joon Miller, Najeeb Haddad, Conrad Price, Jim Alumbaugh, Ron Hanneman, Vivek Bhargava, Dave Harper, Jianzhu Zhang, and Alessandro Maspero.

I want to thank Stuart Feeser at Alta3 for taking the time to review one of my chapters. I also want to thank Bethany Bower who has helped me a great deal during the editing phase.

I'd like to thank the staff at Cisco Press, especially Karen Gettman, Emily Frey, and San Dee Phillips, for being patient while waiting for my chapters. Lastly, I'd like to thank the Lord for providing me the strength and ability for accomplishing this enormous project while supporting a full-time job and taking care of my wife and children.

Contents at a Glance

Introduction   xiii

Chapter 1   The Telephony Service Provider: An Overview   3

Chapter 2   VoIP Network Architectures: H.323, SIP, and MGCP   17

Chapter 3   Offering Wholesale VoIP Services   61

Chapter 4   Offering Bundled Voice and Data Services   73

Chapter 5   QoS Considerations in VoIP Network Design   83

Chapter 6   Implementing the PSTN Switch/VoIP Gateway Trunk   109

Chapter 7   Gateway and Gatekeeper Design Requirements   135

Chapter 8   Security Considerations for VoIP Networks   157

Chapter 9   Network Management: Maintaining an SLA   167

Index   191

Table of Contents

Introduction   xiii

Chapter 1   The Telephony Service Provider: An Overview   3

Motivation for IP and Voice Convergence   4

VoIP Services on the Rise   6
   Wholesale VoIP Service   6
   Retail VoIP Service   9

Successful VoIP Deployments   11

The VoIP Network Architecture: Gateways and Gatekeepers   11

Seven Steps in Designing and Implementing a VoIP Network   13

Summary   13

Chapter 2   VoIP Network Architectures: H.323, SIP, and MGCP   17

H.323 VoIP Network Architecture   20
   H.323 VoIP Services   20
   H.323 VoIP Architecture Components   21
   Gateway   22
   Gatekeeper   28
   Gateway and Gatekeeper Signaling   29
   RAS   30
   H.225   30
   H.245   31
   RTP   31
   Directory Gatekeeper   32
   SS7 Interconnection (PGW 2200 and SLT)   33
   VoIP Application Servers   35

SIP Network Architecture   37
   SIP Network Services   38
   SIP Network Architecture Components   38
   SIP User Agents   39
   SIP Gateways   40
   SIP Servers   41
   SIP Signaling Messages   43
   H.323 and SIP Network Interworking   47

Softswitch Network Architecture   49
    Softswitch Network Services   49
    Softswitch Architecture Components   52
    Softswitch   53
    Call Agent Signaling   54
    Gateways   57
    Aggregation and Edge Routers   58
    Feature Servers   59

Summary   59

Chapter 3   Offering Wholesale VoIP Services   61

Migrating Toward a VoIP Infrastructure   61

Wholesale Peering Arrangements   63
    Call Routing   64
    SS7 Interconnection to the PSTN   65

VoIP Billing Systems   67

Summary   71

Chapter 4   Offering Bundled Voice and Data Services   73

Overview of Managed Voice and Data Services   73
    Integrated Access Architectures   74

Managed Voice and Data Services Using AAL2   75

Fundamentals of AAL2   77

Summary   80

Chapter 5   QoS Considerations in VoIP Network Design   83

IP Network Characteristics   84
    Delay   84
    Jitter   85
    Packet Loss   85

Using QoS to Support VoIP Services   86

Choosing the Right QoS Approach   86
    Overprovisioning   87
    IntServ   87
    DiffServ   87
    QoS Building Blocks   88

Using DiffServ for VoIP Services: The EF Behavior   92

Implementing the EF Behavior   93
    Dial Peer and NBAR   94

CB-Marking   95
    QPPB: QoS Policy Propagation Through BGP   96

Congestion Management Using LLQ for VoIP   98

Avoiding Congestion in VoIP Networks   100

CAC for VoIP Networks   101
    Local CAC   102
    Network CAC   102
    RSVP CAC   103

MPLS Supporting Voice   104

MPLS TE   104

Fast Re-Route for Voice   106

Summary   106

Chapter 6   Implementing the PSTN Switch/VoIP Gateway Trunk   109

Overview of VoIP Gateway to PSTN Connectivity   109
    Circuit Types   109
    Signaling Types   110

Case Study: JIT VoIP Network   111

T1, E1, and DS3 Fundamentals   113
    Using T1s to Interconnect to the PSTN   113
    Using E1s to Interconnect to a PSTN   115
    Using DS3s to Interconnect to the PSTN   115

T1 CAS Trunks   117
    T1 CAS Trunk Template   119
    Signal Type   119
    Line Code Method   119
    Framing Mode   120
    Incoming and Outgoing Digit Format   120

PRI Trunks   121
    Q.921   121
    Q.931   122
    PRI Trunk Template   123
    ISDN Variant   124

NFAS   124
Digit Sending Method   125
Incoming and Outgoing Digit Format   126

SS7 to Interconnect to the PSTN   126
SS7 Trunk Template   127
Mode   128
ISUP Variant   128
Signaling Speed   129
Signaling Channel   129
Point Codes   129
Network Indicator   130
CIC Mapping   130

Troubleshooting Techniques   130
Ensure Line Is up and Correct Synchronization and Clocking   131
Ensure D Channel Is up and Correct PRI Signaling   131
Ensure No Alarms   132
Loopback Test   132
CAS Troubleshooting   133

Summary   133

Chapter 7   Gateway and Gatekeeper Design Requirements   135

Gateway and Gatekeeper Design   135

Traffic Engineering   139
Erlangs   140
Trunk Sizing   140

Zones   141
Dial Peers   141
Normalization Rules   143
Dial Plan Administration   146

Gatekeepers and Directory Gatekeeper Sizing   147

High-Availability VoIP Network   148
Gateway High Availability   148
Gatekeeper High Availability   151
DGK High Availability   153

Troubleshooting Gateways and Gatekeepers   155

Summary   155

Chapter 8   Security Considerations for VoIP Networks   157

    H.323 RAS Authentication   157

    Network Access Security   160

    Device Security   161

    Using IPSec for Additional Security   163

    Summary   164

Chapter 9   Network Management: Maintaining an SLA   167

    Overview of Management Layers   168

    VoIP SLA Management Architecture   170
        Database   172
        Probes and Local Collection Engine   172
        Archive and Reporting Database   173
        Trouble Ticket Application   173

    Collecting the VoIP Management Data   174

    Identifying the Data to Calculate the VoIP SLA Indicators   175
        VoIP Management Data Sources: SNMP MIBs and Traps   176
        VoIP Management Data Sources: Syslog and ASCII Message Collection   179
        VoIP Management Data Sources: Relational Database and Trigger Collection   179
        VoIP Management Data Sources: SA Agent Collection   180
        VoIP Management Data Sources: NetFlow   182

    Filtering and Correlating the Collected Data   183

    Presenting and Reporting the Data   187

    Summary   189

Index   191

Introduction

This book assists the reader in understanding key building blocks of a VoIP network. These building blocks are vital when designing a VoIP network for a service provider. This book includes the following topics:

- H.323, SIP, and MGCP architectures
- QoS design considerations
- Gateway and gatekeeper scalability
- Security considerations
- Supporting VoIP SLAs

Goals of This Book

The goal of this book is to provide a comprehensive overview of important topics on designing VoIP networks. This book focuses on wholesale VoIP networks and highlights other VoIP network architectures. *Voice-Enabling the Data Network* discusses unique VoIP topics, such as supporting VoIP QoS mechanisms and VoIP SLAs, which are timely. This book also discusses newer VoIP technologies such as SIP and MGCP. This book provides a comprehensive view of VoIP from a service provider's perspective and complements other existing VoIP books in an outstanding manner. This book also highlights recent VoIP features in Cisco gateways and gatekeepers that are well suited for a service provider environment. This book, however, does not cover all elements and services supported by VoIP networks. For example, this book does not cover packet voice Virtual Private Networks (VPNs).

Who Should Read This Book?

Voice-Enabling the Data Network is targeted to network designers, managers, project managers, engineers, and CTOs who are involved in VoIP networks and services. This book can also be used for undergraduate/graduate studies that are focused on telecommunications and data networking. The benefits to the reader are the following:

- Facilitate a solid migration path from existing circuit-switched TDM networks.
- Understand the key components of VoIP solutions to help make better business decisions when initiating a VoIP network project.
- Understand the different VoIP technologies available to consider in a design.
- Understand how VoIP has emerged to provide better trade-off analysis in a network design.
- Become better educated on VoIP solutions to help justify the business case for a VoIP network deployment to upper management.

How This Book Is Organized

Chapter 1, "The Telephony Service Provider: An Overview"

- This chapter provides an introduction to VoIP technologies, architectures, and services.

Chapter 2, "VoIP Network Architectures: H.323, SIP, and MGCP"

- This chapter discusses newer VoIP technologies: MGCP and SIP.

Chapter 3, "Offering Wholesale VoIP Services"

- This chapter discusses different aspects of migrating toward a VoIP infrastructure, how wholesale peering arrangements are established, and key aspects of VoIP billing systems.

Chapter 4, "Offering Bundled Voice and Data Services"

- This chapter describes a multiservice architecture for an enterprise environment using ATM AAL2. This architecture is ideal for service providers that already have an existing ATM infrastructure and for managing data traffic between multiple sites for their business customers.

Chapter 5, "QoS Considerations in VoIP Network Design"

- This chapter discusses QoS architectures and mechanisms to consider when provisioning bandwidth in a VoIP network.

Chapter 6, "Implementing the PSTN Switch/VoIP Gateway Trunk"

- This chapter covers common signaling types that interconnect a VoIP gateway to a PSTN switch.

Chapter 7, "Gateway and Gatekeeper Design Requirements"

- This chapter addresses several areas that are essential in understanding how to design and implement a wholesale VoIP network.

Chapter 8, "Security Considerations for VoIP Networks"

- This chapter focuses on the three security measures that need to be implemented in a wholesale VoIP network. These security measures are H.323 RAS authentication, network access security, and device security.

Chapter 9, "Network Management: Maintaining an SLA"

- This chapter is one of the most important chapters, discussing what to consider when implementing a network management system to meet the customer's expectations in terms of quality and reliability of VoIP service.

CHAPTER 1

The Telephony Service Provider: An Overview

This chapter will assist network engineers, technicians, and other necessary decision makers within telephone companies (telcos) and Internet service providers (ISPs) to understand the transition to a Voice over IP (VoIP) network. Because of the extremely competitive environment in the telco and Internet industry today, the entire group of service providers has an interest in providing VoIP services. The service provider market consists of several segments:

- **Incumbent local exchange carriers (ILECs)** are the traditional telcos in the United States, which consist of the regional Bell operating companies (RBOCs) and independent operating companies (IOCs), which are typically located in less inhabited areas of the country.

- **Post, Telephone, and Telegraphs (PTTs)** are the ILEC equivalent in other parts of the world where deregulation has occurred differently than in the United States. Generally, the incumbent carriers, or PTTs, have not been broken apart into local and long distance businesses but have instead been forced to open up interfaces to competitive carriers. This has led to a market of competitive carriers, known as OLOs (other local operators), which are mainly focused on high value business, long distance, and international applications.

- **Competitive local exchange carriers (CLECs)** compete with ILECs for local traffic as a result of the Telecommunications Act of 1996. A CLEC can be a data or voice CLEC.

- **Interexchange carriers (IXCs)** are traditional long distance telephone companies. IXCs have primarily provided telephony-switching services but also provide transport services for other telcos and ISPs. Traditional IXCs have recently been acquiring and partnering with ISPs and CLECs to provide local voice and data access in addition to long distance voice service.

- **ISPs** form the national and international backbones for the Internet. They position their services to large business customers and have bilateral interconnect agreements, also referred to as *peering partners*, with other ISPs. With the addition of voice applications on these networks, ISPs are referred to as *Internet telephony service providers (ITSPs)*.

- **Cable operators'** networks provide high-speed access to homes and businesses for both high-speed data access and second and primary line voice services.

- **Mobile operators** provide a unique telephony service with the huge advantage that users can make and receive calls virtually anywhere in the developed world. Over the past decade, mobile operators have seen incredible growth in both subscribers and traffic volumes.

NOTE   Some service providers that offer global data services are transitioning their networks to support voice services. This allows them to compete with traditional service providers that offer voice services.

Whether a service provider has deployed an IP infrastructure, is starting with no network, or is simply augmenting a *time-division multiplexing (TDM)* voice network, transitioning to a VoIP network is essential. Several service providers provide or plan to provide a bundled package of voice and Internet data services to small to medium size businesses by using an *integrated access device (IAD)* as the *customer premises equipment (CPE)*.

Motivation for IP and Voice Convergence

Service providers are leveraging worldwide IP-based networks to deliver voice traffic and are migrating away from TDM-based infrastructures. An important question is "Why are service providers choosing an IP network to carry voice traffic instead of a circuit-switched TDM voice network?" The answer lies in the substantial savings that comes from leveraging existing data networking infrastructure equipment and increasing the amount of voice traffic over available transmission infrastructures. These options are not available with traditional circuit-switched TDM-based infrastructures.

The immediate cost-saving benefits are not the only thing driving service providers to converge IP and voice services; business strategies are another factor. Telcos are adding data services to grow revenues because TDM services alone are not growing fast enough. Data service providers are adding voice functionality to maintain their customer base because data services alone have become a commodity. By combining voice services with data and new, converged application services, service providers can create a bundled service offering that can preserve and grow its customer base.

Because ISPs typically do not own a circuit-switched infrastructure, the main benefit to ISPs is the added value to offer additional voice services on their existing data network, which effectively leverages their existing nationwide or worldwide network to transport voice calls and their existing data traffic. The main benefit to a telco is the increased network efficiency for handling voice traffic and the added ability to introduce new revenue that is generated by integrated voice and data services.

Besides the savings and strategic reasons for using an IP network for voice and data, VoIP has three other major benefits:

- Voice compression
- Silence suppression
- Statistical gains

VoIP can create additional bandwidth as needed by compressing the voice conversation. Currently, VoIP networks can compress up to 1/12 of the original required bandwidth used in TDM while removing any silence in the conversation.

NOTE	In achieving bandwidth savings, service providers need to carefully calculate the correct level of voice compression to achieve the desired level of voice quality because high compression can degrade the voice quality of a call. In certain areas of the world, bandwidth is inexpensive; therefore, bandwidth savings are not the main concern of the service provider. In these scenarios, voice compression and silence suppression are not used.

Furthermore, IP networks can efficiently use the underlying transport network by transmitting IP packets only when necessary. This method of transport, called *statistical gains*, uses costly transmission circuits only as needed. Unlike IP networks, TDM networks dedicate a certain amount of bandwidth, 64 kbps for each conversation, including any silence, for the duration of the call. The bandwidth is dedicated or nailed up for the duration of the conversation. Thus, a VoIP network can handle a higher volume of calls than a switched-circuit TDM network by using the same transmission infrastructure. This savings is most dramatic on expensive long distance calls because VoIP saves on satellite link costs.

After a VoIP network is deployed, enhanced services, such as Wholesale Minutes, Retail Minutes, Internet Call Me, and Unified Messaging, can deliver additional revenue opportunities to service providers as value-added services.

VoIP benefits to a service provider also include the following:

- Reduced total cost of ownership across voice and data platforms
- Savings in CAPEX, maintenance, and operations costs
- Creation of seamless convergent networks by one switching infrastructure system
- Easy scalability
- Reduced system turn up time
- Bandwidth savings
- Fast creation and rollout of new revenue-generating services

VoIP Services on the Rise

The telecommunications industry has become a highly competitive industry. To survive, service providers must continually find ways to increase revenue and expand services. Voice and data convergence is driving fundamental changes to service providers' business models and networks. For example, many large traditional service providers have supported both voice services by using TDM and data services by using Frame Relay by developing separate organizations within their companies that now have to work together to provide bundled voice and data services. Putting this into practice has been a challenge for many service providers.

Today's service provider VoIP infrastructures support lucrative business models:

- Wholesale VoIP Service
- Retail VoIP Service
- Integrated Voice and Data Access for Small Businesses
- Managed Services for Large Businesses (Enterprises)

NOTE   Integrated voice and data access and managed services are discussed in Chapter 2, "VoIP Network Architectures: H.323, SIP, and MGCP," and Chapter 4.

Wholesale VoIP Service

The exchange of wholesale minutes has been one of the fastest revenue generating services for service providers. This peering relationship is often set up as a bilateral agreement, where service providers commit a certain amount of voice and fax minutes each month and a defined service level to each other. This business model offers telcos and ISPs three advantages:

- Service providers can offer VoIP services more quickly than through traditional methods.
- Service providers can leverage their partners' VoIP infrastructure and minimize the cost of deploying long distance service.
- With the right peering partners, service providers can extend their reach almost anywhere in the world, which eliminates the need to provide their own termination points to complete the VoIP call.

It is important to recognize that long distance calls are subject to access charges that can be significantly high in cost. ILECs and IXCs historically have higher tariffs for long distance calls than transporting these voice calls over a circuit-switched TDM network. However, the Federal Communications Commission's (FCC) current stance is that an IP packet carrying voice is not a conventional long distance phone call. This means that VoIP can have substantial return on investment for a service provider. The growth of VoIP wholesale service has skyrocketed because of the regulatory bypass that the FCC created. For example, a traditional call from Atlanta to New York City might consist of the following fees:

- Local access fee in Atlanta
- Long distance fee
- Local access fee in New York City

VoIP can eliminate the long distance fee and perhaps the local access fees depending upon the pairing arrangements.

For many service providers, wholesale VoIP service is a significant portion of revenues, so the objective within the wholesale market is to increase the number of minutes that are received from a peering service provider. Equally important to this objective is obtaining an efficient level of voice compression while maintaining the *Service Level Agreement (SLA)*. In many situations, small increases in compression of large volumes of traffic can generate millions of dollars of additional revenue per month. For example, a service provider with a VoIP network that terminates 100 million minutes per month with a profit margin of three cents can generate an additional $750,000 by squeezing out 25 percent more bandwidth through compression to carry 25 percent more voice traffic.

The challenge in providing wholesale VoIP service lies in developing strong relationships with the selected partners, whether the terminating partner is a regional telco in the United States or a large ISP in Italy. Wholesale long distance is becoming an aggressive and competitive business because of the growing number of companies around the world that are transitioning to a VoIP network. A good peering partner must possess the following traits:

- Strong SLAs—An SLA needs to be measured by the following parameters:
    - Network uptime
    - Delay variance in end-to-end packets over time
    - Packet loss trends
    - Answer Seizure Ratio (ASR)
    - Post Dial Delay (PDD)
    - Available voice coder-decoders (codecs)
- Competitive termination rates
- Extended reach to strategic termination points
- Volume of originating and terminating VoIP minutes
- Vendor type of VoIP equipment
- Financially stable business

Selecting peering partners can be an overwhelming task. Service providers needs to commit to their SLA for their individual subscribers, which results in the requirements of achieving an equal or higher level of SLA from their peering partners. Service providers use different criteria to select a peering partner. Security and network connection methods can be a major factor in selecting a peering partner. For example, Internet versus private peering can be a deciding factor in peering agreements. Many strategic peering partners are selected based on the amount of IP voice minutes that are reciprocated by the terminating service provider. For example, two service providers can peer together based on expectations that they can increase each other's volume of IP voice minutes. The cost to terminate each other's IP voice minutes can be based on the volume of voice traffic. Many service providers form more than one peering relationship, which permits the service providers to select the most cost-effective rates for terminating their voice and fax calls. Today, service providers determine the least cost route either statically or dynamically. *Least Cost Routing (LCR)* enables service providers to always obtain the lowest termination costs.

NOTE   LCR is important in determining the route that the call traverses, especially with wholesale ITSPs. The peering partners of a wholesale ITSP change rates on a weekly or daily basis. Therefore, every call must be routed to the route with the least cost to enable the ITSP to maximize profits. The billing system calculates the rating of the call route.

Although terminating other service provider's VoIP minutes can be lucrative in the wholesale service market, there are some disadvantages to negotiating bilateral agreements. One disadvantage is that peering relationships must be created with service providers in various regions of the world. Consequently, unique communications interface requirements for interconnection increases lead time for offering VoIP services in the desired countries. Furthermore, the service provider must handle each individual settlement for call accounting with each peering partner.

For this reason, many service providers choose a clearinghouse model to reduce risks and to limit the risk of constant fluctuations of worldwide termination rates. A clearinghouse service provider has established termination agreements with a group of service providers and uses economies of scale to provide cost-effective termination rates to its regional customers by consolidating multiple regional (or global) service providers. The clearinghouse service provider might have a limited VoIP infrastructure or might not have a VoIP infrastructure at all! This is a settlement provider, and (as mentioned) this company might not be an ITSP at all; it might provide only settlement services. More importantly, a clearinghouse service provider extends the service reach of its service provider's customer beyond its VoIP network coverage area. For example, a clearinghouse service provider can route the originating service provider's traffic and terminate this traffic with another service provider's network in the target country or city where the call terminates. Besides handling the complex call routing and call rating, a clearinghouse service provider handles the settlement of the VoIP termination costs for each service provider that uses its service.

Mainly, vendor-specific methods of performing the clearinghouse functionality exist today. This is a disadvantage because the clients of the wholesale service provider must support the same clearinghouse software. This means that VoIP equipment must be identical between the wholesale service provider and its clients. However, this requirement is slowly changing because of an emerging protocol called *Open Settlement Protocol (OSP)*.

OSP is an open standard for performing a clearinghouse service. OSP can create rating and routing tables to mesh together multiple service providers to form interconnections between their VoIP networks by using a standard framework; therefore, a more cost-effective combination of service providers can be produced. OSP uses a standard set of messages and procedures to transfer accounting and routing information from VoIP gateways in a secure manner. Instead of the clearinghouse service provider settling based on terminating minutes by exchanging spreadsheets or database files, OSP provides clearinghouse service providers a standard method and format of call authorization, call accounting, and call settlement for VoIP calls.

NOTE   Call settlement for VoIP calls refers to monitoring and reporting transactions for charging VoIP calls within the network shared by two or more service providers. For example, two service providers might use each other's network to terminate minutes. One service provider might have the ability to terminate voice minutes in China whereas another might have the ability to terminate minutes in the United States at competitive rates. OSP provides the ability to automatically determine how many minutes of voice calls were terminated and charging for the voice calls between service providers in a secure manner.

Retail VoIP Service

The Retail VoIP Minutes model is composed of calling card services. Calling cards can be prepaid or postpaid and have become financially attractive to service providers because the user buys phone cards in various increments, such as $5 or $25, which are prepaid and often not used to their full value. A growing demand for prepaid cards exists with travelers, college students, military service personnel, and low-income families. In addition, many service providers are selling prepaid calling cards in underdeveloped countries where telephone service (especially international) is expensive and in places where telephone service is scarce. With calling card and messaging services, phone service can be provided to people in countries (Russia, China, Africa, India, and so on) that do not have residential phones.

A user starts the call by dialing an access number with a calling card service. A VoIP gateway answers the call and, based on the number dialed, determines whether the user is calling a prepaid or postpaid number. If the user is a postpaid service, the gateway prompts the caller to enter the calling card number and PIN, if necessary. In addition to fraud detection and avoidance, the challenge with prepaid and postpaid services is to achieve a high penetration rate across different niche markets while retaining the subscribers through customer service and voice quality. A VoIP network provides easy and quick access to both prepaid and postpaid services.

Service providers that provide calling card services are beginning to introduce a set of enhanced new services called *unified messaging*, which is the convergence of voice, data, and e-mail. Unified messaging provides new features beyond simple call features offered with prepaid and postpaid calling cards to a service provider's customers. These features include the following:

- Voice messaging over IP
- Forward voice messages as e-mail attachments
- Access e-mail messages from a phone

Figure 1-1 shows the ease of adding unified messaging to a VoIP network. A set of databases and application servers are interfaced to the core IP network through Ethernet connections. These interfaces are based on a framework from Cisco called *Open Packet Telephony (OPT)* that opens the call control function within the VoIP network to software developers to provide enhanced services.

Figure 1-1   *Unified Messaging*

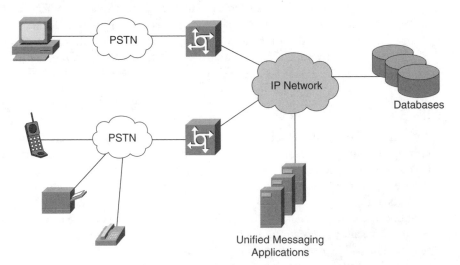

Successful VoIP Deployments

The number of service providers, including ILECs, in the wholesale VoIP market has grown rapidly over the few years. ILECs are responding to the significant competition as the CLECs and cable operators gain access to the local access market. ILECs created a new organization to offer wholesale VoIP services. These ILECs provide wholesale local exchange access based on VoIP. In other words, ILECs are taking part in terminating international retail or wholesale VoIP calls in their particular regions of service. ILECs deploy VoIP gateways to convert incoming IP-based calls into a *public switched telephone network (PSTN)* format. ILECS then provide the final leg of transport and switching of the PSTN traffic to the final destination.

NOTE   The CLEC market has significantly reduced in size after the recent economy contraction. As a result, the competitive landscape for ILECs has significantly changed.

ILECs have always provided IXCs with local access to their subscribers and local switched network. Now, ILECs simply provide the same service by using VoIP technology instead of circuit-switched TDM technology. Some ILECs also provide origination of international minutes, such as handing off to an ITSP. For example, ITSPs can terminate their IP-based calls through an ILEC's regional *points of presence (POPs)*, making use of its gateways and gatekeepers to send voice calls over the PSTN. This eliminates the requirement for these retail and wholesale service providers (ITSPs) to set up their own POPs with links to the Internet and local PSTNs, which results in tremendous savings in capital outlay expenditures.

Service providers such as IXCs, which have traditionally focused on originating and terminating international minutes, are transitioning their networks to support VoIP. Service providers are continuing to establish peering relationships with ILECs and PTTs to extend their reach in the United States, Canada, South America, Western Europe, Eastern Europe, and Asia.

The VoIP Network Architecture: Gateways and Gatekeepers

Large scalable VoIP devices are displacing legacy circuit switches within telco networks. These VoIP devices are called *gateways* and *gatekeepers*, and this section explains their functionality.

NOTE   *VoIP* and *gateway* are general terms that imply that the underlying technology is either H.323, SIP, MGCP, MEGACO, or some combination of these. However, the term *gatekeeper* implies that VoIP is H.323-based only.

Gateways terminate voice, fax, and data traffic, which create a POP for the service provider. Gatekeepers implement the dialing plan and map traditional phone numbers to IP addresses that are understood by the packet network. Gateways perform a translation function between the PSTN network and the IP-based network. Wholesale VoIP service providers strategically position their gateways and gatekeepers to minimize the network costs associated with terminating and originating VoIP traffic. A general rule in designing VoIP networks is to transport all telephone calls over IP unless restricted by local, state, or country regulations.

Voice quality is a critical factor in determining the success or failure of a service provider. A PSTN-level of voice quality can be achieved by using the correct design criteria and techniques to fine-tune the network. The key components in determining voice quality are end-to-end latency, packet loss, and echo and compression. These components are discussed in detail in later chapters. After voice quality is acceptable, VoIP call authentication and call routing can be tested.

NOTE   If the packet network is voice only, as it is for some service providers that provide calling card applications or alternate long distance calling, voice quality is much easier to deal with. Service providers have the challenge to provide consistent and appropriate levels of voice quality in a mixed voice and data network. Chapter 5, "QoS Considerations in VoIP Network Design," discusses this topic.

The main function of the gateway is to translate calls between packet networks and switched-circuit TDM networks. Gatekeepers possess the knowledge to select call routing and call rating, and other vendor specific services. A centralized *Remote Authentication Dial-In User Service (RADIUS)* server and a gateway normally handle caller authentication. Authentication can be based on the originating number without any caller interaction or on the account number and PIN entered by the caller. A sequence of steps exists for caller authentication:

Step 1   *Interactive voice response (IVR)* software collects the caller's card number and PIN. This is called *two-stage dialing*.

Step 2   The gatekeeper authenticates the account and PIN digits entered by the caller. Or the gatekeeper automatically receives an automatic number identification (ANI) without any caller interaction when it is available across a Signaling System 7 (SS7) network, ISDN, or Feature Group D network, or EIR2 network. Authentication based on ANI is called *single-stage dialing*. Step 1 does not occur for single-stage dialing.

Step 3   The ANI or account and PIN digits are passed on to the RADIUS server to authenticate the caller.

After the caller is authenticated, the gatekeeper, based on the phone number dialed, determines the destination route. The gatekeeper has access to a database that contains all authorized call routes. Call routes can be based on all dialed digits or on only a portion of the dialed digits, such as the city code; service providers also have the ability to block certain dialed numbers, country codes, and city codes.

Seven Steps in Designing and Implementing a VoIP Network

Deploying a service provider's VoIP network includes the following seven key steps, which are discussed later in this book:

Step 1   Select the VoIP architecture: H.323, SIP, and MGCP (Chapter 2).

Step 2   Offer VoIP public network services (Chapters 3 and 4).

Step 3   Design a network topology with quality of service (QoS) (Chapter 5).

Step 4   Implement the telco switch/VoIP gateway trunk (Chapter 6).

Step 5   Design and implement the VoIP gatekeeper and gateway (Chapter 7).

Step 6   Implement security (Chapter 8).

Step 7   Maintain an SLA (Chapter 9).

Summary

This chapter provided an overview of VoIP services and benefits in a service provider environment. The remaining chapters provide a discussion of the seven key steps that are required to implement VoIP services in a service provider network.

As TDM voice traffic is replaced with VoIP voice traffic, some service providers are implementing a two-phase approach in migrating toward VoIP and displacing existing TDM networks. This approach presents the following possibilities:

- VoIP networks will support trunking of voice calls across the core of the service provider's network.

- VoIP networks will extend from the core to the access loops to reach the individual subscriber. This phase has occurred with the use of xDSL and broadband cable technologies.

CHAPTER 2

VoIP Network Architectures: H.323, SIP, and MGCP

Historically, VoIP networks have been H.323-based but emerging VoIP technologies, such as Session Initiation Protocol (SIP) and Media Gateway Control Protocol (MGCP), are now providing new IP-based voice services and applications. These new technologies possess numerous business benefits.

H.323-based wholesale VoIP networks have been the dominant VoIP architecture implemented by service providers for the past few years. H.323 VoIP networks have also been the dominant architecture for prepaid services. Prepaid calling card networks process user authentication on the gateway and then carry the voice across the IP network. The purpose of a wholesale VoIP network is to collect traffic from other service providers and transport this traffic by using VoIP to termination points of presence (POPs), which can be in the same or different countries. The originating traffic can be time-division multiplexing (TDM)-based or already encapsulated in IP packets. The terminating POPs can be owned by the same service provider or they can be a peering partner, such as an Internet telephony service provider (ITSP), Post, Telephone, and Telegraph (PTT), ILEC, or IXC.

VoIP technologies, such as SIP and MGCP, bring new IP-based voice services and applications to end users and organizations. These new VoIP services can be rapidly turned into additional revenue streams for a service provider. SIP and MGCP-based networks have been tested and deployed over the last couple of years. Web-based services, Internet phone calls, and mobility applications are easily handled by SIP because of the strong support and use of Internet protocols and technologies. Microsoft's XP operating system provides an application called MSN Messenger to support SIP-based PC to phone calling and other IP-based communication services. This is an example of the industry's support of this new protocol.

Some service providers with existing H.323 VoIP networks, especially ITSPs, combine traditional and newer VoIP technologies to expand the reach of the VoIP network to other locations. They can do this by combining established wholesale networks that have global presence with a core H.323 network interworking with SIP and MGCP networks. Still other service providers, such as incumbent local exchange carriers (ILECs), are currently migrating away from a heritage TDM architecture and toward a centralized softswitch architecture.

A *softswitch* is an interconnection of standards-based software modules that dictates call control, signaling, protocol mediation, and service creation within a converged network. Optimally, the softswitch performs intelligent call handling between media gateways independent of access (e.g., wireline or wireless, narrowband or broadband), medium (e.g., video, data, voice), and speed.

Although there are implementations of only Media gateway controller architectures, they are usually in the scope of endpoint management solutions, such as Access and Trunking gateways and are usually part of a larger network architecture. A softswitch architecture is more of a centralized architecture model and usually incorporates both the Media Gateway Controller and Call Agent functions.

The *Media Gateway Controller (MGC)* function provides the call state machine for endpoints. Its primary role is to provide the call logic and call control signaling for one or more media gateways. The MGC function

- Maintains call state for every call on a media gateway.
- Might maintain bearer states for bearer interfaces on the Media Gateway (MG).
- Communicates bearer messages between two MGs, as well as with IP phones or terminals.
- Acts as conduit for media parameter negotiation.
- Originates or terminates signaling messages from endpoints, other MGC, and external networks.
- Might interact with Application Server(s) for the purposes of providing a service or feature to the user.
- Might manage some network resources (e.g. MG ports, bandwidth, etc.).
- Might provide policy functions for endpoints.
- Interfaces to Routing and Accounting applications for call routing, authentication, and accounting.
- Might participate in management tasks in a mobile environment. (Mobility management is generally part of the Call Agent.)
- Applicable protocols include MGCP and H.248 (Megaco).

The Call Agent function provides signaling protocol management and application protocol interfaces and exists when the MGC handles call control and call state maintenance. Examples of Call Agent protocols and APIs include

- SIP, SIP-T, BICC, H.323, Q.931, Q.SIG, INAP, ISUP, TCAP, BSSAP, RANAP, MAP, and CAMEL Application Part (GSM, 3GPP) (mobile)
- Open APIs (JAIN, Parlay, etc.)

A softswitch architecture enables a service provider to "backhaul" voice minutes through VoIP access onto its existing Class 4/5 TDM infrastructure. This approach facilitates the migration of a TDM voice architecture to an IP-based architecture that can support both voice and data services. Furthermore, a softswitch architecture can bundle data services, such as a Virtual Private Network (VPN) and managed data services, with voice services such as simple, plain-old telephone service (POTS) lines and calling card services.

Important attributes of a softswitch, such as the Cisco BTS 10200, typically include the following:

- Supports call control signaling (e.g., ISUP/H.323/SIP)
- Supports number translations
- Provides routing based on carrier and Time of Day (TOD)
- Controls gateways by using MGCP to establish VoIP call sessions between two endpoints
- Provides call detail records (CDRs) for billing
- Supports Class 5 type services (e.g., Caller ID)

Multiple VoIP protocols such as H.323, SIP, and MGCP can and do coexist. It is not uncommon for a service provider VoIP network to include more than one protocol. A Softswitch, such as Cisco's BTS 10200, supports multiple VoIP signaling protocols: H.323, SIP, and MGCP. A softswitch uses MGCP signaling to centrally control gateways and to interwork with existing H.323 or SIP networks in a transparent manner. At times, a service provider might implement a SIP-based service first and add a softswitch in the future. Softswitch architecture and SIP services are not mutually exclusive.

Routine network design steps must be accounted for when implementing VoIP network architectures. For example, a network designer must understand the existing dial plan and dialing usage. After reaching this understanding, the VoIP components, such as VoIP Media Gateway Controllers and softswitches, must be configured appropriately to interact with the voice dial plan. Key design steps that need to be considered in a service provider VoIP network include the following:

- Create a scalable dial plan.
- Support policy-based routing (e.g., Least Cost Routing [LCR]).
- Allow network to easily grow.
- Maintain Service Level Agreements (SLAs).
- Provide billing.
- Provide security.
- Support fraud prevention.
- Ensure compliance with country specific regulations (e.g., CALEA).

These design requirements are tightly coupled with the VoIP service and architecture. For example, routing policies defined for an ITSP are likely different than policies defined for a local access service provider.

This chapter provides an overview of three types of VoIP network architectures:

- H.323 VoIP Network Architecture
- SIP Network Architecture
- Softswitch Network Architecture

H.323 VoIP Network Architecture

H.323-based VoIP networks have been the commonly deployed VoIP architecture. H.323-based wholesale VoIP networks were adopted by most service providers. One of the reasons for the widespread use is the early acceptance of H.323 products and the immediate Return On Investment (ROI) on wholesale and retail H.323-based voice services.

H.323 VoIP Services

Three common types of VoIP service that use an H.323 VoIP network architecture are

- Wholesale VoIP
- Enterprise VoIP
- Retail VoIP

Wholesale VoIP services are also referred to as *tandem* or *transit* voice services. This service is typically used for terminating international VoIP minutes and to support originating VoIP minutes from calling cards or from another service provider. In many cases, wholesale voice services are considered service providers' underlying service in providing in-country long-distance and international voice calls. Historically, wholesale and retail VoIP services have been the first two services deployed in an H.323 VoIP network architecture. H.323 based networks have proven to be reliable and scalable.

Some service providers are now expanding their wholesale and retail network to provide additional services for enterprise customers. Using a Cisco Gatekeeper, a service provider might offer enterprise VoIP services in conjunction with Cisco Call Manager. The Call Manager is the interface between the IP telephones and the H.323 gatekeeper. This solution enables the enterprise phones to reach destinations on the service provider's VoIP network.

Calling card applications are an example of a retail VoIP service. Remote Authentication Dial-In User Service (RADIUS) servers and interactive voice response (IVR) support within a gateway authorize and rate calls. IVR supports interactive voice announcements, and the gateway supports billing for calling card services. Both prepaid and postpaid calling card services can be supported. This has proven to be a successful method of introducing VoIP services to a service provider network.

H.323 VoIP Architecture Components

The essential H.323 signaling components and devices within a Cisco VoIP network to support H.323 VoIP services include

- Gateway
- Gatekeeper
- Gateway and gatekeeper signaling:
  - Registration, Admission, and Status Protocol (RAS)
  - H.225
  - H.245
  - Real-Time Transport Protocol (RTP)
- Directory gatekeeper
- SS7 interconnection
- VoIP application servers
  - Route Server
  - AAA/Radius Server
  - Billing Server
  - IVR
  - Network Management

Figure 2-1 depicts key components of an H.323 VoIP network.

Figure 2-1 *H.323 VoIP Network Architecture*

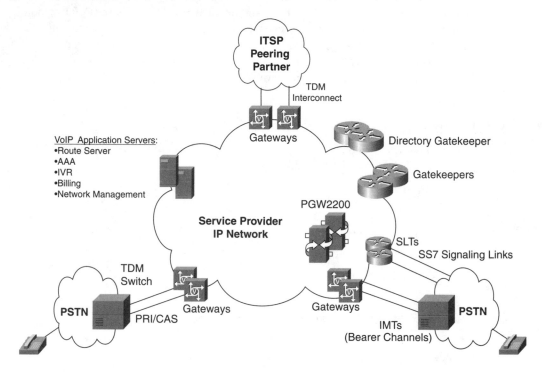

Gateway

One of the main functions of a gateway is to translate functions for call setup and teardown between the IP network and the PSTN networks. A gateway connects two dissimilar networks (for example, an H.323 network and non-H.323 network such as Switched Circuit Network). The gateway performs functions such as protocol translation for call setup and release, conversion of media formats from one network to the other (e.g., TDM to IP), and transfer of information between the networks connected by the gateway. For this process to work, a gateway must have a dial plan in gateways. A *dial plan* defines the locations of phone numbers in the VoIP network so that calls can be established by the gateway. A dial peer, an important concept in Cisco IOS Software, implements a dial plan in gateways. A *dial peer* is the mechanism that determines the direction of the voice packet within the gateway. For example, is the voice packet destined for Atlanta or Tokyo? After the call is set up, standard IP routing can route the voice packets. The two types of dial peers are VoIP peer and POTS peer. The POTS dial peer determines the PSTN destination, and the VoIP dial peer determines the IP destination of the terminating gateway (TGW) that is associated with a call. Both POTS and VoIP peers are needed to establish VoIP connections. In other words, dial peers determine how a VoIP call is set up. Dial peers and call legs are shown in Figure 2-2.

Figure 2-2   *VoIP Dial Peers and Call Legs*

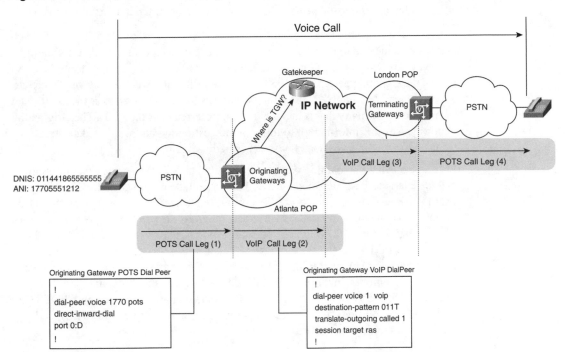

A voice call consists of four call legs. Two call legs are from the viewpoint of the originating gateway (OGW) and two are from the viewpoint of the TGW. All the call legs have the same connection ID, which identifies the call. The CDR uses the connection ID. The dial peer identifies the endpoints of a call.

A dial peer defines characteristics associated with a call leg. These characteristics include the following:

- Coder-decoder (codec) type
- Quality of service (QoS) parameters
- Voice activity detection (VAD)
- Silence suppression
- Fax relay and dual tone multifrequency (DTMF) relay parameters
- Direct Inward Dial (DID)
- Application calls (e.g., Toolkit Command Language [TCL] IVR or Voice XML Application)
- Number expansion or translation

Figure 2-2 shows an example of a call made to 011441865555555. The following steps help you further understand how dial peers and call legs are an integral part of establishing a call:

1 A user in the PSTN dials a number, for example, 011441865555555. The PSTN network routes the call to the ITSP's network. This call is received by the Originating Gateway. The Originating Gateway receives this call over a CAS or PRI interface. As part of the signaling between the PSTN and the Originating Trunk Gateway, the Gateway receives from the PSTN the number that was dialed (referred to as the DNIS) and the number of the party that is making the call (referred to as the ANI). The Originating Gateway uses this information to look up the destination address in a data structure referred to as a dial peer, which was described previously.

2 POTS peers enable incoming calls to be received by a TDM device by defining the call leg characteristics between the TDM device and the Cisco gateway. This dial peer example shows a trunk port (port 0:D) configured to set up a connection with a TDM switch through a trunk interface, such as a T1 or an E1. The POTS dial peer establishes an association with a TDM device, such as a switch, with a range of E.164 telephone numbers. A POTS dial peer is configured, as shown in this figure, to associate a destination telephone number with a particular voice port and to provide the dial peer a unique tag number. In this example, the OGW looks up the destination number 011441865555555 in its list of incoming dial peers that are associated with POTS Call Leg 1. The OGW finds a POTS dial peer that matches either called (DNIS), calling (ANI), or incoming voice port.

NOTE   When a call arrives on the OGW, the OGW issues a dial tone to the caller while collecting digits. The OGW collects digits until the destination dial peer can be identified. At this time, the OGW forwards the call to the next call leg. By using DID (Direct-Inward-Dial), the OGW does not present a dial tone to the caller and does not collect digits—in this case, the TDM switch collects the digits. Figure 2-2 shows the statement direct-inward-dial in the dial peer in the OGW. This informs the gateway to use the DNIS as the destination pattern number to find the VoIP dial peer for the outgoing call leg.

Alternatively, a command could have been inserted into the POTS dial peer to launch a script to authenticate based on ANI or DNIS for all incoming calls from the TDM port 0:D. An IVR or VXML is one of the applications that uses ANI and DNIS information. This scenario is called *two-stage dialing*. *One-stage dialing* is used in this example where the user dials the destination number and the OGW automatically receives this DNIS from the TDM switch.

---

3 The OGW finds a VoIP dial peer that matches the called number (DNIS). VoIP peers point to the TGWs. This is accomplished by associating destination telephone numbers with a specific IP address. In this example, a match for 011T is found. T defines the interdigit timeout interval, which is definable, between the dialed digits. The gateway collects dialed digits as they are entered—until the interdigit timer or the user dials the termination of end-of-dialing key (#). After the dial peer is matched, the session target address identifies the terminating gateway's IP address. The gatekeeper provides the gateway with an address of the TGW so that the gateway can complete the call to the phone with the number 011441865555555. This example has the session target equal to RAS, which instructs the gateway to issue an H.323 Address Resolution Request (ARQ) message to its assigned gatekeeper.

NOTE   If a gateway receives an Admission Reject (ARJ) message back from the gatekeeper after issuing an ARQ message, the next highest priority dial peer is used if one exists. This feature is called *rotary dial peer* in IOS. A rotary dial peer is a hunt-group like function.

A rotary dial peer is assigned a preference value to prioritize matching destination dial peers. Some of the reasons to use rotary dial peers are as follows:

- Provide gateway load balancing when multiple T1 or E1 ports exist to complete a call

- Provide PSTN hairpinning when no TGW exists or is available to terminate the call

Rotary dial peers are further discussed in Chapter 7, "Gateway and Gatekeeper Design Requirements."

4 A setup message is issued to the TGW.

5 The TGW looks up the destination phone number in its list of dial peers. If the matching dial peer exists, it identifies the location of the voice port to send the voice packet to. If a rotary dial peer is used and multiple ports exist that can terminate a call, the gateway tries them in order until the call can be established.

6 The port on the TGW is identified where the called party phone or the terminating PSTN switch is located.

NOTE   It is common for service providers to dedicate gateways to handle only originating or terminating traffic. This helps to maintain and troubleshoot a large scale VoIP network. For example, a service provider's POP in Atlanta might have ten gateways dedicated to accept only incoming traffic from U.S. peering partners and ten gateways dedicated to terminate only traffic destined for the United States.

Translation rules serve an important purpose within the gateway. The gateway uses a pre-defined translation rule to change the ANI or the DNIS for incoming and outgoing calls to normalize numbers to peering partners or local PSTN requirements. Gateways use translation rules to normalize numbers to a standard format. Translation rules can be applied to numbers received from the PSTN before they enter the IP network. Also, translation rules can be applied to numbers received from the IP network before they enter the PSTN.

For example, international dialed numbers can be normalized to the following format in every gateway: Country code + city code + local number. Translation rules are configured on each gateway to handle the local dialing rules in each country. Translation rules enable digits to be manipulated to normalize the numbers before the gateway sends it to the gatekeeper, where call routing is performed. Translation rules can be applied to POTS and VoIP dial peers or can be applied to a physical POTS interface. For example, in Figure 2-2, the OGW assigns the command **translate-outgoing called 1** to the VoIP dial peer to strip the access code 011 for international calls originating in the United States. This command uses a **translation-rule 1** command (not shown in Figure 2-2) to strip off the 011.

Example 2-1 *Translation Rule*

```
translation-rule 1
Rule 0 ^0111.% 1
Rule 1 ^0112.% 2
Rule 2 ^0113.% 3
Rule 3 ^0114.% 4
Rule 4 ^0115.% 5
Rule 5 ^0116.% 6
Rule 6 ^0117.% 7
Rule 7 ^0118.% 8
Rule 8 ^0119.% 9
```

This translation rule enables the digits 011 to be stripped from the international number. The rule accomplishes this by replacing the first four digits (e.g., 0119) of the DNIS, with a single digit. For example, Rule 8 would replace '0119' with 9. The caret (^) indicates that the match happens only at the beginning of the string.

NOTE   Number normalization simplifies the configuration in the gatekeeper and gateways. Number normalization is discussed in Chapter 7.

Cisco IOS Software has extended certain gateway features relevant to a service provider network. The following new concepts are now supported by Cisco IOS gateways:

- **Enhanced number translations**—A newer version of IOS translation rules has been added to IOS. This adds more flexibility in manipulating digits. For example, enhanced number translation rules can be based on trunk groups. This is useful in cases where a selected group of carriers' ANI and DNIS need to be manipulated in a unique way. Enhanced number translations use sed like regular expressions to attain these added benefits; sed defines a set of editing commands to be performed on a text string or on a file; used commonly in UNIX. Furthermore, existing numbers (ANI or DNIS) are preserved after the translation is completed and recorded in accounting transactions. This is beneficial in billing applications.

NOTE   There is a difference between existing IOS translation rules and the new enhanced translation rules. Old and new translation rules should not be used together. A dial plan needs to be revisited when migrating to new translation rules.

- **Carrier ID**—Enables IOS gateways to be connected to multiple carriers. This allows traffic to be identified in terms of which carrier is sending it. Traditionally, only the IP address of the gateway was known. Also, translation can be provided based on the carrier ID.

  The OGW can identify which carrier to use by propagating the carrier ID to a route server. The route server selects the destination carrier based on the carrier ID it received. The gatekeeper can obtain real-time call capacity based on the carrier ID or trunk group.

- **Trunk group**—Similar to a carrier ID. A trunk group groups together circuits that have the same signaling characteristics. IOS supports routing based on this group of circuits, which can be associated with a particular service provider. As a result, trunk groups broaden the selection range of TDM channels and analog ports for an outgoing call. For example, a trunk can consist of a predefined set of DS0 timeslots of a T1, or a group of T1 circuits within a gateway can share the same trunk group.

  Trunk groups enable more advanced algorithms when searching for a channel to send a call to. For example, the hunt scheme uses selection based on a round robin scheme, a selection based on least-used channels (default), a selection based on longest-idle channels, a selection based on least-idle channels, or just a random selection of the channels. Channels can be selected using only even or odd channels. This method prevents glare, which can reduce the network's overall Post Dial Delay (PDD).

  A trunk group label is included in RADIUS records to allow CDR records to contain a trunk label.

- **Enhanced dial peers**—Allow the use of trunk groups and carrier IDs as previously described. Carrier ID and trunk group labels are supported in dial peers. A carrier ID or trunk group is configured in the dial peer for this to work. Access lists can be used in dial peers to block calls based on a source carrier ID/trunk group. Furthermore, user configurable cause codes are supported, which allow a service provider to define what ISDN cause code is mapped to an H.323 cause code received by a peering partner.

Gatekeeper

One of the main functions of a gatekeeper is to provide call routing. Basically, gatekeepers decide what calls go to which gateways in their zone that the gatekeeper is responsible for. Gatekeepers can query another gatekeeper or a directory gatekeeper to help terminate the call. The decision in finding the TGW for a call is influenced by a feature called the *resource availability indicator (RAI)*, which is discussed in Chapter 7. RAI allows for a gateway to communicate the status of its available resources (digital service 0 [DSO] and digital signal processor [DSP]) to its gatekeeper. Thus, RAI assists the gatekeeper in making its routing decision.

The gatekeeper manages the gateways in its zone; this happens by configuring the gateway to register to its designated gatekeeper. For example, the gatekeeper might be responsible for routing calls in a city such as Atlanta. Typically, the gatekeeper is located in a POP along with the gateways serving this city, and routes calls based on the first three or six digits of a ten-digit number. Part of this process includes translating between E.164 phone numbers and IP addresses. Gatekeepers also manage the gateway's resources to help determine the appropriate call route. For example, a gatekeeper can be aware of the available DSOs and DSP resources when attempting to establish a VoIP call. If the gateway is low on or has no resources, the gatekeeper can select another gateway with sufficient resources. This helps with sustaining a certain call success ratio and PDD. Additional SLA information is discussed in Chapter 9, "Network Management: Maintaining an SLA."

Another function of a gatekeeper is to differentiate traffic. This means that a gatekeeper can transport voice mail and fax traffic to different gateways where a voice mail server or a fax server exists. Technology prefixes or Gatekeeper Transaction Message Protocol (GKTMP)-based applications can accomplish this task. GKTMP can be used in a service provider network because of its capability to customize the control of the call control intelligence in the VoIP network to support capabilities such as LCR. In other words, GKTMP can extend the call control intelligence of a gatekeeper by providing an interface to a route application server where advanced call routing decisions can be made. GKTMP is a protocol that enables an external application to exchange information with a gatekeeper through an application program interface (API) that is publicly available. This allows intelligent call routing decisions to be made outside of the gatekeeper IOS, which allows a service provider to fine-tune its call routing decisions according to its defined network policies. A GKTMP-based application can support LCR. For example, all calls made on Sunday to the United Kingdom must use carrier ABC.

Load balancing, redundancy, and high volume call support is commonly performed by a feature called *gatekeeper clustering* that enables up to five gatekeepers to be clustered together and act as one logical gatekeeper. Chapter 7 further discusses gatekeeper clustering.

Gateway and Gatekeeper Signaling

Registering the gateway to a gatekeeper is one of the first steps that must occur before any calls can be set up. The gateway issues a registration request (RRQ) message to a gatekeeper to initiate the registration. The gatekeeper responds with a registration confirmation (RCF) message to accept the registration of the gateway. Figure 2-3 shows the registration messages (shaded) and the sequence of RAS messages that are involved in establishing a voice call between two gateways. The gateway is configured to either auto discover or to be statically aware of the gatekeeper.

Figure 2-3   *Gateway and Gatekeeper Signaling*

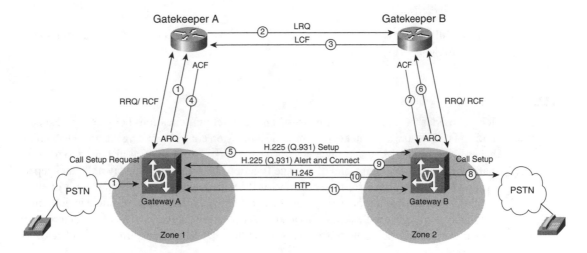

The following steps occur:

1 After receiving a call setup, Gateway A sends an ARQ message to Gatekeeper A. In this example, Gatekeeper A does not find the destination gateway address of the incoming call in its routing table.

2 Gatekeeper A sends a location request (LRQ) message to Gatekeeper B to see if Gatekeeper B has the location of the TGW that controls the dialed number. Gatekeeper A also sends a RIP (request in process) message to the gateway to tell it to wait while it looks for the IP address of the terminating gateway.

3   Gatekeeper B looks in its routing table to try to find a match. Gatekeeper B sends a location confirmation (LCF) message to Gatekeeper A if a match is found.

4   In response, Gatekeeper A sends an admission confirm (ACF) message, which contains the terminating gateway's IP address.

5   At this point, Gateway A sends a setup message to Gateway B.

6   Gateway B sends an ARQ to its local gatekeeper (Gatekeeper B) asking if it is allowed to terminate the call. For a basic call, the gatekeeper ensures that only the bandwidth is available to establish the call.

7   If the bandwidth is available, Gatekeeper B issues an ACF message.

8   Gateway B sets up a call to the destination endpoint.

9   Gateway B issues an alert and connect message.

10 At this point, the procedures defined in H.245 determine the characteristics of the voice session between the two gateways. CODEC type is one of the negotiated characteristics.

11 Finally, the voice conversation begins and packets are exchanged that contain voice samples.

RAS

RAS provides the registration, admission, and status communications between a gatekeeper and an H.323 gateway. Gatekeepers provide admission control by using standard RAS messages, which authorize a gateway to access the network or zone. RAS is also used to perform bandwidth changes, status, and disengage functions between the gateway and gatekeeper. An RAS channel is used for the exchange of RAS messages. The RAS channel is opened before any other channel is opened between gateway and gatekeeper. A gatekeeper defines a collection of registered gateways as a zone. Associating gateways to a zone is determined by various factors, including traffic load distribution, gatekeeper performance, and gateway locations.

H.225

H.225 is used to establish connection between two H.323 end-points. An OGW communicates with a TGW with three main protocol layers: H.225, H.245, and RTP. After the setup message is received by the TGW, using H.225, an alert and connect H.225 message is returned. H.225 provides call control based on the ISDN Q.931 protocol. The alert message identifies that the terminating phone is ringing. The connect message identifies that a connection is established and that voice can be transported. Other supplementary messages, such as call hold, are also specified by H.225, which release and release-complete messages are issued after the call is terminated. All H.225 messages are sent directly between the OGWs and TGWs and do not traverse the gatekeeper. This mode of issuing messages between the gateways is called *direct mode*.

NOTE   An H.323 direct mode gatekeeper does not support billing in a wholesale clearinghouse environment. In this environment, a service provider is interconnected to other service providers, through IP, and the clearinghouse routes their VoIP calls using a gatekeeper. In this architecture, H.225 signaling is sent directly between the OGW and TGW. Thus, call accounting records exist within these devices, which are not owned by the wholesale clearinghouse provider.

An alternative is to have the client gateways issue call accounting records to the clearinghouse provider; however, this dictates that a trusting relationship exists between the two service providers. Another alternate solution that solves this clearinghouse peering issue is to insert another gateway into the wholesale clearinghouse network. At the time of this writing, this solution is currently being released in IOS. This provides the wholesale clearinghouse service providers a demarcation point to interconnect their customers. Gateways now send the H.225 messages directly to this gateway and act as an intermediate point of the call. The wholesale clearinghouse provider can collect RADIUS records to bill its customers.

H.245

H.245 signaling is used to exchange end-to-end control messages governing the operation of the H.323 endpoints. The OGW and TGW initiate a capabilities exchange to agree upon the type of codec to use for the voice session by using H.245, which enables the two gateways to determine how many logical channels to open, which Gateway is the master or slave, how fax will be handled, and whether the DTMF tones are in-band or out-of-band. With H.323 FastConnect, the initial H.225 message contains the H.245 message embedded within it.

RTP

After the completion of the H.245 message, RTP streams are established between the OGW and TGW to transport voice traffic. RTP provides sequence numbering and time stamping to ensure the proper sequence of voice packets because this protocol is responsible for end-to-end transport. An important aspect of RTP is the associated RTP Control Protocol (RTCP) that provides information about the quality of service related to the call or lower) and contains an independent count of the number of packets and bytes transmitted between the gateways.

Directory Gatekeeper

A directory gatekeeper enables an H.323 VoIP network to scale by supporting another level of call routing. This works by having a gatekeeper hand off any H.323 call routing messages to the directory gatekeeper that it has no responsibility for. Thus, if a gateway issues an ARQ to the gatekeeper and the TGW does not reside within the gatekeeper's zone (e.g., it's not responsible for the area code of the incoming DNIS), the gatekeeper sends the request for using an LRQ message to the directory gatekeeper. For this to be supported, the gatekeeper must have the command **lrq forward-queries** as part of its IOS configuration. A directory gatekeeper typically provides international call routing by using the country code, and the gatekeeper provides domestic call routing by using the Numbering Plan Area (NPA) or the NPA and local exchange (NPA-NXX) in North America; NXX is called the prefix. With this hierarchical structure, a directory gatekeeper eliminates the need to fully mesh the gatekeepers. Determining how each directory gatekeeper and each gatekeeper supports call routing is an important aspect of designing the dial plan for the VoIP network. Figure 2-4 shows a directory gatekeeper in a Cisco VoIP network.

Figure 2-4 *Directory Gatekeeper*

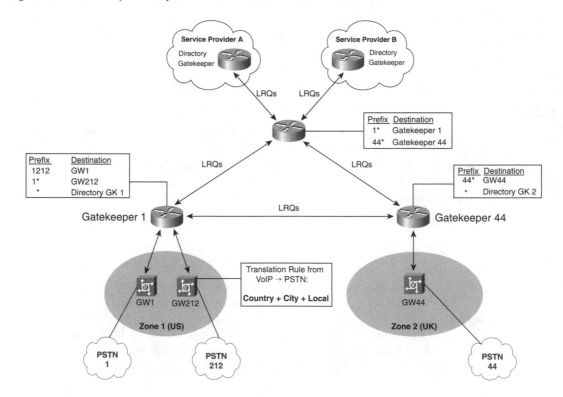

Without the use of a directory gatekeeper, a gatekeeper must be aware of all the other gatekeepers' E.164 prefix tables, called a *zone prefix table*, that are associated with other zones to provide call routing based on the called party's E.164 address. In a fully meshed network, every gatekeeper's zone prefix table needs to be updated in the network if one of the gatekeepers adds a prefix or changes a prefix in its table.

With the use of a directory gatekeeper, the list of phone numbers, that is, prefix tables, is now shifted onto the directory gatekeeper. By using a hierarchical structure, the local gatekeeper is required to be aware of only the phone numbers in its local zone. For example, Gatekeeper 1, in Figure 2-4, handles only dialed numbers for the U.S. (Zone 1). All other dialed numbers (international numbers) are forwarded onto the directory gatekeeper, which knows the locations of different gatekeepers and the NPAs that these gatekeepers are serving. Gatekeeper 44 serves all calls destined for the U.K. (Zone 2). Only the gatekeeper that is adding a prefix or a change in prefix needs to be changed for local exchanges. This eliminates much of the administrative burden in maintaining a large scale VoIP network.

Cisco gatekeepers and directory gatekeepers exchange LRQ and LCF messages. When a LRQ message is received from a gatekeeper, the directory gatekeeper looks in its routing table to determine which gatekeeper is responsible for the dialed number and then forwards the request to the appropriate gatekeeper. If the directory gatekeeper does not find a match, it might forward the LRQ to another directory gatekeeper to process (not shown in Figure 2-4).

Figure 2-4 shows the directory gatekeeper peering with other service providers that are also using a directory gatekeeper. This method of peering uses a direct IP connection rather than the traditional direct TDM connection. Service provider peering that uses a direct IP connection can be implemented by using directory gatekeepers or Open Settlement Protocol (OSP).

SS7 Interconnection (PGW 2200 and SLT)

A common method of interconnecting gateways to the PSTN is through the use of ISDN Primary Rate Interface (PRI) and CAS trunks. Another common method of interconnecting to the PSTN, sometimes mandatory in certain cities around the world, is through the use of Signaling System 7 (SS7), as shown in Figure 2-5. When SS7 is used in the U.S., separate physical links are used for the signaling and the bearer channels. In Europe, SS7 signaling and the bearer channels usually are on the same E1 facility. SS7 is commonly called C7 outside the U.S.

The gateways use Inter-Machine Trunks (IMTs) to connect to the PSTN switches by using TDM trunks, such as T1s, when using SS7 to interconnect to the PSTN. IMTs do not support any call control signaling and carry only user traffic, referred to as *bearer channels*. In some cases, service providers use one of the timeslots of a T1 or an E1 trunk to carry the SS7 signaling.

Figure 2-5 *SS7 Interconnection to the PSTN*

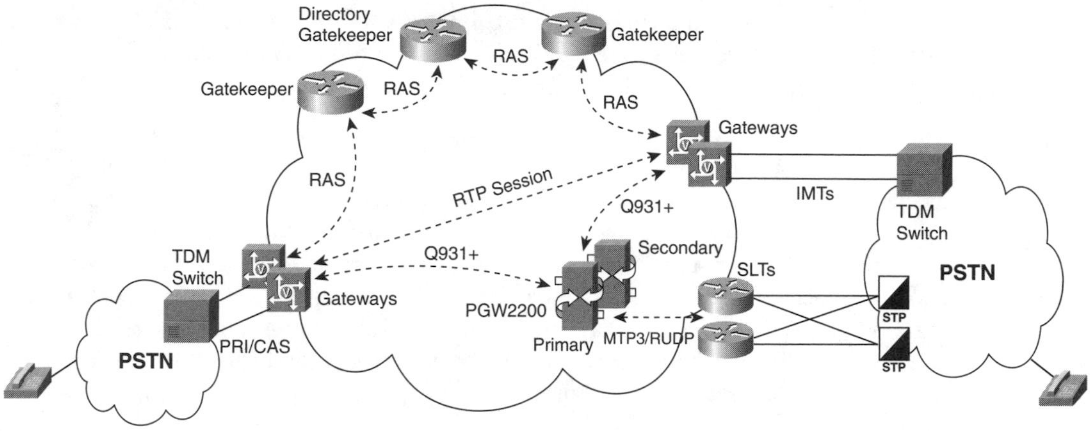

Cisco's SS7 solution consists of two main components:

- The PGW 2200 is a Sun Solaris server running signal control software that provides centralized signaling and call processing services for multiple Cisco gateways. All call control signaling received from the PSTN terminates at the PGW 2200. The PGW 2200 converts the SS7 ISDN User Part (ISUP) messages to Extended Q.931 messages (Q.931+), also called NI2+ (National ISDN-2). The PGW 2200 transports the Q931+ over IP to the gateway. The PGW 2200 is always configured in fault-tolerant pairs (Primary and Secondary). The gateway supports bearer control for calls by inter-preting the Q931+ messages received from the PGW 2200.

  The PGW 2200 supports many different ISUP variants that exist in various countries and transports ISUP messages into Q.931+ over IP. The PGW 2200 also creates a call detail record for each call.

- The Signaling Link Terminal (SLT) is a Cisco 2600 router with IOS software that is capable of supporting SS7. The SLT is always configured in fault-tolerant pairs, which provide multiple communication paths between the SS7 network and the PGW 2200. The SLT provides a direct interface to the PSTN's SS7 network through the signal transfer point (STP), as shown in Figure 2-4. The SLT terminates the MTP Layer 2 of the SS7 ISUP message on either an A- or an F-Link. After terminating the Message Transfer Part (MTP) Layer 2 message, the SLT encapsulates the MTP Layer 3 infor-mation in Cisco's Reliable User Datagram Protocol (RUDP), which is sent over IP to the PGW 2200. The latest IOS gateway software supports an embedded SLT that enables the service provider to terminate an SS7 F-link directly on the gateway.

The PGW 2200 can be geographically separated (e.g., a different POP) from the SLT through a managed WAN. However, strict design requirements need to be followed. End-to-end delay between the PGW 2200 and SLT need to be less than 150 msec and packet loss must not exceed 1 percent. In essence, the use of the SLT enables the PGW to be remoted from the point of interconnect and enables a network design that increases reliability.

VoIP Application Servers

VoIP application servers consist of various applications needed to support VoIP services. These applications are as follows:

- **Route server**—Supports advanced call control to optimize call routing. This is accomplished by using GKTMP between the gatekeeper and route server application. Recently, Cisco has extended the information available on this interface. The enhanced GKTMP interface provides zone routing for carrier ID and trunk group ID. Gateways can provide a gatekeeper the following information:

    — Carrier ID or trunk group ID

    — Current status of use for each circuit

    — Circuit name

  Using this additional information, route server applications can now provide additional call control logic. For example, a gatekeeper can track the usage of circuits and provide LCR and carrier-based routing on this information. A route server can also manipulate DNIS and ANI numbers.

  Cisco has two route server products: Network Applications Manager (NAM) and Campus Switch Router (CSR). A route server sits on top of the gatekeeper that provides the basic routing intelligence. For example, routing can be based on LCR, QoS, TOD, or carrier. A CSR can use a combination of these rules to meet a service provider's policy in making routing decisions. Choosing peering partners' routes based on the cheapest rates is a common method of determining how to route calls. CSR assists in applying and enforcing these rules. Traditionally, it's been common to use TDM switches to apply these rules in a manual fashion; however, with a GKTMP applications monthly routing rates can be captured automatically, which eliminates the need for manual updates.

- **AAA/RADIUS and Billing Server**—Because H.225 call setup and call teardown messages do not traverse the gatekeeper, CDRs reside within the individual gateways and must be sent to an application server that uses the RADIUS protocol. The application server might be a billing application that uses the RADIUS accounting records for billing. These accounting records can also assist with customer performance and fraud detection. RADIUS records include the following elements:

    — Unique per-call identifier

— Calling party number

— Called party number

— Connect time

— Disconnect time

— Disconnect cause code

— QoS of the call

— Start/end times of any fax/modem relay sessions

— codec type used

- **IVR**—An IVR application authenticates calling card users based on ANI and DNIS information, and processes accounting and billing. An IVR application handles inbound calls when a POTS dial peer in the OGW or a VoIP dial peer in the TGW is selected. The dial peer is configured by using the command application. IVR applications are programmed by using Tcl scripts and reside on the gateway. IVR scripts normally reside on a TFTP server. IVR scripts can do the following:

  — Collect account numbers

  — Collect Personal Identification Numbers (PINs)

  — Collect destination phone numbers

  — Play voice prompts

  — Perform authentication, authorization, and accounting (AAA) tasks interacting with a variety of servers (e.g., RADIUS Server)

  — Configuration statements that are needed to reflect the use of SIP, include (other configuration steps are required)

  This caller information authenticates the user and determines the called party number.

- **Network management**—An important component in a VoIP service provider architecture. Network management encompasses fault management, configuration management, accounting management, performance management, and security management. These categories are referred to as FCAPS. Chapter 9 focuses on performance management and discusses some of the mechanisms needed to support SLAs in a VoIP network. For example, Cisco IOS gateways, gatekeepers, and routers can be monitored for fault and performance information through different mechanisms. These mechanisms include, but are not limited to, the following:

  — Simple Network Management Protocol Management Information Base (SNMP MIB) objects and traps

  — RADIUS records containing voice quality metric

  — syslog messages

  — IOS Service Assurance Agent (SAA)

  — IOS Command-Line Interface (CLI)

SIP Network Architecture

VoIP networks that are not H.323 VoIP networks are currently being deployed to support voice services. One increasingly popular technology is Session Initiation Protocol (SIP), which was standardized by IETF in March 1999, as defined in RFC 2543 and updated in June 2002, in RFC 3261. SIP is quickly evolving and maturing in terms of features, stability, and vendor interoperability. Certain H.323 features do not exist in SIP products today; however, SIP is quickly catching up in supporting H.323 features. As an example of its maturity, SIP is being considered to support VoIP wholesale services. Figure 2-6 depicts a SIP wholesale architecture. Cisco uses LRQ messages, not defined in SIP, to implement a SIP wholesale architecture. Other RFCs supporting SIP services follow:

RFC 3262 defines 100rel and PRACK.

RFC 3263 Locating SIP Servers.

RFC 3264 Offer/Answer.

RFC 3265 Event Notification (Subscribe/Notify).

RFC 2976 SIP INFO Method.

RFC 2916 E.164 and DNS (ENUM).

RFC 3204 MIME body types for ISUP and QSIG.

Figure 2-6   *SIP Wholesale Architecture*

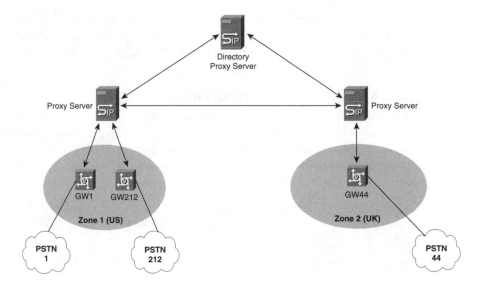

SIP Network Services

Similar to H.323, SIP uses a peer-to-peer protocol that results in intelligence existing in the endpoint devices, unlike MCGP where a master/slave communications model exists. This means that endpoint devices, called SIP User-Agents (UAs), can have various levels of intelligence including the capability to tap into the services available within the network. Thus, endpoint devices can initiate VoIP sessions with other endpoint devices. However, in most cases, a proxy server or softswitch is present to facilitate the VoIP session. Some of these servers, referred to as application servers, can use existing Internet-based protocols and APIs such as Lightweight Directory Access Protocol (LDAP), extensible markup language (XML), Java Telephony Application Programming Interface (JTAPI), or Common Gateway Interface (CGI) to tap into existing network services that are already in place. For example, service providers are actively testing and deploying SIP-based applications that include PC-to-Phone and PC-to-PC communications. Also, some service providers use SIP to support multitenant applications, such as IP Centrex, Hosted IP-Services, IP-PBX services, and wholesale VoIP services.

A wholesale VoIP service is one of the SIP network services that are being tested for deployment by various service providers. The SIP network architecture for this service is similar to H.323 wholesale VoIP service. The same hierarchical structure exists.

- Gateways
- SIP proxy server
- Directory proxy server

In wholesale VoIP architecture, a SIP proxy server is similar to an H.323 gatekeeper where routing at the NPA-NXX level is performed. A directory proxy server is similar to an H.323 directory gatekeeper where routing at the country code level is performed.

SIP Network Architecture Components

The SIP model uses two components, clients and servers, to describe the signaling protocol. Two general categories of SIP components are User Agents (UAs) and intermediaries. UAs are endpoints that initiate or terminate SIP transactions and dialogs, whereas intermediaries are the servers, such as proxy and redirect servers, that help to route calls and provide some value added services, such as security, along the way.

A SIP client simply refers to the entity that originates a request, and a SIP server is the entity that receives a request. A SIP UA and a SIP proxy both consists of a SIP client and a SIP server.

Figure 2-7 shows an example of a SIP network architecture.

Figure 2-7   *SIP Network Architecture*

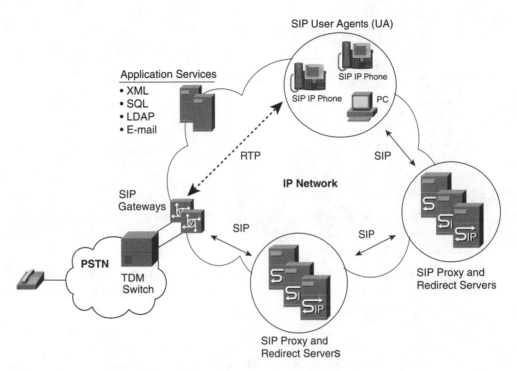

A SIP network consists of the following devices and signaling:

- SIP
- SIP gateways
- SIP servers
- SIP signaling messages

SIP User Agents

SIP is a peer-to-peer protocol that can establish and tear down VoIP calls between two SIP endpoints. These endpoints are called *user agents*. There are two types of user agents: *User Agent Client (UAC)* and *User Agent Server (UAS)*. A SIP endpoint, referred to as a SIP User Agent, normally supports both types of user agents. SIP User Agents originate and terminate SIP requests. These clients typically have both a UAC and a UAS to originate and terminate SIP requests. SIP User Agents can take on various forms, including the following or any device that has Internet connectivity and can support a SIP UA:

- SIP phones

- SIP-based PC clients (e.g., Softphones)
- SIP VoIP gateways
- SIP-based PDAs
- SIP-based wireless devices

Examples of Cisco phones that support SIP include the following:

- Cisco 7940
- Cisco 7960
- Cisco ATA 186

SIP Gateways

Cisco IOS gateways provide support for H.323, SIP, and MGCP. SIP features in IOS include IVR, creating CDRs, Fax relay, and DTMF relay. Cisco is constantly adding new SIP functionality to IOS gateways.

Gateways in the SIP network perform the same functions as the gateways in the H.323 network (described previously); thus, determining the appropriate capacity of the gateway is the same for either H.323 or SIP networks.

For a gateway to talk to a SIP server, the dial peers in the gateway must be configured to use SIP, rather than H.323, which is the default configuration mode in a Cisco IOS gateway. The protocol that the gateway uses is selected through the dial peers on a per-call basis. Configuration statements that are needed to reflect the use of SIP, include (other configuration steps are required)

- Defining to use a SIP server (session protocol sipv2)
- Defining the VoIP protocol (session target sip-server)

A dial peer that is configured for SIP is shown in Example 2-2.

Example 2-2   *Dial Peer Configured for SIP*

```
!
dial-peer voice 770 voip
 session protocol sipv2
 destination-pattern 770…….
 session target sip-server
!
```

Examples of IOS gateways that support SIP include the following:

- Cisco 1700
- Cisco 2600
- Cisco 3600
- Cisco AS5350
- Cisco AS5400
- Cisco AS5850
- Cisco 7200

SIP Servers

Each SIP phone in the network must register with a registrar server to notify the server of the address where it can be reached. A SIP REGISTER message is issued to this server. A Gateway UA, such as a Cisco 5350, cannot send this message to the local SIP server. After registration, a SIP client can issue a SIP INVITE request message to a SIP server. The INVITE request establishes a SIP call. This server can either be a SIP proxy server or a SIP redirect server. Three types of SIP servers exist:

- **Proxy server**—The proxy server performs the routing of SIP messages. Besides controlling call routing, a proxy server performs other vital network functions, including

  — Authentication

  — Authorization

  — Determination of next-hop address

  A proxy server receives SIP messages and forwards them to the next SIP server to establish the end-to-end VoIP connection. Proxy servers can authenticate, authorize, route, and provide security using SIP services. A SIP proxy server is an optional component that supports a SIP-based call. In other words, all the intelligence of creating a voice session between two SIP phones can exist in the phone itself. A SIP proxy server is analogous to an H.323 gatekeeper in that a gatekeeper might not be required in a simple H.323 VoIP network. A SIP proxy server is similar to the H.323 Gatekeeper Routed Signaling (GKRCS) model where all signaling traverses the gatekeeper, except that the SIP proxy server is normally involved only in the call setup. Subsequent signaling is direct between the two UAs unless the SIP proxy server explicitly asks to be on the path (Record-Route).

SIP proxies can insert a Record-Route: header into an INVITE message. Any additional method associated with the established session should use the same Route: header based on the Record-Route header. For example, this ensures that the signaling for a CANCEL or BYE flows through the proxy. This might be required to support billing. SIP proxies can use any database, registrar server, or Domain Name System (DNS) query to determine the location of the next hop of the message.

- **Redirect server**—Provides the SIP client with information about the location of the next hop to get to the terminating SIP endpoint. Thus, a redirect server provides address resolution similar to a Cisco IOS gatekeeper.

   The redirect server provides a lookup for a SIP request. A database lookup can be accomplished when a call comes in. A proxy server is more intelligent than a redirect server. Both of these functions might reside in the same physical box. A SIP server reuses HTTP error messages. The end devices register with the local SIP server.

- **Registrar server**—SIP UACs register their location with the registrar server by using their uniquely assigned SIP addresses. This SIP address can be fully qualified domain names (FQDNs) or E.164 number, or both.

   Examples of these combinations are as follows:

   — sip: "Jim Durkin" <jdurkin@cisco.com>

   — sip:17705551212@gateway.com; user=phone

   — sip:17705551234@10.1.1.1; user=phone sip:jdurkin@10.1.1.1

   When requested, the registrar server provides the SIP client's address to the location server. For example, a SIP user might move to another endpoint. The location server can locate the SIP end user by using an Internet-based protocol such as LDAP.

Adding call routing intelligence to a SIP network can be accomplished with certain SIP proxy capabilities:

- **GKTMP**—GKTMP enables a Cisco SIP Proxy Server (CSPS) interface to a route server. NAM is an example of a Cisco provided routing server.

- **ENUM**—This capability maps E.164 numbers to DNS addresses.

- **H.323 LRQ interface**—This interface provides the ability to interwork with an H.323 VoIP network. Call routing can be off loaded to the H.323 network where H.323 gatekeepers and route servers are fully aware of the available resources in the gateways (e.g., RAI).

Cisco's SIP server is called a Cisco SIP Proxy Server (CSPS). The CSPS is not IOS-based but runs on either a Solaris or Linux server. CSPSs can be grouped together to create a cluster of SIP servers, as shown in Figure 2-8.

Each Cisco SIP server in a cluster is synchronized by grouping SIP servers together, and together they act as one server. This feature is called *farming*. This feature enables all the SIP servers to have their register databases synchronized with each other.

Figure 2-8   *SIP Farming*

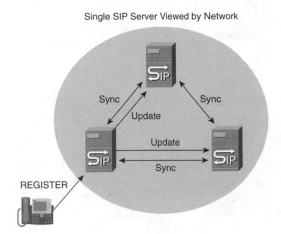

CSPS supports call accounting using a RADIUS interface, unlike an IOS gatekeeper. RADIUS records are created when CSPS encounters SIP-based call establishment and teardown messages. Call accounting records for VoIP calls consist of RADIUS start and stop records. The SIP proxy server on a 200 OK SIP message generates a start record for a VoIP call, and a SIP proxy server on a BYE or CANCEL SIP message generates a stop record.

SIP Signaling Messages

SIP is a signaling protocol that has been defined by the Internet Engineering Task Force (IETF) to support Internet-based sessions that require voice or multimedia. SIP is a point-to-point protocol that uses text-encoded messages rather than binary messages as used by the H.323 protocol. SIP is targeted at Internet-type applications, such as Instant Messaging and VoIP.

One of the advantages of SIP is that it can use Internet-based protocols to complement its signaling protocol. Because SIP specifies only how sessions are created, modified, and torn down, additional functionality is supported by other IETF protocols. For example, SIP uses several IETF protocols, including HTTP1.1, Session Definition Protocol (SDP), RTP/RTCP, Dynamic Host Configuration Protocol (DHCP), and DNS, to accomplish other tasks such as domain name lookup to allow mobility.

Although SIP was not initially designed for interworking with existing PSTN protocols, such as ISDN, IOS gateways that support SIP can provide extensive interworking capabilities, such as SIP-ISDN and SIP-ISUP interworking today. The following are examples of interworking capabilities:

- ISDN Cause <---> SIP Response
- ISDN Present Ind <---> SIP From: Hdr
- ISDN Progress Ind <---> SIP 183 Resp
- ISDN Red't Num <---> SIP Div Hdr
- SIP & RTP IP Address Binding

These endpoints use two processes to perform signaling: UAC and UAS. The UAC process originates requests and the UAS process terminates requests, as shown in Figure 2-9.

Figure 2-9   *SIP End-to-End Call Flow*

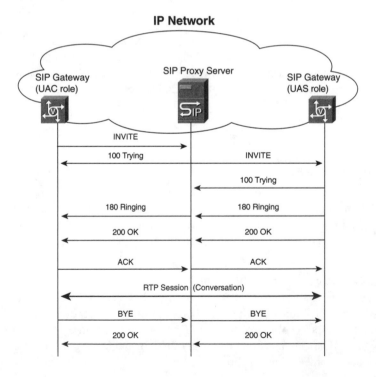

These requests are defined as follows:

- **REGISTER**—This message enables a SIP client to register with the registration server. Key fields found in the REGISTER message are as follows:
  - The first field of the REGISTER message indicates the type of message and the location of the proxy server. Via is used to record route for the purpose of trace-back for responses to that specific request.
  - The next message field is indicated by the word Via—a list of SIP devices and the desired transport protocol. These SIP devices are in the signaling path that leads to the destination device, which is typically the proxy server.
  - The From field enables the Registration Server to identify the originator of the REGISTER message.
  - The To field notifies the proxy server to send all messages with the SIP phone's address. The To header field provides the name you are registering. The Contact header field tells it where to send them to, described next.
  - The Contact field actually identifies the exact location to send any messages destined for the SIP phone.
- **INVITE**—The INVITE request establishes a SIP session. Key fields found in the INVITE message are as follows:
  - The request line in the INVITE contains the ip address or domain name of the next hop for this INVITE, which is usually a proxy server.
  - A SIP body can be SDP, an e-mail attachment, or other data. SDP assists in establishing a call by adding a set of parameters to describe the call as defined in RFC 2327. SDP identifies the type of media, such as voice, and its characteristics. For example, SDP can identify the RTP port and codec type. After the proxy server looks up the called party's address, the proxy server forwards the INVITE request to the called party. RFC 3204 defines SDP for ISUP.
  - The Via field lists all the devices that were in the path of the INVITE request message. This is essentially a stack where addresses are pushed on as a request travels to the destination UA, which then simple copies into the response, with addresses popped off as the response returns to the requestor.
  - The Record-Route field in the INVITE request indicates the SIP proxies that must be in the return signaling path. It's common for the proxy server to include its IP address in this path so that it receives any return signaling messages. Record-Route is copied to Route in subsequent requests to enable them to follow the same set of proxies.
  - After the SIP Phone accepts and processes the INVITE message, it returns a response of 100, which indicates that the INVITE message has been received and stops retransmissions of the INVITE message.

- **ACK**—A message to confirm receipt of a final response to an INVITE message.
- **BYE**—A message sent by either SIP client to end a call.
- **CANCEL**—A message sent by the UAC that sent the INVITE to end a call that is not yet connected.
- **OPTIONS**—A message used outside a dialog to query the capabilities of an SIP endpoint. Also, an options-tag used in an INVITE message can do this concurrently with dialog setup assuming required options are supported. Require: Proxy-Require: and Supported: headers are used to indicate what methods are needed or available.

NOTE	Other SIP request messages have been and are being standardized in the IETF. Furthermore, because of the insecure nature of an open Internet, in many cases, authentication and authorization mechanisms are needed and addressed by SIP as well.

SIP can set up and tear down VoIP calls. SIP also has other capabilities that enable the creation of SIP-based services. These capabilities include the following:

- **Determine SIP endpoint address and availability**—SIP can provide address resolution, name mapping, and call redirection. SIP can determine if the SIP endpoint is not available.
- **Determine capabilities of SIP endpoint**—SIP uses a protocol called SDP that is contained in the body of a SIP message. SDP assists in establishing a call by adding an SDP that assists in establishing a call by adding a set of parameters to describe the call. For example, SDP identifies the type of media to be exchanged, such as voice. SDP enables SIP to determine a common set of services that both SIP endpoints can support.
- **Establish and terminate a call session**—SIP can establish a session to support a voice conversation. SIP can also make changes to the call, such as conferencing other SIP endpoints into a call. SIP uses the BYE message to terminate a call.
- **Call forking**—This allows a SIP proxy to send an INVITE message to multiple SIP endpoints (UAS devices). This SIP capability is useful in providing traditional call center telephony applications, such as sequential or parallel hunt groups. Also, call forking is used in mobility applications such as when SIP services need to follow a SIP user.
- **Transfer a call**—This enables a SIP user to transfer a call. To support call transfer, the dial peer that is matched needs to have the dial peer command **application session** on the gateway that is controlling the transfer.

- **DTMF relay**—Cisco gateways support SIP DTMF relay, as defined in RFC 2833.

- **Fax relay**—Supports the use of T.38 to provide a standards-based signaling and transporting of real-time FAX.

- **Reliable provisional responses**—SIP responses can be used in responding to an INVITE to provide information on call progress. Reliable provisional responses provide end-to-end reliability, whereas TCP provides only hop-by-hop reliability responses can be used for both UDP and TCP.

- **SIP hairpinning**—Hairpinning enables an incoming PTSN call on a SIP gateway to be signaled through the IP network and back out the same gateway.

- **QoS support**—QoS support on SIP gateways is used to indicate to the other endpoint whether sufficient network resources exist to meet the desired QoS requirement. SIP IOS gateways can enable RSVP and synchronize RSVP with setting up a SIP call. In other words, SIP call signaling and RSVP resource management are synchronized so that the appropriate bandwidth, packet loss, delay, and jitter can be established during the duration of the SIP call. SIP supports a message called UPDATE that can be used to indicate if these requirements have been met. This message is issued before the SIP call is set up. NOTE: RSVP must be configured on a dial peer-supporting SIP.

- **SS7 interconnectivity**—Similar to H.323, a SIP network uses the Cisco PGW 2200 to interconnect to the PSTN.

SIP and H.323 signaling differ, but each performs similar call setup and teardown functions. For example, the SIP INVITE message issued to the SIP proxy is similar to the H.323 setup message. It is important to understand that SIP and H.323 have distinct features. For example, call control and redundancy are implemented differently when using H.323 or SIP protocols.

H.323 and SIP Network Interworking

Internetworking H.323 with SIP is one way to translate SIP into an H.323 core network. An advantage of this method is that an ITSP can keep its existing H.323 gateways and gate-keepers because H.323 networks already have mature software procedures and processes in place. This is a longer-term approach because the H.323 and SIP internetworking option needs to ensure that SIP functionality in the translation of H.323 calls is not lost and does not eliminate enhanced or unique call control found in the SIP network.

There is another option to support interworking H.323 and SIP networks. This option, as shown in Figure 2-10, keeps all the components and intelligence, such as RAI, within the H.323 network while creating a bridge to SIP services.

Figure 2-10 *Adding SIP to an H.323 Core Network*

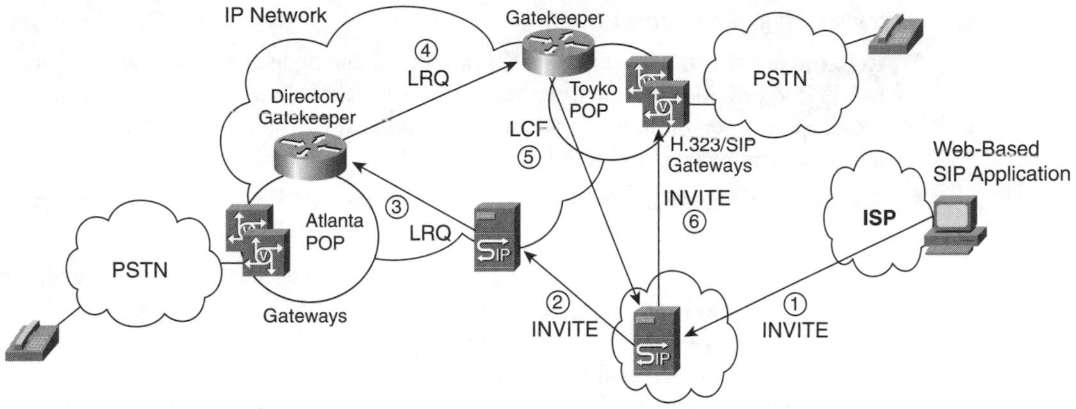

This option uses the same gateways to support both H.323 and SIP. This is one method to combine H.323 and SIP networks. One advantage to this approach is that the service provider can leverage its existing investment in its gateways if it is already supporting H.323 VoIP services and wants to migrate to SIP services. This architecture is a common step in migrating from an H.323 network to a SIP network.

This method is implemented by having the SIP proxy server issue LRQ messages to the H.323 gatekeeper to exchange call signaling. Versions of CSPS as of 1.1 support this capability. However, the RTP session is established directly between the SIP endpoints. A SIP-based service provider, such as an ASP or ISP, can request the use of another service provider's H.323 network (ITSP) to reach additional customers. The sequence of messages to support this interworking (requires that the gateways to support both incoming H.323 and SIP calls), as shown in Figure 2-10, follows:

1 The SIP-based application issues an INVITE message.

2 The service provider's SIP server issues an INVITE message to the SIP proxy server that is owned by the peering service provider, for example, an ITSP.

3 The SIP proxy server accomplishes address resolution by issuing an LRQ request for an endpoint address to a gatekeeper to determine the appropriate gateway to use.

4 The IP address of this gateway is returned through the LCF response message.

5 The SIP server proxies the INVITE to the gateway with the IP address that is obtained by the proxy server.

Softswitch Network Architecture

Many service providers that provide data services today are quickly moving to add voice and IP-based services to their existing service offerings. A softswitch architecture, implemented by a Softswitch, is an architecture that can support this. Two key requirements for a Softswitch are scalability and high availability. The Cisco BTS 10200 Softswitch can scale from a few thousand subscribers to millions of subscribers and provide 99.999 percent availability. This reliability and scalability results from the decomposition of services, as well as from the redundancy designed into the BTS platform or network design.

Softswitch Network Services

A softswitch network can provide multiple VoIP services, including the following:

- Voice and data local access service
- Cable packet services
- Voice transit services

One common service that is supported by a softswitch architecture is voice and data local access to residential and small and medium-sized businesses. Service providers can use a softswitch architecture to provide new services that leverage their existing local access architectures (T1, DSL, or cable) and their core and edge IP and Multiprotocol Label Switching (MPLS)-based networks. For example, a softswitch architecture can provide voice services on an existing data-centric network. It is important to realize that a softswitch architecture can offer a similar capability of a TDM Class 5 switch, but it is not expected to be a replacement of a Class 5 switch. The replacement of a Class switch carriers with it a list of capabilities that does not make sense in a packet network architecture.

A softswitch provides a subset of Class 5 features that are typically offered by Local Exchange Carriers (ILECs, IOCs, and CLECs). A softswitch architecture can bundle data services, such as VPN and managed LAN services, with voice service as part of the services offerings. Voice services can include simple POTS lines, Centrex-like services, and calling-card services. Typical voice services include the following:

- **Basic voice features**
    - Local
    - Long distance
    - Class of service screening
    - Network announcements
    - Billing record generation

- **Toll features**
  - Preferred IntraLATA/InterLATA/
  - International carrier
  - Dial around (101xxxx)
  - International calling (011 + CC + #)
  - Toll free (800/866/877/888)
  - Toll (900)
  - Local Number Portability (LNP)

- **POTS features**
  - Anonymous call reject
  - Call forward (Unconditional, Busy, and No Answer)
  - Remote call forward
  - Three-way calling
  - Call waiting (basic, enhanced)
  - Calling number and name delivery and blocking
  - Caller ID and name display
  - Music on hold

- **Centrex features**
  - Direct inward dialing
  - Direct outward dialing
  - Private dial plans (voice VPN)
  - Multiple line hunt group
  - Call transfer
  - Call hold
  - Automatic redial
  - Speed dial
  - Voice mail
  - Unified messaging

- **Network features**
  - B-number modification
  - Policy-based routing (e.g., LCR)
  - Trunk circuit selection (e.g., least idle)
  - Testlines: 100, 102, 105, 108
  - Busy line verification
  - Operator barge-in
- **Regulatory features**
  - E911 emergency services access
  - 711 telecommunications relay service
  - CALEA
- **Service features**
  - 311 nonemergency assistance access
  - 411 directory assistance access
  - 611 repair services access
  - Operator services

Also, a softswitch architecture can backhaul voice minutes using VoIP access onto an ILEC's Class 4/5 infrastructure.

Softswitch architectures are widely used by multiple service operators (MSOs) to provide data and voice services over their hybrid fiber coax (HFC) network. Cisco's cable modems, such as the uBR925, can operate as Media Gateways. These services can include the same services as defined in the local access solution. VoIP in an MSO network is defined by the PacketCable standards that contain call signaling, QoS, voice transport and encoding, billing, security, and network management requirements.

Voice transit services enable a service provider to offload TDM voice traffic from the TDM circuit switched network across an IP network.

NOTE   There are data service providers today that choose to use H.323 or SIP in networks to implement voice services. These data service providers feel more comfortable with the peer-to-peer or distributed architectures because their existing data services are based on these architectures.

Softswitch Architecture Components

A call agent uses Media Gateway Control Protocols (e.g., MGCP, NCS, and TGCP) to control Media Gateways. These protocols support a call control architecture where the call control intelligence is outside the gateways. In this architecture, the gateway has no knowledge of the call signaling protocols. The softswitch maintains the call state for all endpoint devices. This centralized approach is different from the H.323 and SIP gateways in that these technologies maintain their call states within their gateways, which support a distributed approach. The softswitch separates the call state control from the gateway where the gateway becomes less intelligent, and the call control intelligence is placed in one location: the softswitch.

The gateways are responsible for two things: interfacing to voice circuits from a TDM switch, such as a Class 4 or Class 5 switch, and packetizing voice from these TDM circuits into IP. Because the gateways do not interpret the signaling protocol, the call agent must instruct them to set up or tear down a circuit. The call agent uses MGCP for this function. Another important capability of the call agent is that it provides a signaling path to an SS7 network. For example, Cisco's integrated access device (IAD) 2400 uses protocols such as Point-to-Point Protocol over Ethernet/Asynchronous Transfer Mode (PPPoE/A) to support voice and data services over the service provider's local access network, and MGCP enables a central call agent to provide line side service and to interwork with SS7.

NOTE   MEGACO and H.248 are still evolving and maturing. MEGACO, which was defined in RFC 3015, is being standardized in IETF, and H.248 is being standardized in ITU-T in parallel. MEGACO and H.248 are emerging alternatives to MGCP.

Figure 2-11 shows an example of a call agent architecture that supports local access services.

Figure 2-11 *Local Access Softswitch-Based Architecture*

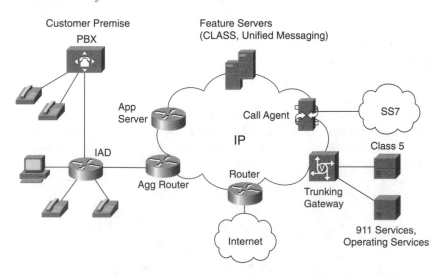

This softswitch architecture example can support data and voice services to small and medium-sized business customers and to residential customers. The following list contains the key functional components of this architecture:

- Softswitch
- Call agent signaling
    - MGCP call model
    - MGCP
    - Softswitch interworking
    - SIP/SIP-T
    - H.323
    - PSTN
- Gateways
    - Residential
    - Access
    - Trunking
- Aggregation and edge routers
- Feature servers:
    - POTS
    - Centrex
    - Tandem
    - AIN
- Network resources
    - Voice mail or unified messaging
    - IVR and announcements
    - CALEA server

Softswitch

The key function of the softswitch is to provide voice call management and control feature mediation and passage. This includes the establishment and the teardown of voice calls through instructions to the gateways through MGCP. The softswitch also processes and controls the connection to the SS7 network (either directly or through a signaling gateway with Signaling Transport [Sigtran] support), supports dial plan management, and has interfaces to Operations Support Systems (OSSs).

Call Agent Signaling

MGCP describes a model that uses an abstracted view of physical and logical resources found in an VoIP network. Two abstracted entities are defined: endpoints and connections. An endpoint is a logical resource that exists within a gateway that is required to support voice or data services. Examples of endpoints are a DS0 channel, analog line, announcement server, or an ATM virtual circuit. Furthermore, an endpoint can be associated with one or more external entities, such as a physical PRI circuit. A relationship must exist between endpoints to complete a call. The connection entity provides for this function. A connection creates a relationship between two or more endpoints to enable a voice or data call to be created in the MGCP model.

MGCP uses a master/slave model that defines the gateway to carry out a limited set of transactions initiated by an MGC or call agent. Although these commands are limited, a large set of call services can be implemented by using the intelligence found within the call agent. This master/slave model is similar to the traditional TDM circuit switch architecture where all the call control intelligence has been developed in a centralized manner, similar to a Class 4 or Class 5 switch. Similar to traditional Class 4/5 switches, MGCP allows for centralized call control. However, unlike traditional switches, MGCP provides an open standard for clear separation between the centralized call control entity and the entities terminating trunks and lines. Thus, the Call control intelligence resides outside the gateways and resides within the softswitch software. The call agent provides an API for inserting new services on top of the centralized softswitch—this process is referred to as *service creation*. This feature server architecture allows for faster deployment of new services.

MGCP is a widely deployed protocol developed by IETF (RFC 2705bis) that enables softswitch devices to control gateways in a VoIP network. Because the call control intelligence resides in the softswitch, the call agent issues standard MGCP commands to control the gateway. Other protocols, such as H.323 and SIP, are used by the softswitch to interface to other services and to interface with other call agents. Figure 2-12 shows an example of an MGCP message establishing a VoIP call.

MGCP uses a simple set of messages, referred to as primitives, as shown in Example 2-3.

Example 2-3 *MGCP Primitives*

```
Create Connection      CRCX    (CA  --> MG)    Create a connection to an endpoint
Modify Connection      MDCX    (CA  --> MG)    Modify connection parameters
Delete Connection      DLCX    (CA  <-> MG)    Delete an existing connection
Notification Request RQNT    (CA  --> MG)    Instructs the gateway to watch for
  specific events
Notify                 NTFY    (CA  <-- MG)    Inform Call Agent when requested
  events occur
Audit Endpoint         AUEP    (CA  --> MG)    Audit an existing endpoint
Audit Connection       AUCX    (CA  --> MG)    Audit an existing connection
Restart In Progress    RSIP    (CA  <-- MG)    Notification that endpoint or
  gateway is restarting
```

Figure 2-12 *Call Agent Call Flow*

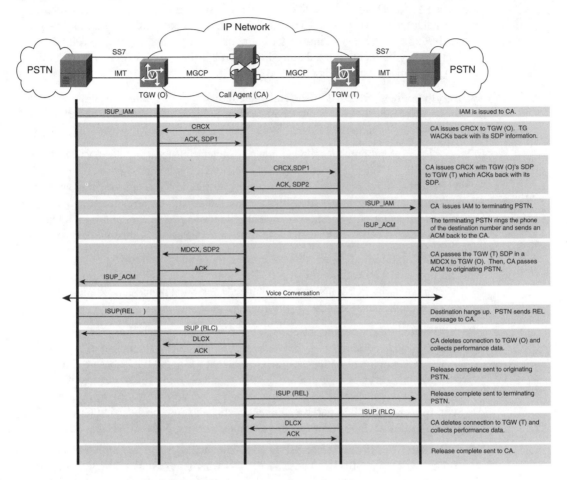

MGCP messages, such as SIP, are in text format. Also, similar to SIP, MGCP uses SDP to define the characteristics of the bearer session. For example, SDP defines the media type (e.g., voice), UDP addresses to use for the RTP session, and available codec types.

Each MGCP message has a defined format. An example of an MGCP message is shown in Example 2-4.

Example 2-4 *MGCP Message Example*

```
CRCX 2389 s0/ds1-2/9@gw1.cisco.com MGCP 1.0
M: sendrecv
C: 678ABC3
L:  a:PCMU, e:on, s:on
```

The first field in the first line in Example 2-4 defines the MGCP message, in this case, create connection (CRCX). The next field defines the transaction ID, which uniquely identifies this particular message for the call agent and the gateway to keep track of multiple messages. S0/ds1-2/9@gw1.cisco.com identifies the endpoint on which the connection will be created. The endpoint syntax is interpreted as in slot 0, port 2 is the targeted DS1, and the ninth DS0 in this DS1 with the gateway is identified as gw1.cisco.com.

The next three lines, provided by the call agent, are additional parameters that are given to the gateway to define the connection characteristics. These parameters are abbreviated with a single uppercase character followed by the value.

In Example 2-4, M abbreviates the parameter ConnectionMode and has a value of send-receive (sendrecv). This parameter value is interpreted by the gateway to create a bidirectional connection. C abbreviates the parameter Call Id and has a hexadecimal value of 678ABC3. This value uniquely identifies the particular call. L abbreviates the parameter LocalConnectionOptions. The LocalConnectionOptions parameter can set up telephony parameters such as codec, echo cancellation, silence detection, and network type.

In Example 2-4, three subparameters are used: a (compression algorithm), e (echo cancellation), and s (silence suppression). The compression algorithm value is PCMU, which refers to u-law PCM, and the echo cancellation and silence cancellation values are on, which indicates that these capabilities are enabled:

- **Softswitch interworking**—Softswitch can interwork with other protocols, such as H.323. One benefit of this is that local access service providers that use a Softswitch softswitch can tie into other VoIP networks that are non-MGCP-based. This expands the possible services and revenue streams that a service provider can achieve. For example, a local access service provider might want to offer VoIP access service to enterprises with H.323 gateways/gatekeepers or to enterprises using Cisco Call Manager. Figure 2-13 shows a call agent interworking with SIP, H.323, and the PSTN.

- **SIP/SIP-T**—Call agents use SIP or a variant such as SIP-T to communicate with other call agents. SIP-T can pass SS7 ISDN User Part (ISUP) messages. This is accomplished by using SIP's capability to carry Multipurpose Internet Mail Extension (MIME) content within its messages. ISUP messages are mapped into a MIME attachment. A call agent can also be used to control SIP phones, for example.

- **H.323**—Cisco BTS10200 and gateway create a logical H.323 gateway. Multiple instances of an H.323 gateway can be supported simultaneously. Essentially, the BTS 10200 sends all H.323 signaling to an H.323 gatekeeper. These H.323 gateway instances register with a gatekeeper.

- **PSTN**—The media gateway terminates voice beaters over PSTN interfaces (e.g., E1 or T1 trunks).

Figure 2-13 *Softswitch Interworking*

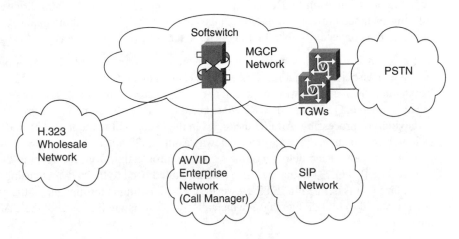

Gateways

These endpoints are referred to as gateways and are classified or positioned according to the services that they provide within the VoIP network. These classifications and examples of these classifications are as follows:

- **Trunking**
  - 3660
  - 5350
  - 5400
  - 5850
  - MGX 8850
- **Access** (Residential and Small-to-Medium Business)
  - 2600/3600
  - IAD 2400
  - ATA 186/188
  - uBR925
- **ETTX**
  - 7960/7940

A gateway can be positioned in multiple locations within a network depending upon the network architecture and the interface being provided. For example, a gateway can reside in the service provider's network and support interfaces relevant to the PSTN, such as IMTs or PRIs, that are typically connected to a telco switch or private branch exchange (PBX).

This is called a *trunking gateway*. A trunking gateway hands off the traffic to a Class 4/5 switch. For example, an MGX8850 or IOS-based gateway such as a 5X00 series can hand off long-distance traffic to an interexchange carrier (IXC). The trunking gateway also provides the connectivity for 911 and operator services.

The gateway can be positioned at a customer premises to interface to a PBX through PRI or channel associated signaling (CAS). This is called an *access gateway*. The PRI signal is backhauled from the gateway to the call agent. The gateway terminates the Layer-2 messages, defined in Q.921, and uses RUDP to backhaul the Q.931 signaling information to the softswitch for processing. All PRI messages in the D channel are tunneled back to the softswitch, rather than terminated on the gateway as in H.323 networks. RUDP provides an in-sequence guaranteed delivery of the signaling information from the agent to the softswitch. The PRI Q.931 signal can also be backhauled back to the call agent using Sigtran, a standard that is defined in IETF. However, CAS signaling is terminated on the gateway and translated to MGCP messages, which allows the softswitch to control the CAS signaling events.

An IAD is an example of an access gateway. The IAD aggregates PBX, data traffic, and POTS phones to provide an integrated access platform. The IAD supports a single link to the service provider network and is managed by the service provider. This particular example uses Cisco's 2400 IAD, which is an important component in this architecture.

Finally, a gateway can also be positioned at a residence or small business that supports a POTS-type interface. This is called a *residential gateway*.

As with SIP and H.323 gateways, an MGCP gateway needs to have its dial peers configured to use MGCP. The VoIP protocol that establishes a VoIP call is determined by the dial peer configuration. An example dial peer configuration for MGCP is as follows:

```
dial-peer voice 1 pots
application MGCPAPP
port 0
```

Aggregation and Edge Routers

Figure 2-11 shows an aggregation router as the point of access to the business customer's equipment. For example, an ESR 10000 can be the aggregation router if a large number of DS1 lines are deployed by the service provider to its business customers. A router, such as a GSR, is required to support the customer with Internet connectivity by interfacing to an ISP.

Feature Servers

The feature servers run the applications that support the service provider's service offerings. The feature server provides enhanced features such as, Centrex, POTS, and tandem to the call agent. These feature servers provide feature support and control through an API.

Summary

This chapter provided an overview of an H.323 architecture, an SIP architecture, and a softswitch architecture. Cisco provides voice solutions that support these three protocols: H.323, MGCP, and SIP. This chapter also covered internetworking of a service provider's H.323 network with another service provider's SIP network. This architecture has become more common because of the maturity of the SIP protocol and the need for traditional wholesale VoIP providers to expand their service offerings. For example, ITSPs want to expand their customer base and add new services. This chapter discussed different methods to accomplish this requirement. Adding SIP capabilities to a network is one method of adding new and enhanced VoIP services, such as web-based voice applications.

CHAPTER 3

Offering Wholesale VoIP Services

This chapter discusses the following topics:

- Migrating Toward a VoIP Infrastructure
- Wholesale Peering Arrangements
- VoIP Billing Systems

This chapter discusses the essential components of Wholesale VoIP services. For many traditional service providers, such as incumbent local exchange carriers (ILECs), migrating from their traditional time-division multiplexing (TDM)-based architecture to a VoIP architecture is the first challenge. This chapter discusses some of the questions to consider when planning this migration.

Service providers establish peering arrangements to exchange VoIP minutes for wholesale VoIP service. Peering arrangements help local service providers to gain worldwide service coverage. In many cases, a service provider must use Signaling System 7 (SS7) to interconnect with the public switched telephone network (PSTN) to provide wholesale and prepaid calling card services. This chapter provides an overview on supporting SS7 within a VoIP network.

A billing system is one essential component for wholesale VoIP services. The key components and architecture of the billing system that supports wholesale and retail VoIP services are discussed.

Migrating Toward a VoIP Infrastructure

Wholesale VoIP service is common among service providers; many reasons exist for providing this service. One reason is that data services for service providers is a high-growth area of their business. These data services are also being delivered by IP. Therefore, service providers are implementing IP networks to support the fast growth of data services, regardless of supporting other services such as VoIP. An obvious benefit of an IP infrastructure is the ability to leverage this same infrastructure to lower network costs and to provide profitable services such as VoIP wholesale and calling card services. The service provider can also add other value-added services. For example, a screen pop application can be implemented in remote/distributed call centers, which allows an organization to quickly add call center seats to handle a product promotion or seasonal burst of activity. Organizations taking calls for Christmas orders can benefit from this application.

The challenge that service providers are faced with today is how to migrate toward an IP infrastructure that supports both voice and data services. Service providers that have traditional TDM voice networks in place must plan for this migration. Of course, to facilitate this migration, many questions must be answered:

- What IP network architecture should be implemented to support this migration?
- What quality of service (QoS) mechanisms are required to support VoIP?
- What extensions to the existing Operations Support System (OSS) are required to monitor and maintain the appropriate level of VoIP Service Level Agreements (SLAs)?
- What provisioning tools are required to support deploying VoIP services in a large-scale manner?
- How will billing be implemented to support VoIP services?

The answers to these questions are based upon the network characteristics of the service provider. Therefore, one answer is not suitable for all service providers. There are different categories of service providers:

- Service providers that own a majority of their network infrastructure. An ILEC is an example of this type of service provider.
- Service providers that own a minority of their network infrastructure. An example of this service provider is an Internet telephony service provider (ITSP).
- Service providers that historically have offered data services only. An example of this service provider is an Internet service provider (ISP).

One possible migration for a service provider that owns most of its network infrastructure and has been a traditional TDM carrier is to replace its Class 4 switches with VoIP gateways. Subscribers that are separated by area codes are always considered a toll call rather than a local call. These telephone calls are always switched at a toll center. The position of a Class 4 switch in a traditional TDM network enables an ILEC to easily provide a first step in migrating to support VoIP services. An ILEC can aggregate all its long distance calls that are directed to its Class 4 switch into VoIP.

NOTE   Historically, the public telephone network has been a hierarchy of telephone switches, which are categorized into different types of switches, such as Class 4 and Class 5. Since the 1984 divestiture, this hierarchy has been flattened because of the deployment of SS7 networks and SONET rings. Flattening the network involved interconnecting Class 5 switches with synchronous optical network rings. It is common for SONET rings to include a Tandem Switch. A Tandem Switch, often called a Class 4 switch, transports calls between central offices (COs). A Tandem Switch is also the entry point into the long distance network and is called the point of presence (POP).

Wholesale Peering Arrangements

Wholesale peering arrangements are required for trading VoIP minutes on a wholesale long distance basis. Many service providers, such as ITSPs, work with other ITSPs to exchange minutes to gain worldwide service coverage. Furthermore, traditional TDM carriers, such as ILECs, are creating wholesale peering arrangements with other service providers. As mentioned earlier, many ILECs are replacing their Class 4 switches with VoIP gateways, thereby eliminating the need to have traditional bilateral agreements with other carriers.

Direct peering and clearinghouse are mechanisms available for service providers to implement their peering arrangements. Direct peering involves the two service providers to negotiate their peering arrangement. A peering arrangement defines SLA guarantees (discussed in Chapter 9, "Network Management: Maintaining an SLA") and settlement procedures. A clearinghouse arrangement involves another party interconnecting the peering partners and providing a settlement. In both peering arrangement cases, price, quality, and capacity are three items that are used in negotiating the peering partner.

Wholesale peering can be accomplished by using direct IP links between carriers. Directory gatekeeper (DGK) peering and Open Settlement Protocol (OSP) are two mechanisms that accomplish this task. With DGK peering, location request (LRQ) RAS messages, as described in Chapter 2, "VoIP Network Architectures: H323, SIP, and MGCP," determine the final route destination. The OSP mechanism requires a server to host the OSP software. This OSP server provides the following three main functions:

- Route resolution
- CDR collection
- Billing settlement

Call Routing

In early VoIP wholesale provider implementations, TDM switches interconnected to various PSTN carriers. These PSTN carriers provided local and backup PSTN routes and interfaced these PSTN carriers to the local POP's VoIP gateways. Besides providing a migration step to a complete end-to-end VoIP network, these TDM switches provided Least Cost Routing (LCR). LCR tables were updated on a periodic basis to capture the changing cost of local and international call rates. Figure 3-1 shows a VoIP wholesale provider interconnecting to PSTN carriers through their own TDM switch that provides LCR.

Figure 3-1 *LCR Using a TDM Switch*

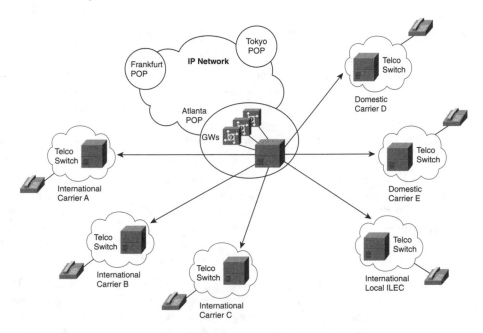

This example depicts a VoIP wholesale provider offering termination for calls to the United States. The VoIP wholesale provider uses its Atlanta POP as its international gateway.

Instead of using TDM switch LCR capabilities, wholesale providers are moving to the LCR functionality as part of the VoIP gateways and gatekeepers. A variety of methods are available to support LCR. The following three methods are discussed:

- Remote Zone Priority
- DGK Routing
- Gatekeeper Transaction Message Protocol (GKTMP)

Remote Zone Priority

As discussed in Chapter 7, "Gateway and Gatekeeper Design Requirements," a Cisco gatekeeper can assign priorities to gateways to facilitate call routing. Priorities can be added to a group of gateways supporting the same E.164 prefix but that are located in different zones. This results in the gatekeeper selecting the highest priority gateway to route the call. The highest priority is associated with the LCR.

DGK Routing

DGKs can be configured to route calls to a particular carrier based on the called number dialed number identification service (DNIS). Thus, a priority list of gateways, each associated with a carrier, is created in the gatekeeper. Therefore, the gatekeeper routes calls based on this list. DNIS-based routing is limited in that routing is based only on the priority list and not on call origination information, such as the originating carrier, or dynamic information, such as link use.

GKTMP

Call routing can be supported by an external software application that interfaces to a Cisco gatekeeper or DGKP by using the GKTMP. The GKTMP method has additional call-routing capabilities from the DGK routing method. Besides routing on DNIS information, IOS 12.2(11)T enhances the GKTMP protocol to support the selection of the egress circuit on the terminating gateway. This enhancement is referred to as carrier sensitive routing. Carrier sensitive routing enables a service provider to select the outbound carrier to route a VoIP call. The outbound carrier is selected based on which carrier originates the call, the time of day, and cost.

Figure 3-2 shows the carrier sensitive routing (CSR) application that is configured to issue any calls to Turkey (country code 90) during Sunday from 8:00 a.m. to noon. The CSR application has Carrier B as the designated carrier during this period and provides a response back to the originating gateway with this information. (Carrier B is inserted into the ACF messages.)

SS7 Interconnection to the PSTN

Two traditional approaches in implementing VoIP wholesale services are

- Linking the IP network to the PSTN without using SS7 interconnection
- Linking the IP network to the PSTN using SS7 interconnection

Figure 3-2   *Example of Using GKTMP*

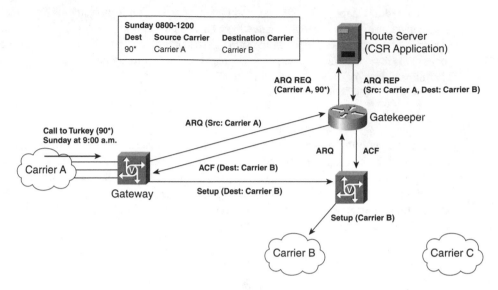

Interconnecting to an SS7 network eliminates the need for Primary Rate Interface (PRI) or channel associated signaling (CAS) connections, which is the first approach listed. Inefficient usage of PRI links exists in many large-scale VoIP deployments. Furthermore, many cities around the world only support SS7 interconnection to the PSTN. Therefore, SS7 access has played an important role in rolling out wholesale VoIP services for many service providers.

The SS7 network transports call control messages for the VoIP network to help establish the end-to-end circuit. Figure 3-3 depicts a VoIP wholesale network interconnecting to a PSTN by using SS7.

Figure 3-3   *SS7 Architecture*

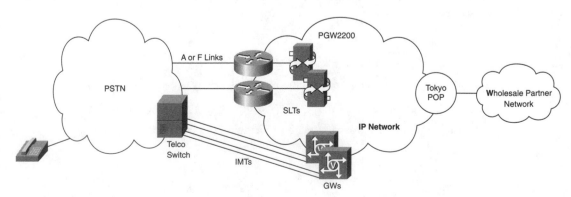

Two main SS7 links interconnect a wholesale VoIP network to the PSTN. Either A-links or F-links can interconnect the gateways to the SS7 network. An A-link provides a pair of links in which each link to the SS7 network is provisioned over diverse routes. The PSTN uses a signal transfer point (STP) as the gateway into the SS7 network; STPs are always deployed in pairs. Using a F-link is a less costly approach to interconnect to the SS7 network. F-links provide a link directly between two telephone switches by using Inter-Machine Trunks (IMTs), which do not require a STP. This approach is called *associated signaling*.

Cisco's solution for wholesale VoIP consists of the Cisco 2600 SLTs, the PGW2200, and a Cisco gateway. The SLT connects to the PGW2200. The PGW2200 and SLT exchange messages using the Reliable User Datagram Protocol (RUDP). The PGW2200 converts ISUP messages into Q.931 and forwards them to the Cisco gateway. In SS7 architecture, the SLT talks to the PGW2200 over IP, and so the SC2200 does not need to physically reside where the A-links are located. As a result, the service provider can deploy a central PGW2200, and remote SLTs at a number of interconnect POPs and multiple peering partners.

VoIP Billing Systems

Billing systems include external PCs or workstations to collect billing records that are produced for each call. The interval to collect these billing records is configured by the service provider. For example, a five-minute interval can be configured to collect these records. These billing records are normally in a format called *Automatic Message Accounting (AMA)*.

NOTE	Telcordia has a standard format for AMA records called *Billing AMA Format (BAF)* used by U.S. service providers.

As with traditional telephony service, billing the call is an important aspect to providing wholesale VoIP services. Two key steps to billing are

- Determining the duration of the call
- Applying the call rate

In VoIP wholesale service, multiple call legs are associated with the bill, as shown in Figure 3-4.

Figure 3-4 *Billing Records*

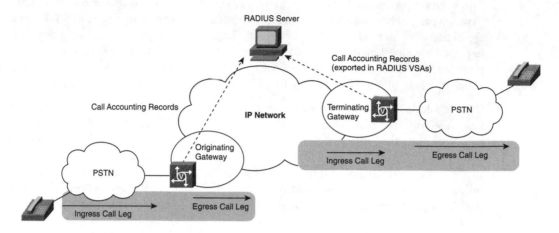

A pair of call legs is associated with each originating and terminating gateway. Each pair consists of an ingress and egress call leg. Each call leg generates a set of accounting records specific to the call leg. These accounting records are called Start and Stop. Cisco gateways use a Network Time Protocol (NTP) server to synchronize their time. This time is used to timestamp the accounting records. The Cisco gateway sends these records to a RADIUS server using Vendor Specific Attributes (VSA). Sending VSAs are supported by the RADIUS protocol. Many VSAs are used to pass a large amount of variables to the RADIUS server. Cisco has defined a substantial number of VSAs to enable tracking and billing for VoIP calls. Thus, VoIP billing systems must be able to process VSAs. Billing systems correlate call legs by using a unique call ID to produce a call detail record (CDR).

The contents of a CDR for a VoIP call leg consists of many fields, including

- ANI
- DNIS
- Call Duration
- Unique Call ID (Connection ID)
- Gateway ID
- Packet voice quality
- IP address of remote gateway
- Packets sent and received

Reconciliation

Service providers that established a VoIP peering partner typically reconcile billing data with each other. Part of a peering relationship is negotiating long distance settlement rates for the relevant countries. For example, peering partners might exchange monthly CDRs or total terminating/originating minutes. One of the wholesale peering partners will have a greater amount of usage after the balance is determined. Thus, a settlement occurs using the agreed upon rates. Figure 3-5 is an example of a set of procedures that might be agreed upon between two peering partners to reconcile billing data.

Figure 3-5   *Reconciliation Procedure Example*

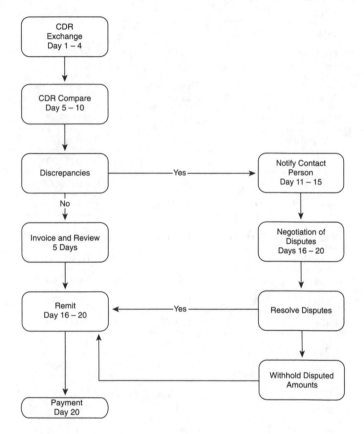

One method for reconciliation is to correlate the source and destination IP address for a call. An external billing system maintains and correlates this information. Another reconciliation method is to use a unique ID in the H.323 SETUP message that is associated with the originating wholesale provider. This unique ID is included in the AAA record, which can be used by the billing system.

Example of a Billing Report

Table 3-1 shows an example of a billing report that indicates the usage per country for Service Provider A's originating traffic and terminating traffic.

Table 3-1 *Billing Report Example*

Service Provider A's Originating Traffic (Calls Rated by Second)

Prefix	Country	No. of Calls	Duration in Sec	Rate (US$)/Sec	Usage (US$)
1	USA	5688	2,883,082	0.001750	5045.39
1	Canada	3506	1,629,227	0.003830	6239.94
44	UK	196	129,734	0.003830	496.88
816	Japan	559	165,374	0.14/min	427.84
351	Portugal	13	3648	0.007500	27.36
353	Ireland	9	3530	0.004660	16.45
356	Malta	7	1333	0.006500	8.66
358	Finland	31	3014	0.005330	16.06
506	Costa Rica	7	2704	0.009670	26.15
598	Uruguay	1	840	0.011000	9.24
972	Israel	25	2935	0.010000	29.35
	Total	**10,042**	**4,825,421**		**12,343.33**

Service Provider A's Terminating Traffic (Calls Rated by Second)

Prefix	Country	No. of Calls	Duration in Sec	Rate (US$)/Sec	Usage (US$)
1	USA	5688	2,883,082	0.001750	5045.39
1	Canada	3506	1,629,227	0.003830	6239.94
44	UK	196	129,734	0.003830	496.88
816	Japan	559	165,374	0.14/min	427.84
86	China	2049	491,990	0.014330	7050.22
90	Turkey	29	5439	0.010500	57.11
222	Mauritania	3	507	0.007830	3.97
351	Portugal	13	3648	0.007500	27.36
353	Ireland	9	3530	0.004660	16.45
356	Malta	7	1333	0.006500	8.66
358	Finland	31	3014	0.005330	16.06
506	Costa Rica	7	2704	0.009670	26.15
598	Uruguay	1	840	0.011000	9.24
972	Israel	25	2935	0.010000	29.35
	Total	**12,123**	**5,323,357**		**19,454.63**

Summary

This chapter reviewed certain key components that are necessary to provide VoIP services. One key component was call routing. Traditionally, TDM switches provided LCR to capture the changing cost of local and international call rates. Today, new capabilities exist in Cisco's IOS Software to support enhanced call routing features.

SS7 connectivity might need to be supported depending upon where a service provider's POP is located. Financial criteria will also be used to determine the need for SS7 connectivity. For example, SS7 interconnection generally results in a different charging regime that is often more favorable to the VoIP service provider. However, SS7 interconnection takes considerable time because of stringent interconnect testing procedures and prolonged commercial negotiations. PRI/CAS, available to any customer, can be implemented quickly but generally results in standard customer tariff structures that might be unattractive.

The service provider also needs to consider the many different variants of SS7 that need to be supported by its network. Another important item that is needed to successfully implement a wholesale VoIP service is the billing system. Many third-party software vendors support billing systems. These billing systems can collect call leg records from a RADIUS server that is connected to each gateway.

Lastly, service providers need to be aware of the current regulatory issues. Various worldwide organizations constantly discuss VoIP regulations. Because the United States offers VoIP service in the United States, the regulatory climate has favored many service providers. However, in some other countries, the regulatory climate has not been so favorable. Changes in VoIP regulations might have a dramatic impact on a service provider's business model.

CHAPTER 4

Offering Bundled Voice and Data Services

Chapter 2, "VoIP Network Architectures: H.323, SIP, and MGCP," describes a managed voice and data service architecture that uses a call agent. A call agent solution is commonly used for the small and medium-sized business (SMB) market. This solution uses an integrated access device (IAD) at the customer premises that supports voice and data using IP or Asynchronous Transfer Mode adaptation layer 2 (AAL2) transport over a T1 access link to the service provider.

This chapter continues the focus on offering managed services to SMBs. Service providers that traditionally use time-division multiplexing (TDM) access and that need to add other service offerings can bundle voice and data services over a single access link to the customer. For example, traditional T1 circuits that are offered to customers to interconnect their private branch exchange (PBX) to interexchange carriers (IXCs) can now be used instead for integrated voice and data traffic, thereby eliminating the need for multiple access links between the customer and the service provider.

Three areas are discussed to help provide an overview of bundled voice and data service architectures:

- Overview of Managed Voice and Data Services
- Managed Voice and Data Services Using AAL2
- Fundamentals of AAL2

Overview of Managed Voice and Data Services

Integrated voice and data is a new service that is offered by service providers. The architecture design to deploy managed voice and data services is based on many factors. One of these factors is the required customer premises equipment (CPE), which is based on the type of business customer.

Two general types of business customers exist. One is a business customer with fewer than 100 users, such as a doctor's office, an insurance agent's office, or a small home office. These businesses are normally single-site locations that require telephony services, Internet access, firewall, and Virtual Private Network (VPN) services. Typically, these businesses do not have older networking protocols, such as AppleTalk or IPX, and they do not have a full-time support staff to maintain their own private network. A service provider can support these services with an IAD on the customer premises, such as a Cisco 2400.

The second type of business customer is an enterprise customer. An enterprise customer has a large installed base of devices that supports many flavors of protocols, sophisticated routing designs, multiple T1s, and back-hauling needs. An enterprise customer needs a multiservice platform, such as the Cisco 2600 and 3600. Many of these enterprise businesses have their own large private networks and their own full-time staff to maintain their multiservice network. However, because of various reasons, such as fast growth and economics, many of these large customers are outsourcing some or all of their services to service providers.

Integrated Access Architectures

Traditionally, service providers offer TDM services that connect a customer's PBX to an IXC Class 4 switch, which provides long distance voice services. Many of these service providers are currently switching from using a TDM-based infrastructure to using a packet-based infrastructure, either IP or ATM. This approach allows for a more efficient method to provide voice transport and also helps to integrate voice and data services over one access link to the customer premises.

NOTE   Many incumbent carriers are adding IP to their core ATM network by inserting Multiprotocol Label Switching (MPLS) technology. This change enables service providers to shift from transport service offerings to IP-based service offerings.

ADSL and T1 ATM are two types of access technologies that can be supported between the SMB and the service provider.

Other Cisco IADs

Other IADs available for SMBs are the Cisco 827-4V and the 1750. Both of these IADs support four Foreign Exchange Station (FXS) interfaces, and the 1750 also supports FX0 and E&M interfaces. The 827-4V supports a fixed configuration that includes Ethernet and DSL WAN-access only, and the 1750 supports a modular configuration that includes Fast Ethernet and multiple WAN options, such as DSL and T1 access. To help further differentiate these two IADs, the 1750 supports dual WAN interfaces for WAN backup or load sharing, hardware Triple Data Encryption Standard (3DES) encryption, and Open Shortest Path

First (OSPF) and Border Gateway Protocol (BGP) routing—these capabilities are not present in the 827-4V. The 827-4V is well suited for small offices that do not require the extra capabilities of the 1750 and are not concerned with expandability, but do require core services such as basic voice (FXS), VPN, and a firewall from their service provider.

Managed Voice and Data Services Using AAL2

AAL2, referred to as VoAAL2 in a voice network, can integrate the voice and data services offered to the customer. Alternatively, a service provider can begin with an IP-based infrastructure and build out a VoIP call agent architecture to support voice and data services to their customers, which is a more common approach today. Both technologies, VoIP and VoAAL2, offer the value of integrating voice and data while achieving efficient bandwidth use.

This section provides an AAL2 architecture that can provide trunking and integrated access services. By using AAL2, many capabilities can be obtained within the service provider's ATM network:

- Dynamically change from voice to fax demodulation
- AAL2 Type 3 cells for reliable dual tone multifrequency (DTMF) relay
- Dynamically change the compression rate to G.711 for fax calls in midcall
- Indicate end of speech burst for background noise generation during silence periods at the egress ATM switch
- Transport up to 248 voice calls with different compression schemes within one or more ATM permanent virtual circuit (PVC)

This architecture provides a Class 4 interconnect replacement, which enables an enterprise to bypass the local Tandem Switch.

NOTE　A *Tandem Switch* is a switch that incumbent local exchange carrier (ILEC) networks use to route calls between COs in the same local access and transport area (LATA). These calls are referred to as intraLATA calls. Trunks at each CO are typically interconnected by a Synchronous Optical Network (SONET) ring. The Tandem Switch also connects to an IXC Tandem Office, which is called a *point of presence (POP)*. A POP houses a Class 4 switch that connects into the ILEC's Tandem Switch. The Tandem Switch aggregates interLATA traffic from multiple COs and a trunk facility. An IXC Tandem Office can have dedicated trunks to an ILEC's CO in cases where a high concentration of traffic exists between the CO and the IXC. An IXC handles interLATA traffic.

A Class 5 switch is located in an end office and a Class 4/5 switch is located in a Tandem Office. A Class 5 switch provides local services in the PSTN to the end user. A Class 5 switch provides enhanced calling features, such as call waiting and three-way calling to end users.

The architecture shown in Figure 4-1 depicts a service provider offering integrated access to business customers and trunking service between two PSTN carriers.

Figure 4-1   *Integrated Access and Trunking Service Using AAL2*

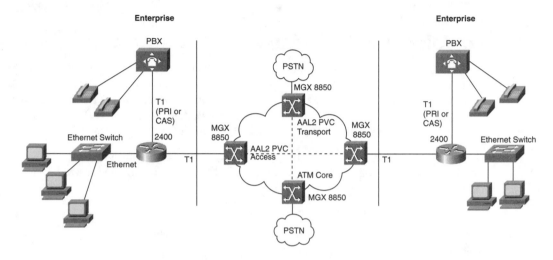

An end-to-end trunking architecture does not require a call agent. This architecture can reduce the complexity of a mesh of narrowband circuits by having only a single integrated voice and data network. IADs can support the transport of data and voice by using AAL2 and AAL5 from the customer premises to the service provider. The architecture in Figure 4-1 includes IAD 2400 at the business customer site, which terminates into a MGX8000 Voice Gateway at the service provider's network edge. The MGX8000 Voice Gateway adds packet voice capabilities to the MGX 8850 that includes VoIP, VoAAL1, and VoAAL2. The voice signaling from the enterprise customer is tunneled through the MGX8000 Voice Gateway to a Class 4 switch by using AAL2 point-to-point trunking. The data is tunneled through to an ATM switch, such as a Cisco BPX 8600.

Figure 4-1 shows AAL2 trunking services, which are indicated by the vertical dotted line. Multiple T1s or E1s with Primary Rate Interface (PRI) or channel-associated signaling (CAS) terminate from the PSTN to the MGX8000 Voice Gateway. The PSTN cloud represents another service provider offloading its voice traffic to another carrier. The integrated access service uses AAL2 PVCs between two MGX 8850s within the service provider's network. In this application, the MGX8000 Voice Gateway uses an ATM User Service Module (AUSM) card. The IAD 2400 aggregates both voice and data traffic over a T1 access line to the service provider.

CAS and PRI signaling can be supported in this architecture. The CAS information is carried in the AAL2 PVC across the network. CAS is a signaling technique that uses robbed bits within a multiframe, such as a D4 Super Frame (SF) or Extended Superframe. These robbed bits, referred to as ABCD, represent various states and transitions of a voice call. These ABCD bits are transported over the same AAL2 channel as the one used for voice because CAS does not use a separate signaling channel, such as in-band signaling; the CAS bits use AAL2 Type 3 packets as they provide CRC checks for reliability whereas voice traffic uses AAL2 Type 1 packets that are without CRC checks. An important feature that this architecture provides is *idle channel suppression*. Idle channel suppression stops sending idle channel bits that are generated from the CAS source (for example, a PBX). This mechanism results in significant amounts of bandwidth savings in the service provider's ATM network; this mechanism has no benefit in common channel signaling (CCS) configurations.

The PRI signaling channels, for example, in T1 the 24th time slot and in E1 the 16th time slot, are carried across the ATM network in the AAL5 PVC while the voice traffic, that is the bearer traffic, is carried by the AAL2 PVC. Thus, two different PVCs traverse the end-to-end network. One carries all the data traffic, and the other carries all the signaling traffic. D-channel information is transported across an AAL5 PVC because the signaling is in High-Level Data Link Control (HDLC) format. AAL2 does not support HDLC but AAL5 does.

NOTE   CCS signaling protocols use HDLC framing, which is a link-layer protocol that provides variable length messages and supports a retransmission error correction capability to ensure 100 percent reliable data delivery. A D channel of an ISDN PRI line uses CCS protocols.

Fundamentals of AAL2

The AAL2 protocol has two layers:

- Service specific convergence sublayer (SSCS)
- Common part sublayer (CPS)

The SSCS encodes different information streams for the transport by AAL2 over a single ATM connection. The information streams might be active voice encodings, silence insertion descriptors, dialed digits, or fax. SSCS can provide error control on critical information (CAS signaling and dialed digits) by using a 10-bit CRC. This is called an AAL2 Type 3 cell. The SSCS segments the information that is being passed from a higher layer application, such as samples of voice from a digital phone into a number of units of data, and submits these units of data to the CPS for transmission. The length of the segmented data can be between one and the maximum length supported by the CPS connection, which is either 45 or 64 bytes. At the SSCS receiver, the units of data are reassembled back into the information before being passed to the higher layer application.

The second layer, the CPS, is specifically responsible for transporting end-to-end connections across the network. The format of AAL2 protocol structure is shown in Figure 4-2.

Figure 4-2 *AAL2 Protocol Structure*

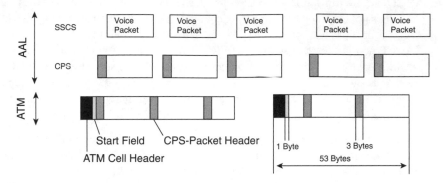

Figure 4-2 shows that AAL2 uses an additional byte of overhead for each ATM cell and an additional three bytes of overhead for each voice packet (e.g., compressed 8 kbps voice). The benefits of the AAL2 scheme are that there is no padding overhead except when there is insufficient data to complete a packet in a prespecified time interval, and the voice channels can be multiplexed over a single ATM virtual circuit.

The content of the Start field and the CPS packet are shown in Figure 4-3.

Figure 4-3 *Start Field and CPS Packet Formats*

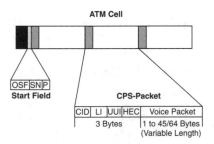

The CPS layer enables the multiplexing of variable length voice packets of end users onto a single ATM virtual channel that is an AAL2 channel. This is accomplished through the different information fields shown in Figure 4-2. Although AAL2 with its three-byte packet header introduces some inefficiency for small packets, the improvement that is reached by having no padding more than offsets this minor inefficiency. Each of the CPS fields and the Start field are described here:

- **Start field**—Enables efficient packing of the voice packets over a single ATM virtual circuit. The Offset field is a six-bit pointer within the Start field that points to the position of the first CPS packet that follows the OSF. A sequence number protects the order of the Offset field. If a Start field parity error exists, all the CPS packets that are associated with the Start field are discarded.

- **CID (Channel ID)**—Identifies the end user, which is referred to as the SSCS entity in the International Telecommunication Union (ITU) AAL2 specifications. The CID allocates the value 1 to exchange layer management peer-to-peer procedures, such as set-up negotiations. CID enables the multiplexing of up to 248 user channels, whereas some CID values are reserved for other uses, such as peer-to-peer layer management. For example, if 8 E1s terminated on an MGX, 240 CID values would be used.

- **LI (Length Indicator)**—Identifies the length of the CPS packet. The default payload length is 45 bytes, and an optional maximum length of 64 bytes can be selected. The maximum length is channel specific.

- **UUI (User-to-User Indication)**—Provides two functions: It conveys specific information transparently between two end points (e.g., CPS or SSCS entity) and distinguishes between the different users, such as SSCS entities and layer management users.

- **HEC (Header Error Control)**—Discards the rest of the CPS packets until the next Start field. As a result, not all voice users residing on the single ATM virtual channel are affected by other end-user errors, which results in a higher end-to-end efficiency.

The CID is an important concept in AAL2. CIDs provide a binding between an endpoint and an AAL2 connection. This is the mechanism that binds the TDM traffic to the ATM traffic. For example, if a service provider needs to provision 100 DS0s between two sites for one of its enterprise customers, 100 CIDs are created across the ATM network. Furthermore, a unique coder-decoder (codec) type is assigned to each individual DS0 because the codec type is assigned to each CID through an AAL2. For example, individual customers in a multi-tenant building can each support multiple compression schemes over a single T1 access link. Each CID is configured and includes the following parameters: codec type, profile type, voice activity detection (VAD), DTFM Tones, and packet period for G.729. For example, to transmit DTMF tones transparently across the ATM PVC, DTMF must be enabled in the CID.

An AAL2 profile is a mechanism that the MGX 8850 uses to assign the compression and encoding scheme of the AAL2 trunking service. A profile is defined by a profile type, which is either an ITU standard or a custom type and a number. These profiles need to match on both ends of the network for the two end devices, such as PBXs, to interoperate. A profile is configured for each CID. For example, if the profile type is ITU and the profile number is 1, you must use G.711. In other words, the profile type and the profile number identify the compression type.

CID enables the use of subcell multiplexing, which provides many of the benefits of AAL2. If you use G.711, subcell multiplexing does not provide any value because G.711 already uses an 80-byte packet. The real advantage of subcell multiplexing is the G.729 encoding scheme. If you use G.729 with a packetization period of 30 milliseconds, three 10-byte packets of payload from one DS0 are packed into one ATM cell. Therefore, the efficiency of packing the voice sample into the ATM cell is increased threefold, and instead of 34 bytes of padding, only 14 bytes exist in the ATM cell. Assuming that VAD provides an additional 50 percent of bandwidth savings, G.729 subcell multiplexing uses approximately 6 kbps of bandwidth per DS0 channel of voice traffic. This is a significant amount of bandwidth savings.

Summary

This chapter provided an overview of managed voice and data services using ATM technology. AAL2 is an important component in providing a managed service using ATM. Because of efficient bandwidth use and the ability to transport different traffic types, AAL2 is used in trunking applications, such as interconnecting mobile wireless sites. Today, many service providers use a pure IP-based architecture to support this service.

CHAPTER 5

QoS Considerations in VoIP Network Design

Appropriate bandwidth provisioning underlies a well-designed Voice over IP (VoIP) network. This chapter discusses QoS architectures and mechanisms to consider when provisioning bandwidth in a VoIP network:

- Using QoS to Support VoIP Services
- Choosing the Right QoS approach
- Using Differentiated Service (DiffServ) for VoIP Services: The EF Behavior
- Implementing the Expedited Forwarding (EF) Behavior
- Congestion Management Using Low Latency Queuing (LLQ) for VoIP
- Avoiding Congestion in VoIP Networks
- Call Admission Control for VoIP Networks
- Multiprotocol Label Switching (MPLS) Supporting Voice
- MPLS Traffic Engineering (TE)
- Fast Re-Route (FRR) for Voice

An IP network is an important element in the design of a service provider's end-to-end VoIP network. In many cases, the IP network is already in place and proper conditioning of this network must occur to effectively support VoIP traffic. In other instances, the IP network is designed and implemented from the beginning to support VoIP traffic and perhaps other traffic. In either case, routers in the network must be configured correctly to handle voice packets to eliminate degraded voice quality because of delay, jitter, and packet loss. If the network is not configured appropriately, voice issues, such as clipping (skips in a voice conversation) and echo, will likely exist.

IP Network Characteristics

The following three network characteristics must align with VoIP services because they determine the quality of VoIP services:

- Delay
- Jitter
- Packet loss

Delay

End-to-end delay, sometimes called *fixed del*ay, is caused by delays in switching, propagation, and serialization in the network. End-to-end delay is an important network characteristic that must be maintained at the correct levels. The target value of 150 msec is commonly used as the one-way delay budget for the threshold of user-perceived delay. The user perceives a decreased voice quality of the call if the 150 msec threshold delay exceeds 150 ms. The objective, therefore, must be to keep the threshold below 150 msecs to sustain high-quality or toll-quality voice calls. Remember that various components, including network and non-network components (e.g., DSP codec processing at endpoints) contribute to end-to-end delay.

This value is defined in the International Telecommunication Union (ITU) G.114 recommendation. The target value to achieve in certain situations, such as within a country, is 150 msec—but not in all cases. Longer end-to-end delays today are in the 200 msec range, while providing acceptable voice quality to many users.

NOTE   The 150 msec and 200 msec delays are applicable to voice payload packets. Different requirements apply to signaling packets. For example, in some cases, signaling protocols such as H.323 and session initiation protocol (SIP) are more lenient, and other signaling protocols such as Media Gateway Control Protocol (MGCP) are more stringent.

Post Dial Delay (PDD) is another category of delay. PDD is defined as the period between the last number being dialed and the distant telephone ringing. Most domestic calls have a PDD of less than one to two seconds, and international calls can have a PDD of up to four or more seconds. The presence of large signaling delays or packet loss of the signaling packets will be a significant factor in increasing the PDD of the call.

Jitter

Delay variance, commonly called *jitter*, has a significant impact on voice quality. On the receiving gateway, a jitter buffer queues incoming packets for playout. If a network has high jitter, you can use a large jitter buffer. However, a large jitter buffer directly impacts end-to-end delay. As users can perceive end-to-end delay that exceeds approximately 150 ms, it is important to use small jitter buffers, which means that the network itself must have a relatively small amount of jitter.

Contributors to jitter include the following:

- A congested queue causes packets to be transmitted onto the outgoing router link with varying delays. This is usually the most significant contributor to jitter.

- Processing of the router and serialization delays of variable-sized packets.

Even in cases where end-to-end delays are small, such as 50 msec, a large swing in delay can produce unacceptable voice quality. Jitter buffers are typically set to 60 ms, which allows a delay variation of 60 ms and increases the voice playout delay by the same amount (60 ms). Adaptive jitter buffers with minimum values can minimize jitter. Adaptive jitter buffers learn the amount of jitter in the network during each voice call and shorten or lengthen the size of the jitter buffer. As long as jitter is less than the size of the receiver's jitter buffer, the jitter is imperceptible to the end user.

NOTE   If a VoIP sample (that is, a Real-Time Transport Protocol [RTP] packet) arrives too early or too late to fit into the jitter buffer, the sample is dropped. This dropped sample has the same negative impact on voice quality as packet loss, which is described in the next section.

Packet Loss

The quality of the VoIP service is somewhat forgiving of end-to-end delay and constrained amounts of jitter. However, packet loss dramatically impacts the quality of a VoIP service. The design objective for a VoIP network should be zero packet loss of the voice packets, including both signaling (MGCP, SIP, H.323) and media (RTP) packets. This is the ideal design goal; in reality, you cannot build any network of any size that has absolutely no packet loss.

Packet loss is typically caused by a poor-quality network, such as high bit error rates (BERs) on links or network congestion. As mentioned in the jitter section, jitter buffer overruns or underruns have the same impact on voice quality as packet loss.

Why is packet loss bad for a VoIP network? Because packet loss severely impacts the quality of the voice call. Packet loss produces clipping. *Clipping* is a skip in the conversation. Packet loss is more severe on fax traffic than on voice traffic—and far more severe on modem traffic than on fax or voice. For example, packet loss on a fax transmission can cause the fax connection to drop. As a result, fax and modem relay techniques should be used on networks with significant packet loss.

Using QoS to Support VoIP Services

When considering the support of QoS mechanisms in a VoIP network, the first question is "Do I really need it?" Why can't a service provider just add extra bandwidth in the network so that delay, jitter, and packet loss are eliminated? Adding extra bandwidth, called over-provisioning, is a design choice in implementing a service provider network to support a VoIP service. However, to properly sustain the quality of the network, there can be no significant congestion anywhere in the network. In most cases, a service provider cannot guarantee that its network will never have any congestion because there will likely be situations where the service provider will not be able to choose the path of its links to its subscribers or to the service provider's points of presence (POPs). Also, subscriber's traffic patterns cannot be predicted. Even though overprovisioning is a design choice in a voice-only network, QoS is used in a voice and data network to support Service Level Agreements (SLAs) with subscribers.

It is important to understand that as soon as data traffic is combined with voice traffic, overprovisioning might not obviate the need for QoS because of the instantaneous and unpredictable nature of data traffic. QoS should be considered in a converged voice and data network to ensure zero packet loss for voice traffic.

This section discusses the various QoS mechanisms that support the proper amount of bandwidth, delay, jitter, and packet loss. These QoS mechanisms must constantly maintain the correct levels of network resources, such as bandwidth and delay:

- Classification
- Policing and metering
- Marking
- Queuing and dropping
- Shaping
- Fragmentation

Choosing the Right QoS Approach

The three main approaches to apply QoS to a VoIP network follow:

- Overprovisioning
- Integrated Services (IntServ)
- DiffServ

Overprovisioning

Overprovisioning, a traditional approach, provides no mechanisms to guarantee QoS parameters such as delay, latency, bandwidth, or packet loss. Overprovisioning is also called *best effort*. The main reason for using best-effort service is that sufficient bandwidth is available for VoIP traffic because of overprovisioning the network—best effort is useful for voice-only networks. This design decision is chosen because bandwidth cost to the service provider is inexpensive or because of limited QoS knowledge.

IntServ

The second QoS model, IntServ, uses a control and data plane architecture. This model has the applications to signal the QoS requirements from the network. Resource Reservation Protocol (RSVP) is the signaling protocol that carries out this request. This model might not scale well in a large service provider network because of IntServ's use of a fine-grained method of providing QoS and the large amount of state information to track all the calls in progress. This fine-grained method is per-flow QoS. A flow is a sequence of messages (e.g., RTP, RSVP) with the same source, destination, and QoS. To eliminate per-flow scaling issues, you can use a combined IntServ and DiffServ architecture. DiffServ is discussed in the next section.

IntServ also provides admission control, which can be based on network policies or available resources. IntServ has built-in signaling mechanisms to determine if QoS resources are available to support a flow. For example, a voice call might not be granted if sufficient delay is not available.

DiffServ

The third QoS model, DiffServ, uses a data-plane-only architecture. Unlike Intserv, DiffServ does not have built-in resource or policy admission control. The lightweight nature of DiffServ, which enables it to scale, is one of the main reasons why many service providers today use this model as their QoS architecture.

Diffserv provides two main functions. First, DiffServ marks packets with the correct traffic class. With DiffServ, the service provider edge router or VoIP gateway marks packets with the correct Diffserv Codepoint (DSCP) value, which classifies the traffic. The edge also polices incoming traffic. These functions that are carried out by the router are also called *traffic classification* and *traffic conditioning*. Second, DiffServ handles these marked packets appropriately by using a defined procedure called *Per-Hop Behavior (PHB)*, which must be implemented in all routers. PHB defines the QoS treatment for every traffic class that flows through a router.

To deploy and build PHB in a router, you must look at traffic types and requirements for the traffic. Obviously, the customer contract or SLA must be supported by this PHB because delay, jitter, and packet loss dramatically impact the voice quality. To do this, routers or VoIP gateways must mark traffic at the entry to the service provider network. This can be accomplished by marking the packets with a code point (DSCP value) that notifies the network how to treat the traffic. The core routers can now easily classify this traffic by using this code point. The egress router traffic is placed in a queue and ensures that this traffic is isolated from traffic in other classes.

DiffServ's two functions are shown in Figure 5-1.

Figure 5-1 *PHB Using DiffServ*

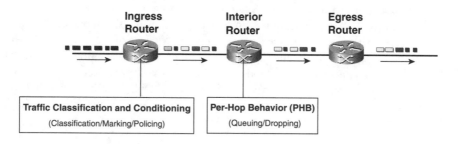

NOTE   DiffServ provides QoS on an aggregate of traffic. Diff-Serv describes how to build a path in IP networks with some guarantees using QoS mechanisms.

QoS classes, also called *traffic* classes, are identified by the DSCP value or IP Precedence value that is defined in the IP header, thereby partially eliminating the need for signaling, such as RSVP; signaling might still be required for admission control purposes. Each packet automatically selects the appropriate PHB in a router by using the DSCP value set by the edge.

A drawback of DiffServ is that it must guarantee all traffic crossing a particular interface in the network, rather than the route or circuit of this path. As a result, DiffServ has no topology-aware admission control mechanism to prevent establishing a call that might degrade all calls in progress.

QoS Building Blocks

Three precedence bits in a standard IP version 4 packet and six DSCP bits are located in the type of service (ToS) field in the header of an IP packet, as shown in Figure 5-2.

Figure 5-2 *IP ToS Field*

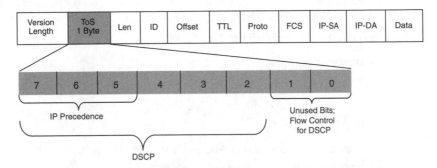

These three precedence bits were originally defined by the Internet Engineering Task Force (IETF), but they were generally not used for their originally defined purpose. Some service providers used these precedence bits to prioritize VoIP packets over data packets in the network, but the lack of a standard made multilateral agreements between service providers using the IP Precedence bits difficult. Another problem was that no standard interpretation of these bits by routers or VoIP endpoints existed.

One reason for the lack of understanding is the lack of standard definitions describing the behavior for each IP Precedence value. For example, RFC 1812 defines that the higher IP Precedence should be forwarded in less time than packets with lower IP Precedence during a certain time interval. This definition is vague. More recently, however, the ToS field has been replaced with DSCP, which is part of the DiffServ architecture, as defined by IETF RFCs 2474, 2475, 2597, and 2598. Unlike IP Precedence, DiffServ describes how to define PHBs, the format of the DS field in the header, certain DSCPs, and the overall architecture for Diffserv as part of an IP network. A service is defined to be a particular set of network characteristics, such as bandwidth and latency, that are associated with the transmission of a packet. Packets of a particular service are referred to as packets of a particular class. Services are implemented in an IP network using PHB.

NOTE   To keep QoS on Ethernet LAN segments, you can translate Layer-3 IP Precedence/DSCP markings to Layer-2 802.1p/802.1q class of service (CoS) bits.

IETF defined DiffServ to standardize QoS in IP networks by using DSCP because the usage of IP Precedence bits was never standardized. Several mechanisms must be in place in the network to implement DiffServ:

- **Classification**—When implementing DiffServ, the first step is to differentiate traffic received into the service provider's network. This process is called *classification*. Classification is necessary to provide QoS. Classification can be accomplished at both

Layer-2 and Layer-3 headers. The decision to classify at Layer 2 or 3 depends on whether Layer-2 traffic, such as Ethernet frames, or Layer-3 traffic, such as IP packets, exist on the link—mapping between the two layers can be accomplished.

Several methods can classify traffic:

— Incoming/outgoing interface

— Traffic is within contracted rate limits or is not within contracted rate limits

— Standard or extended access control list

— IP RTP ports

— Source/destination Media Access Control (MAC) address

— DSCP or IP Precedence value

— MPLS experimental bits

— Network-Based Application Recognition (NBAR)

— Endpoint classification

- **Policing**—Measures the rate of traffic to enforce a certain policy such as rate limiting. Policing meters traffic entering the network to ensure that the traffic does not exceed certain threshold capacities. Packets that exceed a threshold are either marked or dropped. Packets that enter the network and are marked are dropped ahead of nonmarked packets in the network. Policing and marking are normally performed on the edge of the network. This is the most widely used design by service providers. The reason for this design is that the routers in the core of a network are optimized to perform at high speeds and do not have enough resources to perform policing and marking at their line rates.

NOTE   Many service providers use policing only on data traffic and use Call Admission Control (CAC) to carry out policing. Packet drop features, such as Committed Access Rate (CAR) and class-based policing, are not typically used on voice traffic. CAC is discussed later in this chapter.

- **Marking**—Also referred to as *coloring*, refers to rewriting the bits in the header. This is done so that the next-hop device doesn't need to carry out complex classification techniques, such as using lists (ACLs) or mark the header bits. Classification at the edge of entry point of the networks is a CPU-intensive job. As a result of marking at the edge of the network, core routers do not have to perform CPU-intensive classification, but need to perform only simple classification by looking at the marking in the packet header.

Marking also enables the traffic to be prioritized and protected after it leaves the edge of the service provider network. Thus, voice packets can be protected when congestion occurs in the service provider network.

NOTE   Classification and marking should not be confused. Classification is the act of determining out what type of packet is entering the network. This is normally accomplished using ACLs. After this packet is classified, the packet is marked according to the classification (traffic class).

Following is a list of commonly used protocol headers that can be marked:

— IP DSCP

— IP Precedence

— MPLS EXP Bits

— ATM CLP Bit. Using a separate VBR-rt or VBR-nrt PVC for high-priority traffic typically differentiates voice and data packets.

— Frame Relay discard eligible (DE)-Bit

— IEEE 802.1Q/p User-Priority Bits

- **Queuing and dropping**—Queuing and dropping are implemented on the outgoing interface of a router or switch. Queuing refers to holding packet traffic in a queue while transmitting other packets. Normal queuing is First In First Out (FIFO). A variety of mechanisms in IOS exist to optimize queuing. Examples are priority queuing (PQ), custom queuing (CQ), weighted fair queuing (WFQ), modified deficit round robin (MDRR), class-based (CBWFQ), and low latency queuing (LLQ).

A certain amount of bandwidth is allocated to each traffic class, for example, voice. The amount of bandwidth available to each traffic class is implemented as a queue. At some point, a queue gets too large (deep) and packets need to be dropped from that queue. The dropped packets should be data packets, not voice packets—as mentioned previously, voice quality is severely impaired if voice packets are dropped. Weighted random early detection (WRED) (discussed later in this chapter) should be used on data classes to monitor the queues and drop packets selectively. Never use WRED on voice queues. CAC ensures that the voice bandwidth in the voice queues is not oversubscribed so that voice packet loss is never necessary.

Dropping data packets typically occurs at the edge of the network when policing is enforced. Dropping in the core typically does not occur if sufficient bandwidth is provisioned.

- **Shaping**—Shaping, sometimes called *traffic shaping*, is a mechanism that smoothes excess packets in a queue. Shaping does not drop or mark these packets. Shaping is not typically used for voice packets because of added jitter. However, shaping is used in certain scenarios. For example, Frame Relay shaping is typically applied on any PVC that has voice and data traffic on it. Similarly, ATM PVC shaping is always active on ATM virtual circuits.

- **Fragmentation**—Necessary in networks that carry voice and data traffic over low-speed access links. Fragmentation helps reduce jitter that is caused by serializing a large packet onto the access link. The type of fragmentation scheme to use depends on the Layer-2 protocol used on the low-speed access link.

Using DiffServ for VoIP Services: The EF Behavior

In a VoIP network, the PHB is implemented in a router by using the available QoS building blocks previously discussed. A PHB is also implemented for other services that a service provider can implement, such as a premium data service. A premium data service requires its own PHB with its own unique set of QoS mechanisms. Each DSCP value is the mechanism that identifies a traffic class or a traffic aggregate that is assigned a PHB. The PHB implemented for voice traffic, that is VoIP, is invoked by the DSCP value of 101110 (binary value). This value identifies the EF PHB, which is used for delay-sensitive services, such as voice. Routers that do not support DSCP treat the EF DSCP value as IP Precedence 5, bit pattern 101. IP Precedence 5 is the value traditionally used for voice traffic, whereas IP Precedence 6 and 7 (the highest precedence values) are traditionally used for routing and control traffic.

Several DSCP values have been defined. These DSCP values are associated with the following PHB types:

- Default PHB
- Class Selector PHB
- Assured Forwarding PHB

The Default PHB is used for best-effort traffic. The Class Selector PHB is used for backward-compatibility of networks that are already using IP Precedence bits.

NOTE   DSCP is not backward-compatible with the ToS byte definition, as defined in RFC 791.

All the low-order three bits of the DSCP that are equal to zero identify the DSCP value for the Class Selector PHB. The Assured Forwarding PHB is used for premium data services. A service provider that wants to offer a premium data service in addition to its voice services would implement this PHB.

Implementing the EF Behavior

An EF PHB can be implemented on a router by using various QoS mechanisms that are supported by IOS.

The first step in implementing EF PHB is to classify and mark traffic that is entering the network, as shown in Figure 5-3.

Figure 5-3   *EF Mechanisms*

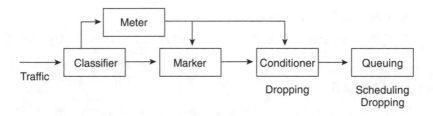

Classification identifies which class of traffic a packet belongs to. Marking colors packets by applying a unique value to an available marker, such as DHCP, to identify the class of traffic so that the correct PHB implementations in the router can be applied.

When service providers handle both voice and data traffic in their IP network, classifying and making traffic needs to occur as it enters the edge of the network.

Many mechanisms exist to accomplish classifying and marking traffic:

- Incoming/outgoing interface
- Predefined class-maps
- Standard or extended source/destination access list
- TCP or UDP ports
- DSCP
- IP Precedence value
- QoS group IDs (0–99) (discussed in QPPB section)
- NBAR
- Ethernet CoS value
- MPLS experimental bits
- Frame Relay DE bit

EF is Cisco's recommended treatment technique for voice traffic. Later in this chapter, the MPLS experimental bits are discussed in supporting DiffServ in a MPLS core network. The DSCP is also the mechanism that marks the packet, as previously discussed. Other methods of marking packets for voice service exist, including IP Precedence, QoS group ID, COS value, MPLS Exp, FR DE, and ATM CLP. EF is the recommended value for voice using DSCP. Multiple layers of protocols might be required to be marked to provide consistent DiffServ service end-to-end.

Various mechanisms can classify and mark traffic. Examples of these mechanisms follow:

- Dial Peer
- NBAR
- Policy-Based Routing (PBR)
- Class-Based (CB) marking
- QoS Policy Propagation through Border Gateway Protocol (BGP) (QPPB)

Dial Peer and NBAR

In many cases, voice gateway traffic is marked on the dial peer because of the lightweight nature of this mechanism. If the gateway doesn't belong to the service provider, NBAR (also called *stateful inspection*) can be used at the service provider's edge box. NBAR is a classification engine in Cisco IOS Software that can recognize and classify different web-based or client/server applications ranging from Layer 4 to Layer 7. After the application has been classified, appropriate QoS policies can be applied to the traffic classes.

PBR

PBR injects a route map to make a forwarding decision that is based on information other than the normal destination-based forwarding function of a router. While performing this task, PBR can color IP packets by marking the IP Precedence or QoS group. The two steps in implementing PBR follow:

Step 1 Create a route map.

Step 2 Apply the route map to an input interface.

NOTE The route map contains a match statement to match the source or destination IP address of a packet. Also, the route map can match any other parameter that can be matched by a standard or extended access list.

Unfortunately, PBR has two disadvantages. First, PBR cannot mark DSCP. Second, PBR has performance limitations with complex access lists that depend upon the router platform used. Access lists are one of the most CPU-intensive classification methods in IOS and are normally applied to low-speed links at the edge of the network. As mentioned earlier, the edge of the network is where packets are classified and marked. Classification in the core typically uses the DSCP or IP Precedence value of the IP packet. It is more common to use a mechanism called QPPB to classify and mark packets in a service provider network.

CB-Marking

CB-marking is another technique for classifying and marking traffic. CB-marking has extended marking capabilities compared to QPPB. CB-marking is capable of using the following extensive list of markers:

- IP Precedence
- DSCP
- MPLS experimental bits
- QoS group
- ATM CLP bit
- Frame Relay DE bit
- IEEE 802.1Q or Inter-Switch Link's (ISL's) CoS
- Using another class-map
- Input interface
- Source MAC address
- Destination MAC address
- RTP (UDP) port range

CB-marking is part of a modular QoS command-line interface (CLI) that is supported by IOS. This modular QOS CLI (MQC) separates classification from service policy. As a result, MQC allows any supported classification to be used with any QoS mechanism. Historically, the QoS mechanisms in IOS have supported their own unique set of classification methods.

The three steps in using MQC are as follows:

Step 1   Configure a class-map. This creates a classification to create a certain traffic class.

Step 2   Configure a policy-map. This associates the traffic class with one or more QoS features by using the **policy-map** command. The policy-map defines PHB.

Step 3   Create a service-policy. This applies the policy-map to an interface or PVC by using the **service-policy** command. Frame Relay and ATM are attached to the PVC.

The configuration listings in Example 5-1 show the creation of a class-map by using IP Precedence and DSCP PHBs.

Example 5-1   *Example of a Class-Map*

```
class-map VoIP
match ip precedence 5
!
class-map Best-effort
match ip precedence routine
!


class-map Voice
match ip dscp ef
!
class-map Best-effort
match ip dscp default
!
```

DSCP marking supports backward-compatibility with IP Precedence values. This is accomplished by using the Class Selector values, which are the most significant three bits of the DSCP value. The Class Selector supports DiffServ PHBs in a service provider network when using QPPB. Thus, a DSCP value EF is mapped to IP Precedence 5. It is not uncommon to include support routers that do not support DiffServ. This is especially true for service providers that upgrade their core to support DiffServ and that leave their edge routers to mark packets based on IP Precedence.

Besides using IP Precedence or DSCP, a QoS group can be used as another marker. Although a QoS group has the advantage of assigning up to 100 classes, there is a drawback of using a QoS group. This drawback is that a QoS group marking must be performed on every router because this value is only locally significant to a router. Therefore, after a packet leaves a router, the QoS group value is lost. The QoS group feature can be used in conjunction with mapping MPLS experimental bits to a DSCP value. Therefore, by using QPPB, BGP can automatically propagate the QoS group values, where class maps implement this on the router.

Creating a service policy is the second component of MQC. Policy-maps configure a service policy, which creates the PHB in a router. In other words, the service policy defines how the QoS mechanisms are applied to the traffic classes, as defined by the class-maps.

QPPB: QoS Policy Propagation Through BGP

Service providers have the dilemma of configuring hundreds of routers with the proper QoS characteristics to support voice traffic. Applying certain QoS mechanisms does not scale in a service provider network because access lists are required. For example, applying and maintaining access lists in a large-scale service provider network is not feasible because of operational costs.

Service providers can overcome this scaling issue with QPPB, which uses BGP attributes to disseminate QoS information within a network. BGP attributes assist in the task of classification and marking. Either the community attribute or autonomous system (AS) path can carry out this task. Community attributes normally encode the service provider's QoS policy and propagate this policy throughout the network. QPPB also marks packets with IP Precedence or a QoS group that is based on the QoS policy obtained through the BGP. Figure 5-4 provides an example of using QPPB to classify and mark packets that are going to a service provider's customer network. The packets received from the customer network are classified and marked by using class-based marking.

Figure 5-4 *QPPB Example*

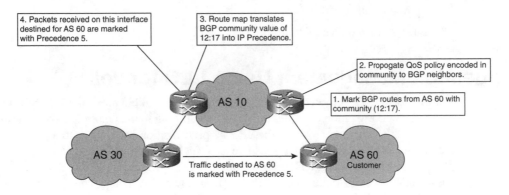

QPPB is carried out in four steps:

Step 1 All routes from a customer network (AS 60) are tagged with a community of 12:17 in the edge router in AS 10 that connects to AS 60. The QoS policy defined by the service provider is encoded into the 12:17 community value, which is a 32-bit value. The 32-bit community value is split into two 16-bit values. The first 16-bits, called the *high order bits*, defines the AS number. The second 16-bits represents the QoS policy.

Step 2 This edge router announces the community 12:17 through its neighbor statements.

Step 3 The QoS policy encoded in the community 12:17 is translated into either the IP Precedence or QoS group. This step occurs when the BGP route update is inserted into each router—all routes inserted in the routing table are processed against the route map. The QoS policy can be applied to source or destination IP addresses and networks.

Step 4 Packets are marked according to the value associated with its prefix held in the Forwarding Information Base (FIB) table. QoS mechanisms discussed previously use this type of classification to enforce their policies that are created on the router's interface.

Remember that Cisco Express Forwarding (CEF) and packet marking must be enabled on each interface on routers that perform marking. Any router not supporting marking does not have to support QPPB. These routers need to support only BGP. In summary, the following items need to be configured on QPPB-supported routers:

- Enable CEF.

- Create a route map. A route map translates the selected BGP attribute into the IP Precedence or QoS group.

- Apply the route map to process BGP routes before these routes are entered into the routing table.

- Enable per interface marking.

Congestion Management Using LLQ for VoIP

Historically, IP RTP prioritization has provided LLQ in combination with WFQ for VoIP traffic. RTP prioritization classifies the packets according to the UDP port, and measures and polices the amount of VoIP traffic. IP RTP prioritization provides a strict priority queuing scheme that allows delay-sensitive data, such as voice, to be sent before packets in other queues. In summary, RTP prioritization is a QoS mechanism in IOS that combines classification (that is, looking at the IP/UDP header) with queueing. This feature can be used with either WFQ or CBWFQ on the same outgoing interface.

With the use of MQC, RTP prioritization has been replaced with LLQ and a classification mechanism. As noted previously, MQC allows any supported classification to be used with any QoS mechanism. Therefore, LLQ provides a priority queue and also uses a policer on traffic to limit the bandwidth associated with the traffic class. This is required to implement EF so that EF PHBs can bind delays on links. Similar to RTP prioritization, LLQ can guarantee bandwidth for VoIP traffic. An EF PHB is invoked by the DHCP value of 101110. This value provides the classification of the traffic that is entering the router.

As discussed earlier, multiple classification methods exist to identify voice traffic that is entering a service provider network. IP Precedence and DSCP values are commonly used. In other cases, the **match ip rtp** command can match packets in cases where traffic is entering the network in conjunction with other traffic over a single interface. The **match ip rtp** command is typically combined with LLQ, as shown in Example 5-2. This method is similar to IP RTP prioritization—the pre-CBQ mechanism—which is defined in IOS.

Example 5-2   *Example of Class-Map Classifying by RTP Port Range*

```
class-map RTP
match ip rtp 16384 16383
!
class-map RTP
match ip rtp 16384 16383
!
```

After classifying the voice traffic by matching the RTP port range, LLQ can be applied. LLQ is a mechanism that can prioritize traffic. For example, CBWFQ creates multiple queues that are each associated with a particular traffic class. A scheduler is applied to these queues to guarantee bandwidth to each class. LLQ is an extension of CBWFQ in that it creates an additional queue that voice traffic can use. This additional queue is called a *priority queue*. It can be used for voice traffic, which is processed first by the scheduler. This process is shown in Figure 5-5.

The first stage of the LLQ process is classifying the traffic into different classes. For example, voice traffic can be classified by matching the IP Precedence to equal 5. Voice traffic is placed in the priority queue, while the other traffic is placed in other queues. Each of these queues is capable of being configured for a specified bandwidth. If the voice traffic exceeds its specified bandwidth, the voice traffic is dropped only if the remaining bandwidth has been used up by the traffic classes with guaranteed bandwidths (Class 1 and Class 2). This prevents starvation of other nonvoice traffic classes that are associated with the other queues. It is important to configure enough bandwidth to the priority queue to handle all the voice traffic.

Figure 5-5   *LLQ Process*

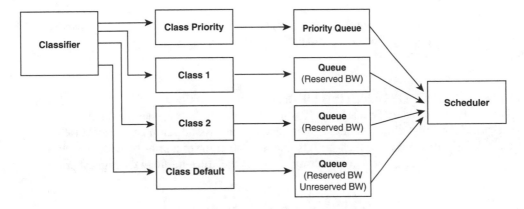

The Class Default traffic class is used by traffic that is not classified. Instead of reserving bandwidth, the Class Default queue can be set up so that the unclassified traffic uses any remaining bandwidth not used by the priority queue or the queues assigned with a guaranteed bandwidth. An example of configuring LLQ for voice traffic is shown in Example 5-3.

Example 5-3   *Example of Configuring LLQ for Voice Traffic*

```
class-map voip
match ip precedence 5
!
class-map premium
match ip precedence 3 4
```

continues

Example 5-3 *Example of Configuring LLQ for Voice Traffic (Continued)*

```
!
policy-map policy1
class voip
priority percent 20
class premium
bandwidth percent 30
class class-default
fair-queue
!
```

The **priority** command in this example creates the priority queue for voice, and the data traffic (class premium) is in a nonpriority queue. The **priority percent** command allocates a portion of the total link bandwidth to the voice priority queue. In this example, 20 percent of the available link bandwidth is assigned to VoIP traffic. Automatically, a policer is invoked that drops any packets that exceed this bandwidth. Alternatively, the absolute option, instead of the percent option, can allocate a fixed amount of bandwidth in kbps to the priority class.

NOTE   The preferred approach is to use a fixed amount of bandwidth (absolute bandwidth) for voice and to use percent for data.

The Cisco GSR 12000 uses MDRR (similar in function to WFQ for non-GSR platforms) to prioritize traffic that maps IP traffic to different CoS queues that are based on IP Precedence bits. These queues are then serviced on a round-robin basis except for one high-priority queue. The high-priority queue is either in strict priority mode or alternate priority mode. Strict priority mode always services the voice traffic in the highest priority.

Avoiding Congestion in VoIP Networks

Congestion avoidance techniques monitor network traffic loads to avoid congestion at potential bottleneck points in the network. Congestion avoidance is accomplished through packet dropping techniques. By default, a simple tail-drop is used on all queues in the event of congestion. More complex dropping mechanisms can perform a differentiated drop based on the IP Precedence or DSCP value. Specifically, WRED provides this capability. This technique is supported as part of MQC and is called CB-WRED. IOS, by default, implements 8 default values that are defined for precedence-based WRED and 64 values that are defined for DSCP-based WRED.

WRED should be used to control congestion on nonvoice queues to help prevent congestion on the link. Voice bandwidth should be controlled with CAC, not with queue tail-drop or policing.

CAC for VoIP Networks

The edge link from the edge gateway to the aggregation router in a service provider network is typically the area where bandwidth is most constrained. CAC is required if the edge gateways can generate more voice traffic than these links can support. The following items determine this condition:

- Call capacity supported by the gateways
- Voice codecs and packetization rates
- Available bandwidth on the link

Call admission is required for a network when worst-case bandwidth required per call times the number of DS-0s supported by the edge gateway is a significant percentage of the edge link bandwidth.

Call admission for VoIP calls is similar to call admission used by the public switched telephone network (PSTN). Before each call is made, the PSTN verifies that resources (DS-0s) are available to complete the call using out-of-band signaling, such as Signaling System 7 (SS7). For example, where a call is attempted during a busy calling period, such as Mother's Day, a fast busy is returned to the caller. A fast busy indicates that the call could not be completed because of lack of resources.

With call admission for VoIP, you can use other alternatives if resources are insufficient. For example, instead of returning a fast busy to the caller, the call can be rerouted to gateways that have sufficient resources, or part of the call can use the PSTN to complete the call.

Different mechanisms support CAC. This section focuses on the following three mechanisms:

- Local CAC
- Network CAC
- RSVP CAC

Local CAC uses the local gateway to determine if it has sufficient resources available (current VoIP connections, digital signal processors [DSPs] or memory) to support the call. Sufficient memory is also required to support Fax over IP because each gateway platform has specified upper limits in terms of calls per second and the maximum number of call connections. Network CAC validates network characteristics to determine if the network resources are available to support the call. These characteristics can include delay, packet loss, and jitter. Lastly, a reservation approach can support CAC. This approach keeps the resources available until the call is complete. RSVP is the protocol, defined by IETF, that sets up this reservation.

Local CAC

One way to apply local CAC is through trunk conditioning, which provides the capability to busy out a voice port. CAS ABCD signaling and Advanced Voice Busyout (AVBO) are two trunk conditioning mechanisms that you can use.

Analog telephony connections and digital T1/E1 on Cisco gateways use ABCD channel associated signaling (CAS). A telephone company (telco) switch using a certain ABCD bit pattern can indicate an Out-of-Service (OOS) condition. OOS condition signaling must differ from busy or seized signaling on the telco switch for this method to work. This capability is useful for assisting service providers in maintaining the SLA of a network. Thus, when network conditions degrade in the IP network, an OOS condition can be applied to selective gateway ports and ultimately signaled to the telco switch. For example, if a network connection to one of the service provider's destination partners degrades, the OOS condition can eliminate any further call attempts to this destination. This forces the telco switch to select an alternative path to route calls, and it safeguards the service provider by minimizing a customer's degradation of voice calls.

AVBO enables voice services to use the PSTN in the event of an IP network failure. The purpose of AVBO is to ensure that VoIP calls maintain a high level of voice quality in the event of network link failure. For example, if a locally connected interface on a VoIP gateway fails, the voice ports associated with that interface are busied out. This issues a signal to the telco switch to reroute the call to the PSTN.

AVBO actually monitors links to remote IP interfaces by using Cisco's Service Assurance Agent (SAA). AVBO enables individual voice ports on the gateway to change to a busyout state in the event that loss of IP connectivity is detected. Loss of IP connectivity is defined as a threshold for packet delay and packet loss, which must be established.

NOTE   SAA is discussed in Chapter 9, "Network Management: Maintaining an SLA."

Network CAC

Network CAC involves probing and checking the network to determine the state of the network resources needed to support a call. In fact, a near real-time check can be made on the call path before the call is actually established. This check can determine the network characteristics (delay, packet loss, and delay variance) and determine if the call can be made. If the results are not acceptable, an alternative path can be checked. In the event that no IP network paths are available to sustain the required SLA of the provider for the call, the call can be redirected to the PSTN. This action is called *PSTN fallback*.

For PSTN fallback to work, the service provider must define the necessary congestion thresholds to determine the quality of the network resources in establishing a call. These thresholds must correspond to the service providers' SLA. The Calculated Planning Impairment Factor (ICPIF) is a measurement that PSTN providers use to calculate congestion. The standard ITU G.113 defines that ICPIF measures the quality of the network in supporting voice. ICPIF supports a variable called *total impairment value* that is composed of delay, packet loss, and codecs used. A probe conducted by the SAA obtains the total impairment value. One of the drawbacks with this approach is that a new SAA probe, which simulates a voice call, needs to be established for every call.

RSVP CAC

RSVP can reserve and guarantee the delay and packet loss for each call in an end-to-end manner. The challenges of doing this are similar to setting the IP Precedence to a high priority to ensure the proper handling of VoIP packets. All routers in the call path must recognize and handle the IP Precedence in the same manner. Typically, this is difficult to achieve in a service provider network that attaches to multiple peering partners. RSVP can encounter the same problem. RSVP copes with the fact that some routers don't support it, and this is an acceptable way to use RSVP if congestion isn't a problem in the backbone.

Another well-known drawback of RSVP is scalability because it maintains state information per call flow. This issue arises in the core instead of the edge of the network. To resolve this issue, the service provider creates one reservation on the backbone. This feature is called *Aggregate RSVP*.

NOTE   The IETF standard for aggregating RSVP is RFC 3175. Aggregate RSVP enables a single reservation on behalf of a group of individual call flows in a DiffServ network.

RSVP has hooks into different queuing mechanisms, such as PQ and LLQ, to support CAC. RSVP CAC and SAA can be used together. RSVP is used for call-by-CAC, and SAA probes can provide trunk conditioning and AVBO. SAA probes can determine if trunks should be turned off. For example, a high threshold can be configured to activate turning off trunk ports. This eliminates trunks being turned on and off too often.

RSVP also provides for a mechanism to handle end-to-end signaled QoS for handling Voice, as well as video calls. Another important requirement for handling voice traffic is providing preemption capabilities. Any VoIP implementation will require a mechanism to handle emergency calls such as police, fire, or hospital services. RSVP provides an excellent mechanism to ensure that these calls get through, even if they need to drop off lower priority calls.

MPLS Supporting Voice

MPLS is a recent technology that has gained popularity with service providers. MPLS uses labels to switch IP packets in a network. Using this technique and other MPLS features, new services are available within the IP network. Traffic engineering and creating Virtual Private Networks (VPNs) are two key services that MPLS provides to an existing IP network. A service provider can create traffic-engineered tunnels that are based on existing traffic analysis to support load balancing across different network paths. A service provider can also create VPNs within their IP network by using MPLS, which eliminates the need to support dedicated point-to-point network connections. MPLS VPNs can support overlapping IP address space, which enables a service provider to have multiple customers using the same IP address.

MPLS TE

Traffic engineering is the MPLS application that assists in supporting voice services. Traffic engineering allows a service provider to efficiently use the bandwidth available in a network by using nonshortest paths as well. MPLS traffic engineering (MPLS TE) combines the fundamental mechanisms of routing (by introducing OSPF and ISIS extensions) and QoS (by introducing RSVP extensions) to ensure that VoIP traffic can traverse a path that is most suitable to least delay, jitter, and packet loss. MPLS traffic engineering (MPLS TE) sets up tunnels between two points to satisfy a certain bandwidth requirement. For example, a MPLS-TE tunnel can exchange VoIP traffic and data traffic between two locations over an IP network, while supporting QoS requirements of the VoIP traffic, as shown in Figure 5-6.

Figure 5-6 *Creating a Voice Trunk Using MPLS TE*

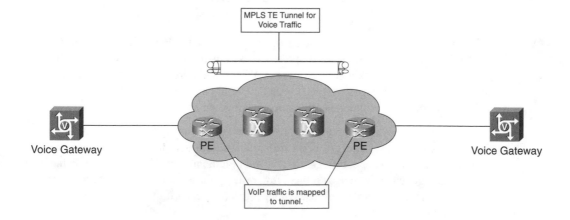

A voice trunk across the MPLS network is implemented by using a MPLS-TE tunnel. The tunnel can either be set up manually or configured dynamically. RSVP with MPLS extensions dynamically configures the tunnel. The Interior Gateway Protocol (IGP), either Open Shortest Path First (OSPF) or Intermediate System-to-Intermediate System (IS-IS), advertises unallocated capacity on network links to support automatically setting up a tunnel. When a tunnel is established, the bandwidth capacity requirement, administrative attribute, and class of traffic that dictate a certain policy determine which path to take between the two endpoints. This step overrides the default process of setting up a default tunnel that is based on the shortest path that IGP calculates. The class of traffic parameter is checked during the constraint-based path computation of the tunnel.

A new capability called *Diffserv-aware Traffic Engineering* or *DS-TE* extends the current MPLS-TE capabilities to be aware of the class of traffic when computing the path of the tunnel across the MPLS network. This capability is necessary to engineer voice and data traffic differently. This is accomplished by assigning a different pool of bandwidth to voice than the data traffic. Traditionally, MPLS TE supports only a single bandwidth pool on the link for traffic inside a tunnel. Therefore, MPLS TE can perform only admission control and QoS mechanisms on the aggregate bandwidth. As a result, data and voice traversing this tunnel uses the same bandwidth pool and cannot be engineered as two classes of traffic, only a single class. This means that the bandwidth used by the voice cannot be guaranteed and be overridden by the data traffic.

To overcome this limitation, DS-TE provides constraint-based routing on a per class basis. One of the mechanisms to accomplish this is to create two bandwidth pools on each link in the network and associate the voice traffic bandwidth pool to an LLQ. RSVP also assists in reserving the voice traffic bandwidth. Therefore, using DS-TE, voice traffic can be routed over links that have the least amount of packet delay, while ensuring that nonvoice traffic is routed over links that have greater delay. Each pool of bandwidth can be independently allocated and matched with the lower-level queues. This allows for flexibility in a DS-TE deployment by ensuring that voice traffic is not oversubscribed, while nonvoice traffic might be oversubscribed. DS-TE enables LLQ to be applied to voice traffic to ensure that bandwidth requirements are met. Admission control is performed over this pool of bandwidth.

NOTE   A *bandwidth pool* represents the bandwidth of the link or the bandwidth that the service provider wants to use on this link. This helps better control bandwidth use on network links. Many intercontinental service providers support expensive links between different continents or countries, which requires them to efficiently use the bandwidth on these links. Voice traffic (EF traffic) needs to be certain that it does not traverse a link with high-traffic use, which can introduce high delay. DS-TE can create a tunnel for EF traffic, which has sufficient bandwidth to meet the constraints; however, the DS-TE might not find the shortest path when initially establishing the tunnel.

Fast Re-Route for Voice

MPLS has a new capability called Fast Re-Route that introduces Synchronous Optical Network (SONET)-like restoration into MPLS networks. This mechanism does not exist in IP networks where restoration is accomplished by routing protocol convergence, which might not be fast enough for voice services. Fast Re-Route introduces a local restoration mechanism that enables a quick SONET-like restoration to route around a failed link or node. In normal IGP routing such as OSPF, after the failure detection, IGP must reflood with new updates to the other routers in the network. Fast Re-Route sets up a tunnel before the failure, which enables support for SONET-like restoration times.

Summary

This chapter discussed QoS components and architectures to consider in supporting VoIP services:

- Fundamental QoS mechanisms
- Congestion avoidance
- MPLS-based VoIP network

Fundamental QoS mechanisms that are supported by Cisco routers include classification, policing, marking, and queuing. A router implements a DiffServ PHB by using these mechanisms to support voice and data services. A specific type of PHB called EF supports voice traffic. EF PHB requires traffic to be classified and marked and uses mechanisms such as IP Precedence, DSCP, QoS Group Ids, and MPLS experimental bits to accomplish this. Classifying and marking traffic in a large service provider network is a challenge. QPPB, which leverages BGP routing, can classify and mark traffic in a service provider network.

Avoiding congestion in VoIP networks is an important design component. CAC is an important congestion avoidance technique. Multiple mechanisms exist to help implement these capabilities, including local CAC, network CAC, and RSVP CAC.

DS-TE and Fast Re-Route, recent features in MPLS, are key ingredients in supporting voice in a service provider MPLS network. Many service providers are currently testing and evaluating these features.

CHAPTER 6

Implementing the PSTN Switch/VoIP Gateway Trunk

This chapter covers different circuit types and signaling types used to interconnect a Cisco gateway to a PSTN switch. The PSTN switch can be either a Class 4 or Class 5 switch. This chapter covers three common signaling types—T1 CAS, PRI, and SS7—that can interconnect a VoIP gateway to a PSTN switch. Each signaling type has a set of parameters used to implement the PSTN Switch/VoIP gateway trunk. This set of signaling parameters is referred to in this chapter as a template. This chapter provides an overview of key signaling parameters that need to be established when interconnecting a gateway to a PSTN switch. This chapter also identifies key troubleshooting techniques to use when interconnecting a VoIP gateway to a PSTN switch.

Overview of VoIP Gateway to PSTN Connectivity

Interconnecting to the PSTN has been the standard architecture for service providers that offer VoIP services. However, some service providers do not need to interconnect to the PSTN. Service providers that provide clearinghouse services have interconnectivity to other peering partners by using direct IP links rather than time-division multiplexing (TDM) links. Direct IP interconnect over the past couple of years has become more common because of the fast adoption of VoIP services by service providers and the fast growth of large enterprise customers that use VoIP-based private branch exchange (PBX) services.

Two elements define the PSTN interconnection types:

- Circuit types
- Signaling types

Circuit Types

Circuit types can be categorized into two types of standard carrier systems:

- Traditional digital carrier systems
- Optical-based digital carrier systems

Traditional digital carrier systems define types of circuits that can be used for trunk connectivity. These types of circuits are defined in a hierarchy of digital transmission rates. The two most common circuits that North American service providers use are DS1 (1.544 Mbps) and DS3. DS3 is 672 DS0s or 44.736 Mbps, which is typically called 45 Mbps.

NOTE   Digital signal hierarchy is based on the American National Standards Institute (ANSI) T1.107-1995 guidelines, which use the terms DS1 and DS3.

Other regions of the world, such as mainland Europe, the U.K., and South America use a different hierarchy of transmission rates. Other transmission rates that commonly define circuit types are E1 (2.048 Mbps) that is defined in ITU-T G.703/704 and E3 (34.368 Mbps) that is defined in ITU-T G.751. DS3 is an exception. Besides North America, DS3 is available in mainland Europe and the U.K.

Optical-based digital systems define optical circuits such as OC-3 and OC-12. OCs are used when higher transmission rates than DS3 are required. Service providers commonly use optical transport systems, especially incumbent local exchange carriers (ILECs), in transporting DS1 and DS3 circuits between central offices (COs) and interexchange carriers (IXCs).

Signaling Types

The connectivity between a VoIP gateway and a PSTN switch is referred to as a *trunk*. Logically, a trunk is viewed as a talk-path between switching machines. The number of trunks that are supported is defined by the capacity of the circuit between the gateway and the PSTN switch. For example, a T1 can support 24 trunks while a T3 can support 672 trunks. A digital trunk can provide two main types of PSTN signaling:

- **In-band signaling**—Any signaling that uses the same physical facility as the voice traffic and that interleaves the signaling message with the voice payload. For example, channel associated signaling (CAS) is in-band because the signaling is carried in the same DS0 as the speech path. In-band signaling includes CAS, Multifrequency tones (MF), and dual tone multifrequency (DTMF). In-band signaling types travel over E1 facilities for countries outside of North America and over T1 in the United States and Canada.

- **Out-of-band signaling**—Also called *common channel signaling (CCS)*; the separation of signaling and bearer traffic. As an example, voice traffic is carried on the bearer channel (B channel), and the signaling is carried on the data channel (D channel) in ISDN. The two main signaling systems in this area are Signaling System 7 (SS7) and Primary Rate Interface (PRI). Both of these systems can be classified into two main instances of signaling systems, Facility Associated Signaling (FAS) and Non-Facility Associated Signaling (NFAS). NFAS signaling is where the signaling channel is not carried over the same physical facility as the bearer information. FAS is exactly the opposite. In North America and Canada, SS7 is usually an NFAS application. NFAS is discussed in further detail later in this chapter. The signaling channel is carried on a physical circuit separate from the bearer traffic. In fact, a separate network is dedicated to carrying SS7. This separate network is mostly composed of signal transfer points (STPs) that provide a routing capability for voice signaling traffic. Service providers commonly use SS7 to interconnect to the PSTN or to peering partners. The Cisco PGW2200 can be used to interconnect to the PSTN using SS7. In this case, the PGW2200 provides the SS7 signaling connection, and the VoIP gateway connects to the partner switch by using Inter-Machine Trunks (IMTs), which do not carry any signaling information, only bearer traffic. An IMT is a DS0 and normally are multiplexed into a T1 or T3.

The service provider, in most cases, uses SS7 for network interconnection between CLASS 4/5 switches. PRI is normally used to connect the service provider to an Enterprise PBX. The use of in-band signaling is primarily because of the lack of an out-of-band method and is prominent in the areas of 911 and operator services. Many PBXs require an in-band trunking interconnection because some COs are not equipped for PRI services, only CAS.

Later sections in this chapter focus on three common PSTN interconnection types:

- T1 CAS trunks
- PRI trunks
- SS7 interconnection

A template is defined for each interconnection type to ensure that the appropriate parameters are chosen. This helps to ensure interoperability between the VoIP gateway and the PSTN switch. This template can be used to help identify the key parameters associated with a certain interconnection type, such as SS7. Before discussing these templates, review the fundamentals of T1, E1, and DS3.

Case Study: JIT VoIP Network

Figure 6-1 shows a network of a fictitious service provider called Jim's International Traffic (JIT).

Figure 6-1 *JIT's VoIP Network*

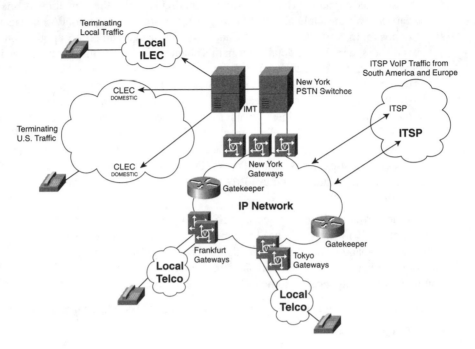

JIT's VoIP network is drawn here to show a sample of different trunk interconnection scenarios.

JIT's initial services include terminating international voice traffic to United States-based ILECs and aggregating voice traffic bound to international-based carriers and Posts, Telephones, and Telegraphs (PTTs). JIT's network consists of two PSTN switches that are located in the service provider's New York facility to serve as its main United States point of presence (POP). JIT owns PSTN switches to facilitate routing decisions among different peering partners and soon will be transitioning to a GKTMP based route server to implement routing decisions. Cost and service levels established with peering partners are two key factors in determining the route.

A peering partner has been established with a South American and European Internet telephony service provider (ITSP). The South American and European ITSP originates and terminates VoIP traffic. JIT's network provides a direct connection to local ILECs and competitive local exchange carriers (CLECs) for terminating local area traffic and interlocal access and transport area (LATA) traffic, respectively. T1s, E1s, and DS3s interconnect their VoIP gateways to the PSTN switches that are located at the ILECs, CLECs, and PTTs.

NOTE	LATAs are telephone service areas in the United States that were negotiated during the breakup of the Bell telephone system in the early 1980s. Toll calls within an LATA are called *intraLATA toll calls* or *local toll calls*. Toll calls between LATAs are called interLATA toll calls. Most states have several LATAs; therefore, not all interLATA toll calls are state-to-state.

JIT's network uses three types of trunk connectivity between a VoIP gateway and a PSTN switch: T1, E1, and DS3.

JIT's decision on which trunk type to use is influenced by its peering partner. JIT has recently started a wholesale VoIP service and plans to leverage the existing PSTN switches that support T1 and E1. JIT uses DS3 trunks to connect its VoIP gateways to its peering partner because of large amounts of projected traffic. The next section provides a review of these three trunk types.

T1, E1, and DS3 Fundamentals

Using T1s to Interconnect to the PSTN

T1 is normally a four-wire circuit that uses two wires for transmit and two wires for receive. These four wires are normally terminated by an eight-position connector that is called an RJ-48C interface, which is then connected to a channel service unit/data service unit (CSU/DSU) device. Referencing the pin layout of an RJ-48C connector is helpful because one of the first obstacles in bringing up a T1 connection is identifying the correct transmit and receive pairs on each end.

A termination punchdown block, such as a BIX, 66, or 110 block, connects the T1 wiring from each end point when a service provider provides a large number of T1 circuits. An RJ-21X, commonly called an Amphenol connector, is a 50-pin connector that can be used with a punchdown block. Most punchdown blocks have a wire-wrap interface on the rear where the T1 connections are terminated from the telephone company (telco) and gateway sides. Some punchdown blocks support RJ-48X jacks where the customer plugs equipment. RJ-48X jacks have loopback, unlike RJ-48C jacks. This makes the RJ jack loop the signal back toward the network when the customer disconnects equipment. This type of punchdown block prevents *loss of signal (LOS)* alarms on the service provider's TDM switching equipment.

Another common method of terminating T1 circuits is through a *digital signal crossconnect (DSX)* panel. DSX panels can be described as containing In, Out, and Monitor jacks on the front of the panel. Each In and Out jack provides direct access to the T1 input and output signals by using a passive design. These signals are terminated on the DSX panel by wire-wrapping the T1 wires on the back of the DSX panel. The front of a DSX panel enables a T1 send/receive pair to be patched to another T1 send/receive pair by inserting a bantum cable (called a *bantum jack*) into the In and Out jacks. This mechanism quickly transfers to backup T1 circuits or backup VoIP gateways during testing, or for troubleshooting and restoring services. For example, the Monitor jack can access the T1 signals and is analyzed by a T1 analyzer device.

A T1 circuit is a digital stream of 24 channels of 64-kbps each, which equals a total capacity of 1.536 Mbps. Each timeslot is called a DS-0, which is sampled 8,000 times per second by using an 8-bit word to represent the sample, thus, yielding 64-kbps per channel. However, most people refer to T1 as 1.544 Mpbs of bandwidth. Where is the extra bandwidth coming from? T1 circuits multiplex the 24 channels into a frame and then add a framing bit before transmitting the channels for frame synchronization. This framing bit produces a 193-bit frame (8 bit sample of each 24 channels + 1 frame bit). Because there are 8000 frames per second, and a T1 frame is 125 usecs, this results in an additional 8 kbps for the T1 frame bit. Therefore, the 1.536 Mbps increases to 1.544 Mbps because of the T1 framing bits. The 1.544 Mbps signal is referred to as a DS-1 regardless of the physical media that carries the signal. A T1 circuit is the most widely used method to carry the DS1 signal; the T1 further defines a digital transmission system that makes use of the DS1 rate.

NOTE   Sometimes, DS1 and T1 are used interchangeably in the industry; however, there is a distinction between the two terms.

A service provider might terminate its line with a device called a *smart jack*, which can be located at the customer premises in a locked enclosure. The PSTN switch incoming signal, which traveled perhaps up to 3000 feet of wire after leaving the last repeater, enters the customer premises at a low level. The smart jack typically is not set up to regenerate the signal, so it continues on to the extended demarc jack and the CSU at this low level. A smart jack is similar to a CSU in that it provides diagnostic and loopback capability, which the carrier can control remotely. This enables the carrier to diagnose most problems without the customer intervening. A CSU is actually customer-owned and provides four main functions:

- Loopback
- Signal regeneration
- Keepalive signal
- Extended Superframe (ESF) statistics

Similar to the smart jack, the CSU provides other loopback capabilities. The CSU creates a loopback of the full T1 if a certain sequence of bits are issued to it. The CSU regenerates the signal that is received from the network and regenerates this signal. This particular interface is called the DSX-1 interface. The keepalive signal is generated by the CSU when customer premises equipment (CPE), such as a VoIP gateway, is disconnected or is malfunctioning. This state generates an *alarm indication signal (AIS)*, also known as a *blue alarm*. The CSU sends a continuous stream of unframed 1s to identify an AIS. Lastly, the CSU collects performance information produced from the ESF in-band signaling and is normally saved within Simple Network Management Protocol Management Information Base (SNMP MIB) tables.

A DSU converts data signals into a T1 format, which ensures the proper line encoding and proper timing. A DSU generates a signal called a DSX-1, which is a short-haul T1 signal that is capable of driving the signal 655 feet. DSX-1 levels are typically used when connecting a Cisco router directly to a PSTN switch that is also using a DSX-1 interface. CSU and DSU functionality is integrated on many routers. For example, Cisco's Multichannel DS1/PRI port adapters integrate CSU functionality, DSU functionality, and DS-0 channel support into the Cisco router. The Multichannel DS1/PRI port adapter provides two, four, or eight independent T1 connections through RJ-48C connectors.

Using E1s to Interconnect to a PSTN

E1 physical connectors and distribution frames are the same as T1. For example, RJ-48C can be used as the connection to terminate within a router. The difference in E1 is that it has 32 channels, six more than T1; numbering begins from timeslot 0 to timeslot 31. Similar to a T1 frame, taking 8 bit samples of 30 channels every 125 microseconds creates the E1 frame. As a result, a 2.048-Mbps line rate can be achieved; however, 1.92 Mbps (30×64 kbps) is the usable bit rate. Two of the 32 channels are dedicated for framing, synchronization, and signaling information. Timeslot 0 contains framing and synchronization information to indicate the start of each frame. Timeslot 16 is used for channel-associated signaling and is also used as the D channel in E1 PRI. Unlike T1, which must steal bits from user channels, E1 uses a separate channel (such as timeslot 16) for call setup.

Similar to a Super Frame (SF), E1 supports the concatenation of 16 multiple E1 frames. These 16 E1 frames are referred to as a multiframe.

Using DS3s to Interconnect to the PSTN

DS3 is equivalent to 28 T1s. DS3 within a VoIP network enables increased port density, lower per port cost, ease of deployment, and ease of provisioning. Because of much higher call volumes being seen in wholesale VoIP, DS3 is typically more cost effective than buying separate T1s.

The three common framing methods for DS3 are M13 and M23, C-bit parity, and unframed.

NOTE   The type of DS3 framing affects the interpretation of the error statistics.

One method of creating a DS3 signal is called M13, which consists of two steps:

Step 1   The 28 DS1 signals multiplex into seven separate DS2 signals; each DS2 signal contains four DS1 signals. This process is called *M12 multiplexing*.

Step 2   The seven DS2 signals are combined to create a DS3 signal. This process is called *M23*.

M23 multiplexing, followed by M12 multiplexing, is accomplished to obtain T1 lines from a DS3. Similar to T1, framing bits that are referred to as F-bits, and multiframing bits that are referred to as M-bits, assist in identifying the framing within the DS3 signal. DS3 also supports C-bits that control bit stuffing.

The C-bit parity method of creating a DS3 eliminates the need for using the C-bits for stuffing. This method is possible because of more accurate clocking sources available in today's networks. The C-bits are used for end-to-end performance monitoring and in-band data-link control messages, similar to the T1 ESF methods. The C-bit method is much more popular than the M13 method because M13 cannot provide end-to-end, in-band control messages. The C-bit parity method can be automatically identified if the first C-bit, called the *indication bit*, is set to 1, and if the framing is set to automatic detection on a DS3 port on a router. If the C-bit indication bit is 0, the DS3 controller sets the framing to M23.

Unframed, also referred to as *clear channel*, DS3 connections enable a service provider to provide subrates or tiered services to an ITSP. Providing subrates, such as 20 Mbps, enables an ITSP to match the traffic capacity more closely to the required transmission bandwidth. Providing subrate service requires the same DS3 DSU equipment on both ends of the link because subrate service is a proprietary procedure. Also, a near-full unchannelized DS3 capacity can be supported at 44.210 Mbps with certain framing bits, such as the C-bits, to ensure compatibility with DS3 equipment.

DS3 defines a set of codes called *far end alarm and control (FEAC)* that enable a DS3 port to send alarm or status information and DS3 idle and loopback requests. C-bit framing, one of the framing types of DS3, provides provisions for control of the local facility loopback by the far end by the in-band FEAC channel. Similar to T1, DS3 can be turned to an idle state to indicate to the far end that the line is administratively down but not in a fault state, which eliminates any alarm conditions on the DS3 circuit. DS3 also supports a Facility Data Link (FDL) communications channel for the purpose of exchanging data-link control messages by using the Link Access Procedure on the D Channel (LADP) protocol.

A common type of physical interface that is found on Cisco routers and gateways for DS3 is the DSX-3 interface, with two female 75-ohm BNC coaxial connectors per port (separate receive and transmit). If the DS3 interface supports long-range build-outs, the DS3 distance can be extended to as much as 450 feet. The DSX-3 long-range distance, referred to as long-range build out (LBO), is 450 feet. Similar to T1 termination panels, DS3 also uses DSX panels to provide a mechanism for easily testing and redistributing DS3 signals. The following are the typical characteristics of a DS3:

- **Common framing**—Unframed, C-bit, M23
- **Line coding**—bipolar 3-zero substitution (B3ZS)
- **Error checking**—16- and 32-bit cyclic redundancy checks (CRCs) supported
- **FEAC codes**—Yes
- **Alarms supported**
  - AIS—Indicates an upstream error condition
  - LOS—Indicates Tx signal is not present
  - OOF—Out of frame
  - LCV—Line code violation
  - EXZ—Excessive zeros
  - FERF—Far-end receive failure
- **Common Serial Encapsulation**
  - HDLC—High-level data link control

A common method of delivering DS3 service is through a Synchronous Optical Network (SONET) ring. SONET equipment, such as the Cisco ONS 15454, can easily drop and insert subrate DS3 or full DS3 service to a service provider through fiber optics. For example, an ITSP can purchase its own SONET equipment or have a carrier-managed SONET multiplexer at its POP. This scenario enables the ITSP to use one carrier to transport its data and its local or long distance voice traffic. In these scenarios, the voice traffic is backhauled to the service provider's CLASS 5 switches over a SONET ring that can support up to OC-192.

T1 CAS Trunks

The establishment and release of calls in telco networks are invoked by signals. Here is an example of the sequence of events that occur in starting and ending a call:

1 The gateway seizes a trunk to its local PSTN switch.

2 The gateway signals the digits of the called party to the local PSTN switch.

3 The local PSTN switch determines which trunk to route the call based on the called-party number and attempts to establish a connection to the called party through the PSTN (details not described here).

4   Assuming that the called party is not busy, the called PSTN switch returns an ACM (Address Complete Message), which is passed back to the originating PSTN switch. Because a bearer channel already exists all the way back to the calling party, the called switch also returns a ringback tone. The originating PSTN switch is operating in RECEIVE-ONLY mode, so the calling party can hear ringing from the remote end. In some occasions, a ringback tone is locally generated.

5   When the local PSTN switch is signaled from the PSTN that the called party has answered, the local PSTN switch sends an answer signal to the gateway. The local PSTN switch also switches to SEND-RECEIVE mode.

6   A call is established.

7   A set of signals is exchanged when the call is released.

Various T1 CAS schemes are used for signaling. Depending upon the type of T1 framing, either A and B bits or ABCD bits emulate analog signaling. Loop-start and ground-start are two seizure-signaling methods that can be emulated by T1. Several types of ear and mouth (E&M) signaling also are supported, including the following:

- Immediate start
- Delay dial
- Wink Start

E&M is the most common trunk seizure-signaling method used on telco trunks. E&M is referred to as CAS, which transmits signal information in the same channel as the voice call, which is also referred to as *in-band signaling*.

NOTE   DTMF tones are commonly carried in-band with the audio.

CAS interleaves signaling bits within voice bits over the 24 channels in a T1 circuit, which allows 24 channels to be available. However, the cost of using this method is that the least significant bit (LSB) of every byte in frames 6, 12, 18, and 24 is used for signaling in ESF. Thus, CAS is a signaling technique that uses robbed bits within a multiframe, such as a D4 SF or ESF. These robbed bits, referred to as ABCD bits, represent various states and transitions of a voice call. Only bits A and B are used in a D4 SF that provides fewer signaling and control states than in ESF. However, in most cases, service providers use only the A and B bits regardless of D4 (SF) or D5 (ESF) framing, and the C and D bits go unused.

After seizing the trunk, some flavors of CAS signaling also can receive automatic number identification (ANI) and dialed number identification service (DNIS) information. This supports authentication billing functions. ANI refers to the sending of the calling number that identifies the origination address. DNIS is the sending of the dialed number that identifies the destination address. In all the E&M protocols, off-hook is indicated by A = 1 and B = 1, and on-hook is indicated by A = 0 and B = 0.

T1 CAS Trunk Template

Protocol/trunks: T1 CAS

Signal characteristics: Wink Start, DTMF, DNIS

Line code method: Alternate mark inversion (AMI)

Framing mode: D4

Incoming digit format: country code (CC)+ dialed number (DN)

Outgoing digit format: 1 + 10 digit DN (for CC = 1). All other CCs use 011 + CC + DN.

Signal Type

Signal type indicates the type of robbed-bit signaling. Cisco's E&M implementation includes support for the following signal types:

- Feature Group B using DTMF signaling with DNIS support
- Feature Group D using DTMF signaling with DNIS support
- Immediate-Start

Line Code Method

The line code method defines how the digital signals on the physical link present the data, which is called Layer-1 line encoding. Four common types of line codes follow:

- Bipolar 8-zero substitution (B8ZS)
- AMI
- High density binary 3 (HDB3)
- B3ZS

NOTE   B3ZS is used only with DS3.

HDB3 is used in Europe. For example, E1 circuits are normally assigned HDB3 by PTTs. Similar to a T1 64-kbps clear channel that uses B8ZS, E1 supports a 64-kbps clear channel that uses HDB3.

ESF is associated with B8ZS coding and D4 SF is associated with AMI.

Framing Mode

T1 uses more than one type of framing format. The most commonly used framing formats are as follows:

- SF

- ESF (ANSI and International Telecommunication Union [ITU] G.704)

- Unframed

An SF consists of 12 individual T1 frames. A common type of SF is D4. The D4 SF uses a framing pattern to support both voice and data. Signaling information is contained within frames 6 and 12 of a SF. The 8th bit from each sample taken in frames 6 and 12 provides these signaling bits, which are referred to as the A and B bits. This bit robbing decreases the channels to 56 kbps of capacity. One of the disadvantages of using D4 signaling is that the A and B bits support only four states of signaling, which limits the amount of signaling information to be transferred in-band.

Today, most T1 trunks use ESF, which consists of 24 individual T1 frames. The 24 framing bits are grouped into three functions called *channels*:

- Framing and synchronization (6 bits used, consuming 2 kbps)

- Detection of errors that uses a CRC-6 check (6 bits used, consuming 2 kbps)

- Data-link control messages (12 bits used, consuming 4 kbps)

The International Telecommunication Union Telecommunication Standardization Sector (ITU-T) has standardized the SF and ESF as an international standard called the G.704. G.704 is essentially equivalent with a couple of minor differences in the communication of alarm information. In the G.704 version of SF and ESF, the ITU-T standard changes the 12th frame signaling bit from a 0 to a 1 to indicate the AIS, and the SF and ESF uses unframed all-1s to indicate the AIS. The G.704 also has no provisions for indicating a yellow alarm. A yellow alarm is a remotely detected failure, whereas a red alarm is a locally detected failure. A red alarm, which might be invoked by a loss of signal and loss of frame locally, will cause a yellow alarm at the remote end.

The unframed mode indicates that the T1 circuit does not support the 24-channel frame structure. Even though an unframed T1 does not have a structured signal, it still needs to support a method of line encoding such as AMI or B8ZS.

Incoming and Outgoing Digit Format

PSTN switches route incoming digits in a proprietary manner. PSTN switches normally select the outgoing route based on the called-party number received from the gateway. Most PSTN switches expect all incoming calls in the format of country code + dialed number (CC + DN). Another method to select the outgoing route is to use the carrier identification code (CIC). All long distance carriers, and many long distance resellers, have their own unique CIC. Each code starts with the digits 101, followed by a unique four digit number. For example, if a carrier's CIC is 0222, its code would be 1010222. This seven digit code overrides a presubscribed long distance carrier on a per-call basis. The seven digits is collectively called the Carrier Access Code (CAC).

PRI Trunks

A VoIP gateway must be selected that supports a channelized T1 controller that is capable of ISDN PRI. PRI signaling is the most widely used type of CCS, which refers to signaling systems in which all signaling is transported in a separate, dedicated signaling channel that can be shared by a group of voice channels. For example, a DS1 circuit can use one 64-kbps timeslot to carry the signaling information that serves all other channels on the DS1 circuit. Because a separate channel is used for signaling, you cannot use one DS0 for voice transmission, which decreases the available T1 channels to 23 voice channels. These voice channels are commonly referred to as the B channels. The signaling channel for PRI is referred to as the D channel, which conforms to ITU-T Q.921 for the Layer-2 protocol and ITU-T Q.931 for the Layer-3 protocol. This single D channel can control other PRI circuits with NFAS. With NFAS, a group of PRIs can be established so that only one D channel from one of the PRIs is used. This allows the other PRIs in the NFAS group to use all 24 DS0s as B channels. NFAS is described in more detail later in this section.

The next sections describe Q.921 and Q.931 because understanding the fundamentals of ISDN signaling can help troubleshoot many signaling problems by using a T1/E1 ISDN analyzer.

Q.921

The Q.921 protocol provides a full-duplex, reliable data link between a gateway and a PSTN switch. Figure 6-2 shows a sequence of Q.921 messages that occurs on a PRI to establish the Layer-2 data link.

Figure 6-2   *Q.921 Layer-2 Establishment*

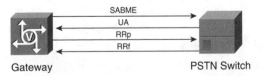

Set Asynchronous Balanced Mode Extended (SABME), disconnect (DISC), disconnect mode (DM), and unnumbered acknowledgment (UA) messages, as defined in Q.921, start and end the Layer-2 connection between the gateway and the PSTN switch. The gateway or the switch sends a SABME to establish the data-link connection. The service access point identifier (SAPI) is set to 0 to indicate that the data link is being used for signaling. The SABME needs to be acknowledged by a UA frame. After the data-link connection is established, Layer 3 INFO frames, as defined in Q.931, can be exchanged. INFO frames are acknowledged by other INFO frames or by RR frames. The INFO and RR frames function as a keepalive message, and verify that the link is up. If no INFO frames are exchanged, the status of the data link can be checked by the periodic exchange of RR frames; this procedure is optional. If no response is received from an RR, the sender tries again until it finally gives up and reinitializes Layer 2.

A DISC message is issued to indicate to the remote site to disconnect Layer 2. A DISC message is followed by a DM response from the other device.

Q.931

Q.931 messaging on the D channel controls the connections of ISDN calls. These messages contain call setup, call clearing, and various status messaging. Figure 6-3 shows the basic call flow between a gateway and PSTN switch.

Figure 6-3   *Q.931 Layer-3 Establishment*

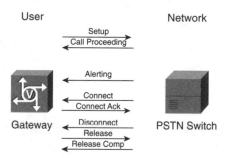

It is important to realize that the Q.931 protocol is used between the gateway and the local PSTN switch, not end-to-end. Q.931 has many variants. These variants are called *switch types*. As a result, both the gateway and the PSTN switch must choose a common switch type. Different switch types that are selected by the gateway and by the PSTN switch normally result in generating immediate call releases after a call setup request.

The SETUP message is sent by the gateway to indicate to the network that it is placing a call. The setup message includes, at a minimum, the bearer capability, channel identifier, and called-party number. The bearer capability defines the call type, which is speech, audio, video, or data. The channel identifier specifies the specific interface and channel to provide the requested service. The called-party number is the phone number that you want to connect to.

When the PSTN switch receives a gateway SETUP message, the switch processes that message and determines if it can establish the call. If the PSTN switch cannot process the request or if some of the fields in the request are invalid, the gateway receives a RELEASE COMPLETE message that indicates the call was refused for a specified reason, which is called a *cause value*. These cause values can provide useful information during trouble-shooting:

- The CALL PROCEEDING message is returned by the PSTN switch to confirm the receipt of the SETUP message and to indicate that the call is now in progress through the network.

- The call is received by the called-party switch and a SETUP message is sent to the called party. The PSTN switch is informed by the PSTN that the call has been handed off to the user and that the user has been alerted.

- The PSTN switch then sends an ALERTING message to the gateway.

- When the called party answers the call, the PSTN switch returns a CONNECT message to the gateway.

- The gateway returns a connect acknowledgment (CONACK) message back to the PSTN switch.

- When disconnecting a call, a DISCONNECT message is originated from the side that wants to terminate the call.

Figure 6-3 shows the called party terminating the call. The PSTN switch sends a DISCONNECT message to the gateway after the switch receives a message that the called party has hung up. The gateway responds with a RELEASE message, and the switch acknowledges the release with a RELEASE COMPLETE message.

PRI Trunk Template

Protocol/trunks: T1 PRI

Line code method: B8ZS

Framing mode: ESF

ISDN variant: National ISDN 2

Network/user mode: Network

NFAS: None

Digit sending method: Enbloc

Incoming digit format: CC+DN

Outgoing digit format: 1 + 10 digit DN (for CC = 1). All other CCs use 011 + CC + DN.

ISDN Variant

Several variants of ISDN connectivity are determined by the carrier switch type. The most popular of these variants, which are also supported by Cisco, are as follows:

- National ISDN 2
- 4ESS
- 5ESS
- DMS-100
- Euro-ISDN
- Australia
- Japan

NOTE	For PSTN switch connections, the gateway is typically defined as *user side*, and for PBX connections, the gateway is typically defined as *network side*.

Cisco routers can support ISDN variants on a per interface basis. Following is an example of a configuration of an AT&T ISDN switch type for the first T1 controller on a Cisco router:

```
controller t1 0
  framing esf
  linecode b8zs
  isdn switchtype primary-4ess
```

NFAS

ISDN FAS is defined as using a single D channel by controlling the PRI interface on which the D channel resides. ISDN NFAS enables two or more T1 lines to share a single D channel. NFAS can also support a backup D channel in the event that the primary D channel fails. As a result, rollover to the backup D channel automatically occurs when the primary NFAS D channel fails, which enables all voice calls to remain active. Overflow of voice calls to other PRI interfaces also occurs if the primary interface is completely used. The benefits of using NFAS is that one additional B channel on each interface is made available to carry other traffic because the D channel is not used. This is a cost-saving benefit because adding more D channels can be expensive. A greater number of PRI interfaces also can be supported on the PSTN switch.

NOTE	NFAS applies only to T1 PRI—not to E1 PRI.

Configuring NFAS on a Cisco gateway first requires the setup of the primary and secondary D channel on the first two channelized T1 controllers. These commands are as follows:

```
voipgateway1# pri-group timeslots 1-24 nfas_d primary nfas_interface number
  nfas_group number
voipgateway1#pri-group timeslots 1-24 nfas_d backup nfas_interface number nfas_group
  number
```

NOTE   A backup D channel is not displayed in the configuration because the attributes are identical to the primary D channel.

The second step is to configure a 24 B-channel interface on other channelized T1 controllers.

The command follows:

```
voipgateway1# pri-group timeslots 1-24 nfas_d none nfas_interface number nfas_group
  number
```

The third step is to assign the voice port associated with the PRI interface with the primary D channel. The command follows:

```
voipgateway1#port 0:D
```

Digit Sending Method

Overlap and enbloc modes of address signaling, sometimes referred to as the type of out-pulsing, define how to set up a call. Enbloc mode does not start any analysis of the dialed number by the calling party until all digits of the called number are complete and received. The PSTN switch interfaced to the VoIP gateway transmits all the dialed digits together to the next PSTN switch in the path. The key principle of enbloc is that the PSTN switch does not determine the route that the call will traverse until all digits are accepted. Overlap mode enables the PSTN switch to select the route before the last digit is dialed.

The following configuration shows that the overlap receiving feature is turned on for a Cisco gateway:

```
interface Serial0:15
 no ip address
 no ip mroute-cache
 isdn incoming-voice modem
 isdn overlap-receiving T302 5000
 no cdp enable
```

The T302 timer sets the interdigit timeout for the digits of the dialed number that is received by the Cisco gateway from the PSTN switch. After the value expires, the digit collection ends and the VoIP call leg is eventually established. This timer value is important because it defines how slow the user can dial the digits of the called party.

Incoming and Outgoing Digit Format

The standard ITU-T recommendation E.164 defines the number plan used in public networks around the world. E.164 divides the world into eight zones:

1	North America
2	Africa
3 and 4	Europe
5	Central and South America
6	South Pacific
7	USSR
8	Far East
9	Middle East and Southeast Asia

Each country is assigned a country code that is either one, two, or three digits in length, beginning with the zone digits. The international number consists of the country code and the national number. The country code plus the national number cannot exceed 12 digits in length. PSTN switches cannot always determine when the user completed called-number digits because lengths of international numbers vary. Whether enbloc or overlap outpulsing is used, a timer can be set within the switch to determine when the number is considered complete. Many switches use a four-second timeout.

As part of the ITU-T number plan, a North American Numbering Plan (NANP) exists. NANP consists of a ten-digit dialing plan where the first three digits are the *Numbering Plan Area (NPA)*, also called the *area code*. An additional seven digits identify the central office PSTN switch and the end-user telephone attached to the CO switch.

The incoming digit format identifies which digits will be exchanged by the switch and the VoIP gateway. A standard format used by many service providers is: CC+DN. This format eliminates any access codes, such as 9, from the dialed number. This provides a uniform format between the switches and VoIP gateways.

SS7 to Interconnect to the PSTN

SS7 is a packet-based signaling network that supports the call establishment and call tear-down of a circuit-switched network that transports voice traffic. Because SS7 is packet-based, new features, such as Caller ID, are made possible that were not possible using in-band signaling techniques.

SS7 is defined as CCS because it performs the signaling of voice calls on separate circuits. SS7 signaling connects a service provider's network to the PSTN over various types of links. SS7 forms a WAN that links the PSTN call control logic and is primarily dedicated for setting up and tearing down phone calls. PRI extends SS7-like control out to CPE, such as PBXs, which permits these devices to share in the rapid call set up and teardown of SS7.

NOTE   In many situations, SS7 trunks to the PSTN are less expensive than PRI trunks, more readily available at times, and sometimes can be the only available signaling interface from the PSTN. This is especially true in Europe.

An overview of an SS7 architecture is discussed in Chapter 3, "Offering Wholesale VoIP Services."

SS7 Trunk Template

Protocol/trunks: T1 SS7

Mode: Fully associated

Variant: ANSI ISDN User Part (ISUP)

Signaling speed: 64 kbps

Signaling channel #: 24

Point codes:

MMCS: 005-027-184

FCI: 005-014-235

Network indicator: 2 (National)

Circuit identifier code (CIC) mapping: If 8 configured T1s (for voice), the CIC numbers range from 1 to 192

Line code method: B8ZS

Framing mode: ESF

Digit sending method: Enbloc

Incoming digit format: CC + DN

Outgoing digit format: 011 + CC + DN

Mode

SS7 has two distinct signaling modes:

- Fully associated signaling
- Quasi associated signaling

Fully associated signaling is when a signaling link exists for each circuit that is carrying voice traffic. An example of fully associated mode is with an E1 circuit where channel 16 can carry the signaling. This is called a fully associated link (F–link). F-links are used when a service switching point (SSP) cannot be directly connected to the signal transfer point (STP) in the case where access links (A-links) are not economically feasible. It is common for the F-link to be combined with voice traffic on the trunk where a 64-kbps channel is dedicated for the SS7 signaling messages.

The second mode can statically route the signaling traffic on a link other than the actual traffic between two PSTN switches. This mode is called the quasi associated mode of signaling.

NOTE   *Quasi associated* is a type of a nonassociated mode of signaling. This is referred to as an *A-link*.

A-links are used between the SSP and STP to provide access into the SS7 network. Typically, ITSPs have at least two A-links, one for each of the STP-mated pairs. Nonassociated signaling provides significant savings on switching interface costs because fewer D channels are required. Using nonassociated signaling means that all the T1 and E1 channels are used for voice and data and the associated signaling is carried separately over the SS7 network.

ISUP Variant

Similar to many other telecommunications standards, ISUP has many variants. SS7 networks worldwide have their own unique ISUP messages and procedures defined. There are many variants of ISUP messages, including variants defined by national standards organizations, such as the American National Institute (ANSI) and Telcordia. Some major difference between the U.S. version of ISUP and other countries include the following:

- **Supplementary services**—These services are country specific and normally access codes invoked by a # on a DTMF telephone keypad. Examples of popular supplementary services are call waiting service, call forwarding service, caller ID, distinctive ringing, and three-way calling. These access codes turn on or turn off these services. Access codes and the procedures to turn on and turn off vary worldwide.

- **Transit Network Selection**—used by a local exchange to identify the IXC when a direct trunk to the IXC network does not exist. A transit network selection parameter is part of the ISUP call control message called the Initial Address Message (IAM). The transit network selection parameter uniquely identifies the IXC. The IAM includes the information (such as the called number) necessary to set up a call. The IAM is the first message sent in setting up a call. The transit network selection parameter, as defined in ANSI T1.113, contains multiple fields that identify the national network (010 for the U.S.), the IXC provider's network (CIC), and whether the call is international.

- **enbloc**—U.S. ISUP signaling must be enbloc, which defines that all address information must be included in the initial setup message. ITU-T SS7 standards define that subsequent address messages can be used.

- **Cause codes**—A cause code value indicates why a call has been terminated. ITU-T defined a list of standard cause code values. ANSI and Telcordia also defined additional cause code values.

Signaling Speed

Signaling data links in SS7 networks can operate at different speeds. Examples of link speeds include

- 56/64 kbps
- 1.544 Mbps

Signaling Channel

The signaling timeslot must be identified when you use fully associated signaling.

Point Codes

Each signaling point, referred to as an SS7 node, is identified with a unique address that is called a point code. A point code identifies a signaling point in an SS7 network, which is assigned by an organization in each country. For example, North American point codes are 24 bits and international point codes are 14 bits. Point codes are carried in SS7 messages that are called Message Transfer Part Level 3 (MTP3) messages, and are exchanged between signaling points to identify the source and destination of each message. MTP3 routes SS7 messages that are based on the point code. The MTP3 message contains an originating point code, a destination point code, and a signaling link selector. The signaling link selector (SLS) helps route and load share SS7 MTP3 messages across links. Every switch in an SS7 network has an assigned point code. The general practice is to connect each switch to two different STPs. Thus, every MTP3 message is sent across one of the two mated STP links.

The point code in North America is broken up into the following three components:

- **Network code**—Identifies a signaling network
- **Network cluster**—Identifies a cluster of nodes belonging to a signaling network
- **Network cluster member**—Identifies a single signaling point within a cluster

In the SS7 trunk template, the point code 005-027-184 for one of the mated STPs consists of the following elements:

- 005 is the network code.
- 027 is the network cluster ID.
- 184 is the end node that is connected to the network cluster.

Network Indicator

The network indicator identifies the type of call that is being established:

- Calls with an indicator of 0 are international bound and are routed to an STP pair that is an international gateway.
- Calls with an indicator of 2 are national calls and are routed appropriately.
- Sometimes, the network indicator of 3 is used in some countries to differentiate carriers that share point codes. For example, Carrier A and Carrier B can both share the point code 005-027-184, but Carrier B uses a network indicator of 3.

CIC Mapping

A CIC field identifies the circuit that each SS7 message is associated with. Each CIC must be mapped to a specific voice circuit in the SS7 trunk interface. The receiving PSTN switch that is terminating the signaling link uses the CIC. The CIC must be agreed upon between two service providers because there is no standard method of allocating CIC numbers. Certain SS7 configurations can allocate only the CIC internal to an ITSP SS7-capable PSTN switch and an ITSP SS7-capable VoIP gateway.

Troubleshooting Techniques

Several troubleshooting steps can be identified to assist the service provider in implementing VoIP gateway trunk:

- Ensure line is up and correct synchronization and clocking.
- Ensure D channel is up and correct PRI signaling.

- Ensure no alarms.
- Provide loopback test.
- Use CAS troubleshooting debugs.

Ensure Line Is up and Correct Synchronization and Clocking

Always verify the physical integrity of the T1 line to ensure that no errors exist because of clocking or synchronization problems. Issue the **show controller T1** command to view the T1 controller status:

- **Status of the line**—The line status identifies if the T1 is up, down, or administratively down.

- **Linecode and pathcode violations**—Linecode violations are the occurrence of either a bipolar violation (BPV) or an excessive error event. These errors can occur because of an AMI/B8ZS problem. For example, there might be devices along the transmission path that do not have all the linecoding parameters set correctly. A path coding violation error is a frame synchronization bit error in the D4, or a CRC error in the ESF formats.

- **Slips**—Because of synchronization issues, input buffers on a trunk overflow and cause a frame slip. The presence of excessive slips on a trunk line indicates a clocking problem. It is important to view both trunk endpoints.

- **Alarms**—Alarms indicate that a performance problem exists. An alarm might indicate that certain counters, such as errored seconds, have exceeded a threshold. For example, an alarm indication signal (AIS) is an "all ones" signal condition to notify the downstream equipment of a loss of signal or an out of frame (OOF) condition. A LOS condition occurs when a device determines that no pulses, either positive or negative, exist within a certain timeframe. An OOF condition occurs when a certain number of frame errors occur within a certain timeframe.

NOTE	An incorrect linecoding parameter setting is a classic problem when interconnecting between service providers. Often, the problem is that one service provider is using AMI while the other is using B8ZS linecoding.

Ensure D Channel Is up and Correct PRI Signaling

After ensuring that Layer 1 has no problems, the next step is to look at the following:

- **Layer 2 is operational**—Verify that Layer 2 is operational by using the **show isdn status** command.

- **Layer 3 is operational**—Verify that Layer 3 is operational by using the **show isdn service** command. This command displays the status of the B channels. Layer 3 controls call setup and teardown. Using debug commands for ISDN Q931 is also recommended.

Ensure No Alarms

Ensure that no alarms exist. If alarms do exist, confirm that framing and linecoding parameters are configured correctly.

Loopback Test

A T1 loopback test is performed on the gateway if the PSTN switch and gateway trunk cannot be established after verifying the previously mentioned steps. A successful loopback test helps to verify that the gateway hardware is not at fault.

Complete the following steps to create a loopback plug for a T1 CSU/DSU:

Step 1 Connect pins 1 and 4 together.

Step 2 Connect pins 2 and 5 together.

NOTE The RJ-45 jack pins are numbered from 1 through 8. Pin 1 on the RJ-45 jack is the left-most pin with the metal pins facing up.

Step 3 Set up the router.

To run the loopback test on channelized T1s, you need to use the **channel-group T1 controller** command to create one or more serial interfaces that are mapped to a set of timeslots in the channelized T1. If the T1 is configured as a PRI, you need to remove the pri-group before using the **channel-group** command. Also a Layer-1 loopback test on the T1 can be done without changing the router configuration to a channel-group.

Step 4 Clear the interface counters by using the **clear counters** command.

Step 5 Perform an extended **ping** test.

CAS Troubleshooting

The **debug serial interface** command can gain additional details of E&M signaling.

Summary

This chapter focused on implementing the PSTN switch to the gateway trunk. Following are three types of trunk signaling implementations that are commonly used in VoIP networks:

- T1 CAS
- PRI
- SS7

This chapter defined a trunk template that helps facilitate the planning and implementation of interfacing VoIP gateways to PSTN switches. As with any project, the more time spent planning, the less probability of problems during the implementation phase. The last section of this chapter discussed examples of troubleshooting techniques that can be used on the PSTN switch and gateway connection.

CHAPTER 7

Gateway and Gatekeeper Design Requirements

This chapter discusses the design and implementation guidelines for gateways and gatekeepers in a service provider H.323 Voice over IP (VoIP) network. Protocols that gateways and gatekeepers use in an H.323 VoIP network are discussed in Chapter 2, "VoIP Network Architectures: H.323, SIP, and MGCP." This chapter addresses several areas that are essential in understanding how to design and implement a large scale VoIP network:

- Gateway and Gatekeeper Design
- Traffic Engineering
- Zones
- Dial Peers
- Dial Plan Administration
- Gatekeepers and Directory Gatekeeper Sizing
- High-Availability VoIP Network
- Troubleshooting Gateways and Gatekeepers

Gateway and Gatekeeper Design

This section identifies important elements of designing and implementing a service provider VoIP network using H.323 gateways and gatekeepers.

This section uses an example to help identify these important elements. A service provider, called Jim's International Traffic (JIT), has points of presence (POPs) in the United States and Germany, as shown in Figure 7-1.

As with any good network design, it is important to provide a set of requirements for deploying a service provider VoIP network. Sufficient resources need to be dedicated to define these requirements to reduce the risk of re-engineering the network after it is operational.

Figure 7-1 *Gatekeeper and Gateway Design Example*

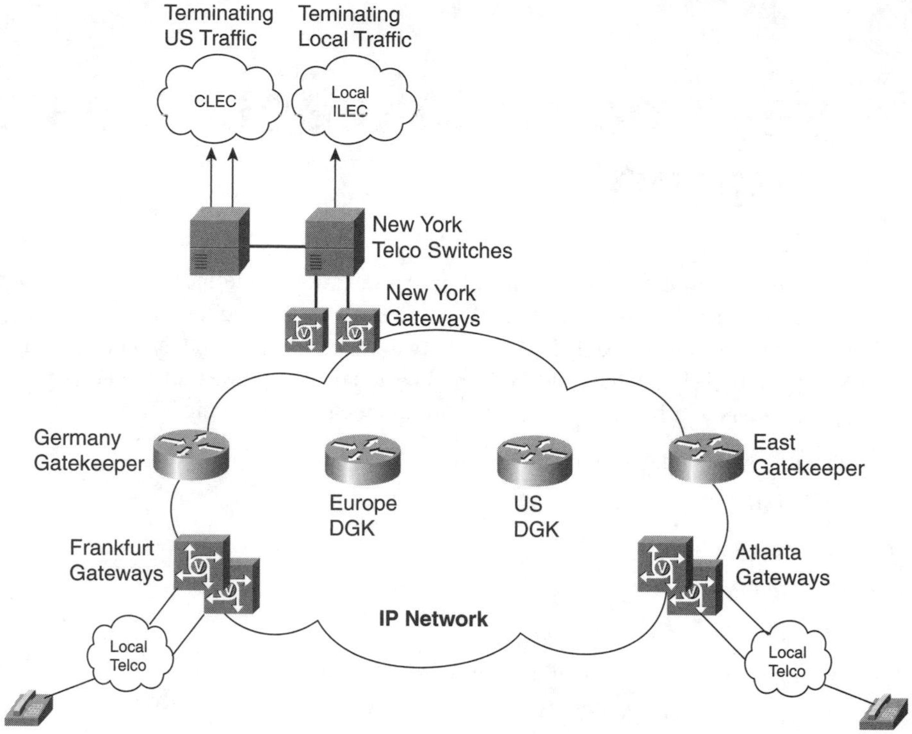

The following items and requirements table is an example of a set of key requirements for designing a VoIP network using Cisco gateways and gatekeepers. This provides a sample set of requirements that might be gathered by a VoIP service provider:

- **General network overview**—JIT uses Cisco VoIP gateways that reside in Atlanta and New York to provide U.S. termination for Germany. JIT also provides European termination by using the Cisco VoIP gateways and gatekeepers in Frankfurt. These gateways are connected to a public switched telephone network (PSTN) switch. An international interexchange carrier (IXC), XYZ, is selected as the carrier responsible for transporting the VoIP traffic on a private network from Germany to New York. A local competitive local exchange carrier (CLEC), ABC, is the carrier responsible for transporting the VoIP traffic from New York to Atlanta.

- **Atlanta POP projected minutes**—Atlanta PPP needs to support 30,000 minutes per day. Busy hour is defined as 20 percent of the total calls in a day. Average hold time is defined as 3 minutes, and Grade of Service is 5 percent. Busy hour is discussed in the next section.

- **Voice characteristics**—JIT uses a G.729 coder-decoder (codec) that supports two frames per packet.

NOTE   The bandwidth required to support a selected codec is determined by the frequency of the voice packets transmitted across a link. This packet frequency determines the bandwidth required and also determines the quality of the voice call.

Table 7-1 provides the total bandwidth required by codec types G.729 and G.711 with different parameter values taken into account. Other voice codec schemes and Layer 2 combinations are available.

Table 7-1   *G.729 and G.711 codecs*

Codec Type	Voice BW kbps	Frame Size (Bytes)	Voice Payload (Bytes)	IP/UDP/ RTP Header (Bytes)	L2 Type	Layer 2 Header (Bytes)	Total Bandwidth Kb/Sec no VAD	Total Bandwidth Kb/Sec VAD (35%)
G.729	8	10	20	40	Ethernet	14	29.6	19.2
G.729	8	10	20	40	PPP	6	26.4	17.2
G.711	80	160	160	40	Ethernet	14	85.6	55.64
G.711	80	160	160	40	PPP	6	82.4	53.56

As shown in Table 7-1, a G.711 codec requires more bandwidth than a G.729 codec. Calculating the total bandwidth for a G.729 call for a Point-to-Point Protocol (PPP) connection follows:

Known information:

— Layer-3 overhead for IP/User Datagram Protocol (UDP)/Real-Time Transport Protocol (RTP) headers = 40 bytes

— Layer-2 overhead for PPP header = 6 bytes

— Digital Signal Processor (DSP) generates a frame every 10 milliseconds

— Two frames per packet (2 × 10 bytes) = 20 bytes

Bandwidth per voice call = voice packet size * voice packets per second

$$= (L2 + L3 + \text{voice payload}) * 8 * (8 \text{ kbps codec bit rate}) / (\text{voice payload} * 8)$$

$$= (6 + 40 + 20) * 8 * (8000 / 20 * 8)$$

$$= 26.4 \text{ kbps}$$

$$= 17.2 \text{ with voice activity detection (VAD)}$$

VAD reduces the bandwidth required for VoIP traffic. Because voice conversations might contain up to 50 percent silence, VAD provides the ability to send RTP packets only when voice conversation is present. Table 7-1 shows that the bandwidth is reduced by 35 percent with VAD turned on. Further bandwidth reduction can be obtained by compressing the RTP header (cRTP). Note: VAD, cRTP, codec type bit rate, and the voice payload size all affect the bandwidth requirements and the quality of the voice call.

- **Normalization rules**—Cisco gateways support a wide variety of rules. In this example, the Cisco gateway supports the following normalization rule: country code (CC) + dialed number (DN).

- **Authentication**—All calls passed to the Cisco gateways in Atlanta and Frankfurt are pre-authenticated by the telephone company (telco) switches in New York and Frankfurt. As a result, the Cisco gateways need to support only single-stage dialing.

- **Growth**—Growth of the Atlanta-Frankfurt link requires strategic planning. Expansion of this link is accomplished by adding bandwidth in 1 Mbps increments between Frankfurt and New York.

- **Billing**—Billing is accomplished by using data from the gateways. VoIP billing is discussed in Chapter 3, "Offering Wholesale VoIP Services."

- **Network management**—A key requirement for VoIP network management is to support and maintain a Service Level Agreement (SLA) for JIT's peering partners. An SLA defines a specified minimum level of VoIP service level that the customers will receive. Chapter 9, "Network Management: Maintaining an SLA," discusses these requirements.

- **Operations acceptance**—The following items must be performed before the operations department accepts the network:

  - Test gateways for 2×24 hours using a traffic simulator.

  - Conduct subjective or listening tests for noise.

  - Conduct subjective or listening tests to determine acceptable echo suppression levels.

  - Determine the Post Dial Delay (PDD) from a call made from the network. The difference between the time that the last digit is dialed and the distant telephone ringing equals the PDD from the VoIP network. Results must not be greater than 15 seconds.

As part of the design phase, a common task is to create a list of VoIP network requirements for each POP. Table 7-2 is an example of a partial list of key network requirements for the Atlanta POP.

Table 7-2   *Partial List of VoIP Network Requirements for the Atlanta POP*

JIT Requirements	Description
Service offerings	Wholesale VoIP
Codec type	G.729
Total minutes per day	Day one: 30,000 minutes
Number of call attempts in the busy hour (BHCA)	2000
Average Hold Time (AHT)	Three minutes
Call blocking	Five percent
Number of VoIP gateways	To be determined by the density of the gateway and the number of minutes traversing the network
Fax capability	Yes
VoIP normalization rules	CC + DN

Traffic Engineering

This section discusses how to size the number of gateways that are required for a POP.

The key objective in traffic engineering is for the network to have low blocking, which dictates the grade of service, and to handle peak traffic spikes. A big part of traffic engineering involves analyzing the traffic to determine the amount of bandwidth per circuit and the number of circuits needed to carry the voice traffic load.

Three key design elements are required to properly traffic engineer a voice network:

1 Grade of service for network

2 Projected number of calls described as call attempts and the AHT of calls to determine the traffic load

3 Capacity requirements of the network elements including the number of trunks and trunk size

Grade of service is defined as the probability of calls being blocked during the time when the traffic volume is the highest, which is called the *busy hour*.

NOTE	An important term used in traffic engineering is *busy hour*. Traffic load is typically measured during the busy hour. A common practice is to estimate the busy hour that might range from 5 to 20 percent of the total calls in a day—20 percent being the most conservative estimate. The result is a traffic load measurement called *Busy Hour Call Attempts (BHCA)*, which defines the number of calls that a network can handle during the busiest hour of the day.

Grade of service can also be expressed as the proportion of the number of answered calls to the number of seized calls. The Answer Seizure Ratio (ASR) is a common way to identify the current grade of network service. The general range of grade of service that service providers use ranges from 1 to 3 calls in 100 calls being blocked.

Erlangs

Use Erlangs to determine the trunking requirements for a VoIP network. There are two steps:

Step 1   Define the traffic load in Erlangs.

Step 2   Determine the total trunks required to support busy hour usage.

An Erlang describes the total traffic volume during one hour. For example, one attempt that lasts 1 hour is Erlang (1 hour × 3600/3600 = 1). As shown in this example, an Erlang is expressed as a percentage of an hour. The equation to calculate Erlangs is as follows:

```
Erlang =    (BHCA x AHT) / 3600
```

This equation can also be written as follows:

```
Erlang = (Total minutes per day x busy hour) / 60
```

Traditionally, the Erlang B model calculates the number of trunks between telephone systems. Traffic engineers commonly use Erlang traffic tables to determine the number of circuits needed to carry a given amount of voice traffic with a specified grade of service.

Trunk Sizing

The JIT network traffic engineering requirements are as follows:

- 2000 BHCA
- 180 secs AHT
- 5 percent call blocking (Grade of Service)

Erlang = (2000 × 180 secs) / 3600 secs

   = 100

   = 105 lines (Using Erlang B Table and 5 percent Grade of Service)

Therefore, 4 E1 trunks or 5 Primary Rate Interface (PRI) trunks are required to support 105 lines.

A number of items must be addressed to complete this table:

- Zones
- Dial Peers
- Normalization Rules

- Dial Plan Administration
- High-Availability Strategy
- Network Capacity Planning

Zones

A *zone* is a collection of gateways registered to a single gatekeeper in a VoIP network. A Cisco IOS router can control several zones. In other words, two or more virtual gatekeepers can exist on a Cisco IOS router. For example, in Asia Pacific, an area is assigned to each city; as a result, each virtual gatekeeper can control the dial plan for one city. Therefore, one physical gatekeeper with several logical gatekeepers inside can control the dial plan of several cities.

Prefix information needs to be configured in each zone. A *prefix*, also referred to as a *zone prefix*, is defined as part of a called number, usually the Numbering Plan Area (NPA) or NPA-NXX. The prefix identifies the zone where a call terminates. Zone prefixes need to be statically configured because no protocol is available today for gatekeepers to advertise which zone prefixes can be accessed from their zones.

NOTE   The Internet Engineering Task Force (IETF) is currently working on such a protocol, as defined in RFC 3219. This protocol is referred to as Telephony Routing over IP (TRIP) . TRIP's main function is to advertise the reachability of telephony endpoints, such as a VoIP gateway. TRIP also advertises attributes of the routes to the telephony endpoints. TRIP is modeled after the Border Gateway Protocol (BGP) and supports many similarities. Also, TRIP is flexible in that this telephony routing protocol does not care about the signaling protocol being used. For example, TRIP can work with H.323 and session initiation protocol (SIP)-based networks.

New zones can be easily added to a VoIP network. None of the other zones need any modifications when new zones are created. New area codes are added to the local gatekeeper and the directory gatekeeper (DGK) but not to the remote gatekeepers.

Dial Peers

Dial-peer matching determines the next leg of the call after the gateway receives a call from the PSTN. If the matched dial peer specifies a session target of RAS, the gateway presents the called number in an Admission ReQuest (ARQ) message to its gatekeeper for address resolution. The gatekeeper either replies with an admission confirmation (ACF) message or an admission rejection (ARJ) message. Before sending one of these two messages, the gatekeeper first tries to resolve the E.164 address to an IP address for the gateway to use. The gatekeeper uses an E.164 to IP address resolution table to determine the hop-off zone and gateway to be used.

The hop-off zone is determined by the zone prefix. If the zone prefix that matches is from a remote zone, a location request (LRQ) message that contains the dialed number is sent to the remote gatekeeper. Otherwise, no LRQ message is generated for a local zone match. If no zone is found to match, the gatekeeper returns an ARJ or uses a local zone for the hop-off, which is the default action. Alternatively, the gatekeeper can issue an ARJ and lets the call fail. As a result, the call uses the next matching dial peer that specifies that the call will be hairpinned to the PSTN.

The gatekeeper selects a terminating gateway after the zone is selected. The selection process is based on the priority assigned to the gateway in IOS release 12.0(5)T (refer to Example 7-1). The default priority is 5, the highest priority is 10, and 0 indicates that the gateway cannot be used.

Example 7-1 *Gateway Priorities*

```
router-atl(config-gk)# zone local gkatl wholesale-minutes.com
router-atl(config-gk)# zone prefix gkatl 404....... gw-pri 10 gw404
router-atl(config-gk)# zone prefix gkatl 770....... gw-pri 10 gw770
router-atl(config-gk)# zone prefix gkatl 678....... gw-pri 10 gw678
router-atl(config-gk)# zone prefix gkatl 706.......
```

NOTE   Prior to 12.0(5) T, prioritizing gateways was unavailable. The selection of gateways was made randomly from all the gateways registered within the same zone.

Example 7-1 shows three gateways: gw404, gw770, and gw678. Each gateway is registered in the same zone, called gkatl. Area code 706 does not have any priorities defined, which means that all gateways can be chosen with equal chance for area code 706. All calls to area code 404 are routed to the gateway with the ID gw404 because it has the highest priority. In cases when gw404 is handling high call volumes and is out of resources to handle more calls, 404 calls are routed randomly to gw770 or gw678. When a service provider does not want a gateway to route a certain prefix, a zero priority command is issued. Example 7-2 shows the output of the command **zone prefix** issued at the gatekeeper, which indicates that gw404 handles all calls to area code 404.

Example 7-2 *Zone Prefix List*

```
router-atl(config-gk)# zone prefix gk404 404....... gw-pri 10 gw404
    router-atl(config-gk)# zone prefix gk404 404....... gw-pri 0 gw770 gw678
```

Normally, if a priority is not configured for a particular gateway and zone prefix, the priority will default to 5 and calls will be routed to that gateway. As a result, a zero priority must be configured for any gateway and zone prefix combination where calls should not be routed. However, there is an IOS command to change the default priority on a per prefix basis. The default gateway priority of 5 can be changed using the command **zone prefix gkatl 770555* gw-default-priority 0**. This command enables calls to be routed to certain gateways for that prefix. This command can be used when one or more gateways (and future gateways) in a zone should not handle calls for a certain prefix. In this case, it is not necessary to configure a 0 priority for these gateways issuing the command zone prefix at the gatekeeper.

The gatekeeper uses the configured list of zone prefixes to determine where to route the call. The call is routed to an alternate off-network like the PSTN (hairpinned) if no zone prefixes match the ones listed. The command **arq reject-unknown-prefix** can be issued in the gatekeeper to prevent this action. The service provider can use this command to restrict local gateway calls to a known set of prefixes. This command can intentionally fail calls so that an alternate choice on a gateway's rotary dial peer is selected.

Additional routing capabilities exist. Cisco IOS 12.2(11)T enables you to route on more than just a destination pattern. For example, an incoming tag can be tagged on an ingress POTS peer with a trunk group or carrier ID. This ID is sent through RAS to the gatekeeper, which can then query a route server application through GKTMP for a target trunk-group or carrier ID based upon the source trunk-group or carrier ID. This enhanced routing capability is discussed in Chapter 2, "VoIP Network Architectures: H.323, SIP, MGCP."

Normalization Rules

Dial plans are statically configured and maintained on Cisco gateways and gatekeepers. Until TRIP is introduced in H.323 networks, service providers must keep track of their dial plans, which can become large and cumbersome if not designed correctly. One of the components to help alleviate the dial-plan administration is the directory gatekeeper. In a good dial plan, gateways handle the local dial rules, and the gatekeepers and directory gatekeepers handle the global routing rules. Gateways also provide a standard pattern in handling the translations of the incoming and outgoing digits. This task is called *normalization* and is required to support local PSTN dialing rules.

NOTE   All digit manipulation techniques, such as translation rules, can be carried out on the gateways. However, Cisco gatekeepers when used in conjunction with an external route server and certain non-Cisco gatekeepers can support digit manipulation techniques. Furthermore, there are certain restrictions concerning the number of translations and matching pattern rules that are associated with digit manipulation techniques. For example, more than 11 rules within a translation rule are allowed. Digit manipulation techniques are enhanced by using translation profiles and regular expressions in IOS 12.2(11)T. These enhancements include supporting regular expressions in defining translation rules. This enables flexibility and the ability to manipulate incoming and outgoing digits.

A dial plan defines the digit patterns to be handled by the gateway. The design objective of a dial plan is to normalize the number entering the gateway into a standard format, such as country code, area code, and local access number. For example, the following dial plan can be used by every gateway in a VoIP network:

```
Country Code (CC) + Dialed Number (DN)
```

There might be a variety of digit patterns when digits arrive from the PSTN into the gateway. Depending on the originating and terminating country that the call is associated with, the digit length can vary from 10 to 15. For example, when a call arrives from an international POP, the local gateway might strip off the international access number and any other associated numbers. A standard 10-digit number is sent into the core and the gateway is able to match this number. To define translation rules for a gateway, the local PSTN dialing rules need to be identified in each country. For example, a gateway in the U.S. might apply the following number translation rules to handle local PSTN dialing rules and to normalize the destination numbers to a standard pattern (CC + DN):

- Local rule: Use 1 + area code + 7 digits
- Long distance rule: Use 1 + area code + 7 digits
- International rule: Strip off 011.

Example 7-3 provides an example of a number translation rule defined in a gateway.

Example 7-3 *Number Translation Rule Example*

```
Hostname ATL-GW

!
translation-rule 2
 Rule 0 ^2...... 17702
 Rule 1 ^3...... 17703
 Rule 2 ^4...... 17704
 Rule 3 ^5...... 17705
 Rule 4 ^6...... 17706
 Rule 5 ^7...... 17707
```

Example 7-3   *Number Translation Rule Example (Continued)*

```
  Rule 6 ^8...... 17708
  Rule 7 ^9...... 17709
  !
translation-rule 1
  Rule 0 ^0111.% 1
  Rule 1 ^0112.% 2
  Rule 2 ^0113.% 3
  Rule 3 ^0114.% 4
  Rule 4 ^0115.% 5
  Rule 5 ^0116.% 6
  Rule 6 ^0117.% 7
  Rule 7 ^0118.% 8
  Rule 8 ^0119.% 9
  !
dial-peer voice 1770 pots
  destination-pattern 17705551000
  port 1/0/0
  !
dial-peer voice 1 voip
  destination-pattern 011T
  translate-outgoing called 1
  session target ras
  !
dial-peer voice 2 voip
  destination-pattern 1T
  session target ras
  !
dial-peer voice 3 voip
  destination-pattern [2-9]T
  translate-outgoing called 2
  session target ras
  !
```

Example 7-3 is a partial configuration example that has two translation rules defined. Translation rule 1 strips the 011 access code on numbers that begin with 011. This translation rule is applied to dial peer 1, which matches all numbers beginning with 011. The T acts as a wild card that supports an interdigit timeout, which enables the digits to be collected when the user does not enter a DTMF tone within a certain time period.

Translation rule 2 takes any seven-digit number that begins with 2–9 and adds a 1770 prefix to that number. This translation rule is applied to dial peer 3.

NOTE   No translation rule is necessary for long distance calls within the U.S. because the digit pattern is already in the desired format. Therefore, dial peer 2 is configured with no translation rule applied.

The following two IOS commands are used when testing translation rules:

* **debug translation detail**
* **test translation-rule**

Using Gatekeeper Transaction Message Protocol

Additionally, some service providers use a front-end switch (PSTN Class 5 switch) to carry out digit manipulation rather than the gateway. In large-scale H.323 VoIP networks, it is normally recommended that the service provider use a *Gatekeeper Transaction Message Protocol (GKTMP)* route server to carry out complicated digit manipulation, such as international call distribution. This allows the network to be more easily managed.

An external application can use GKTMP to communicate to the gatekeeper's application program interface (API). This enables additional intelligence to be built external to the gatekeeper and allows further control in setting up a VoIP call. For example, advanced LCR and advanced digit analysis and translation can be performed by the external application. GKTMP uses a set of request and response messages, based on H.225 Registration, Admission, and Status Protocol (RAS), to exchange information over a Transmission Control Protocol (TCP) connection between an external application and gatekeeper.

Dial Plan Administration

Every gatekeeper controls a particular zone or given number of zones and all prefixes within these zones. The directory gatekeeper (DGK) resolves anything that does not match within the prefix table within the gatekeeper. This occurs by the gatekeeper sending an LRQ message to the DGK. The DGK handles any received dialed numbers that are not handled by the local zone.

As a result of using the DGK, each gatekeeper is responsible for less of the dial-plan configuration. Thus, a hierarchy design exists by taking much of the intelligence for the dial plan out of each gatekeeper and placing it in the DGK. The benefit of this type of architecture is that by adding new zones or NPAs the dial plan administration and provisioning are drastically reduced. A DGK contains zone-prefix tables for the total network. This means that each gatekeeper needs to be configured only with its own locally handled zone prefixes and the IP address of the DGK for all other prefixes. So, when a gatekeeper receives an ARQ with a called number that is not assigned to its own zones, the gatekeeper issues an LRQ message to the DGK.

The DGK uses its own zone-prefix table to find the appropriate gatekeeper to handle the call. After a match is found, the DGK issues an LRQ message to this gatekeeper. In the case of the JIT network, the DGK routes all calls that begin with a country code of 1 to the gatekeeper in Atlanta. The Atlanta gatekeeper then examines the NPA or NPA-NXX of the dialed number to route the call to the terminating gateway in the United States.

Gatekeepers and Directory Gatekeeper Sizing

Certain questions must be answered to complete the sizing of a VoIP network:

1 How many gateways are associated per gatekeeper?

2 How many gatekeepers are required to build a network to carry a certain capacity?

3 How many zones are in the network?

Calls per second (CPS) and CPU utilization use are the two parameters required to calculate the number of gatekeepers in a VoIP wholesale network. Similar to calculating the number of gateways, you use the peak traffic hour to determine the number of gatekeepers. The calls that constitute BHCA can be either intrazone or interzone type calls. Furthermore, Cisco recommends that the average CPU use calculated over a five-minute window should not exceed 65 percent CPU use.

Given:

- Not exceed 65 percent CPU use for DGK

- AS5300 = Maximum 2 CPS

- Total gateways = 8 gateways/POP × 3 POPs = 24 GWs

- Number of AS5300 gateways × 2 CPS = Max CPS on GK

Calculations:

- Total GWs in US × GW max CPS = 24 × 2 = Maximum 48 CPS.

- Performance numbers associated with 3660 indicate that 48 CPS is within performance range.

Because DGKs do not keep track of the state of active calls, DGK processing requirements are less than a gatekeeper. The processing requirements for the DGK can be calculated as a percentage of the local gatekeepers. For example, identify the busiest local gatekeeper and apply 10 percent of the CPU use of this gatekeeper for the DGK.

Given:

- Not exceed 65 percent CPU use for DGK.

- Hot Standby Router Protocol (HSRP).

- Gatekeeper uses approximately 10 percent of the DGK's CPU.

Calculations:

- Recommend six gatekeepers to one DGK; therefore, one DGK is required.

High-Availability VoIP Network

A service provider must have a highly scalable VoIP network to allow for growth on a worldwide basis. This requirement has been met by introducing the DGK. A high-availability VoIP network is another important requirement for any service provider. Such a network entails supporting the following components:

- Gateway High Availability
- Gatekeeper High Availability
- DGK High Availability

Gateway High Availability

Three mechanisms in Cisco IOS are discussed that support gateway high availability:

- Gateway Priority
- Resource Availability Indicator (RAI)
- Hunt Group

These mechanisms help to ensure that the call is completed, which results in a high call completion ratio.

Gateway Priority

The gatekeeper can assist in providing gateway high availability by choosing a gateway within a pool that is based on priority. Therefore, if one gateway cannot be accessed for any reason, the next highest priority gateway is chosen. Part of this selection process can be based on whether the gateway has resources available. The gateway's availability is communicated to the gatekeeper through an RAI message.

Without the priority feature, all gateways that are registered to a gatekeeper are handling the same destination pattern, and the gatekeeper gives each gateway equal priority during the selection processes. For example, if a call arrives for 678-555-1111, the gatekeeper goes through the list of gateways that are handling this particular prefix and chooses the gateway in a round-robin fashion. The gatekeeper goes round robin through the gateways for every subsequent call for the same destination pattern.

Using the priority feature, a gatekeeper can select the gateway that has the lowest cost termination rates, for example, a gateway with no intra-LATA toll charges. Example 7-4 shows how a gatekeeper prioritizes gateways.

Example 7-4 *Gateway Priority List*

```
gk#show gateway gw-type-prefix
GATEWAY TYPE PREFIX TABLE
=========================
  Zone gk.atl prefix 770555* priority Gateway list(s):
   Priority 10:
    10.10.250.1:1720 atl1-gw
   Priority 5:
    10.10.250.2:1720 atl2-gw
  Zone gk.atl prefix 770777* priority Gateway list(s):
   Priority 10:
    10.10.250.2:1720 atl2-gw
   Priority 5:
    10.10.250.1:1720 atl1-gw
  Zone gk.atl prefix 678* priority Gateway list(s):
   Priority 5:
    10.10.250.1:1720 atl1-gw
    10.10.250.2:1720 atl2-gw
```

RAI

In service provider networks, RAI enables a gateway to inform the gatekeeper that its resources, specifically the time-division multiplexing (TDM) channels or DSPs, are low. When the gatekeeper is informed through the RAI message, the gatekeeper will place the gateway at the bottom of the selection list. This means that this gateway will be selected if there are no other gateways available to select.

NOTE   The gateway resends an RAI message to the gatekeeper when its resources become available again.

The IOS command, **resource threshold**, enables a gateway to use RAI. The command to set a gateway to a high resource threshold equal to 90 percent and a low resource threshold equal to 70 percent is **resource threshold high 90 low 70**. Figure 7-2 graphically defines these thresholds.

Figure 7-2 implies that an RAI message is sent to the gatekeeper when either the DSP or DS-0 resources reach 90 percent use and then when either the DSP or DS-0 returns to 70 percent use.

The gatekeeper places all gateways that have sent an RAI at the bottom of the gateway selection list that the gatekeeper maintains.

Figure 7-2   *Resource Availability Indicator*

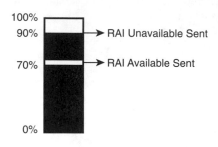

NOTE   The gatekeeper randomly assigns calls based on configured priorities if all gateways in the zone have an RAI equal to true. Furthermore, if there is only one gateway in the zone to choose from, the gatekeeper routes the call to the gateway even though its resources are low, unless a hunt group is configured in the originating gateway.

Hunt Group

Gateways can also handle failover scenarios with a *hunt group*. If a gateway receives an ARJ from the gatekeeper, the next highest priority dial peer is used in the hunt group. A hunt group, called the *rotary calling pattern* feature in Cisco IOS Software, can be configured, which enables the originating gateway to influence the selection of the destination gateway. The rotary feature enables several dial peers to be associated with a destination pattern. Each dial peer is assigned a configurable preference (0–9); zero (0) is defined as the highest value and nine (9) is defined as the lowest value. The gateway uses the highest preference dial peer. If no priority assignment is made, the default priority of the dial peer is 0. If the call cannot complete for any reason, the originating gateway retries the call to the next highest priority dial peer. The dial peer is selected based on the longest matching destination pattern.

Three kinds of hunt group concepts exist in Cisco gateways:

- **Dial peer rotation** hunt groups can use a preference command to specify their priority, but when the call fails in the first dial peer and hunt to the second dial peer, it still uses the same conf-id. This means that there are two radius records for this call. One is a call duration equal to zero, and the other has a longer than zero call duration, but all of them use the same conf-id. In this scenario, some billing software cannot recognize two radius records. This billing software considers that the call duration is zero, which decreases the service provider's revenues.

- **POTS dial peer** hunt groups are configured on an AS5x00 pots dial peer because every As5x00 has more than one T1/ E1 controller. This means that more than one T1/E1 controller can terminate the call. The IOS default operation is to have the call randomly try one T1/E1 controller first. If it cannot hop off the call, IOS lets the call try the second T1/E1 controller. The command **hunt stop** can turn off this feature. In a service provider environment, this feature is normally turned off.

- A gatekeeper can return multiple IP addresses of terminating gateways to the originating gateway. This capability exists when a Cisco gatekeeper uses a GKTMP route server or a non-Cisco gatekeeper that has this capability. The originating gateway sends a setup to the first terminating gateway, and if this request is rejected, the originating gateway sends a call setup message to the second IP address.

Gatekeeper High Availability

So far, high availability has been discussed at a gateway level. What if the gatekeeper or DGK fails? Losing a gatekeeper or DGK has significantly more impact on reducing the call completion ratio than losing a gateway. Therefore, adding an alternate gatekeeper and alternate DGK can introduce high availability at the gatekeeper and DGK level.

Alternate Gatekeeper

After a primary gatekeeper fails, the endpoints reregister with the secondary gatekeeper before issuing any new call setups. An alternate gatekeeper mechanism exists so that there is redundancy at this level—since 12.0(7)T IOS. An alternate gatekeeper enables a gateway to use up to two alternate gatekeepers as a backup in case of a primary gatekeeper failure. Unlike HSRP where the other gatekeeper must be on the same LAN segment, the alternate gatekeeper can be at a geographically remote site.

A static registration statement is configured on each gateway. A secondary registration statement is also configured with a lower priority in each gateway. As a result, a gateway tries issuing another registration request (RRQ) message (after five seconds) to the primary gatekeeper. If there is no response after another five seconds from the primary gatekeeper, the gateway tries the alternate gatekeeper. Example 7-5 shows a gateway configured to use an alternate gatekeeper.

Example 7-5 *Alternate Gatekeeper Configuration Example*

```
hostname atl1
!
!
interface Ethernet0/0
 ip address 172.1.1.1 255.255.255.0
 h323-Gateway voip interface
 h323-Gateway voip id NA-GK ipaddr 172.1.1.2 1719 priority 1
 h323-Gateway voip id NA-ALTGK ipaddr 172.1.1.3 1719 priority 2
 h323-Gateway voip h323-id US-GW1
!
```

Each gatekeeper must have identical configurations. Gateways can register with the primary or the alternate gatekeeper.

NOTE   If the gatekeeper issues back a failed location confirmation (LCF), the originating gate-keeper still waits for a second LRQ message. To route calls properly, the primary and backup gatekeepers must have an entry in their prefix table that identifies each other. However, the preferred approach is to use the Cisco gatekeeper cluster feature.

Gatekeeper Load Balancing

Gatekeeper clustering can replace the alternate gatekeeper's architecture to also provide high availability. Gatekeeper clustering uses load balancing to provide higher calls per second within a zone by enabling the call processing to be evenly distributed among a collection of gatekeepers. The maximum number of gatekeepers that can be supported in a cluster is five. When a call arrives for a gatekeeper, one of the gatekeeper members issues an LRQ message to the DGKs, which then forward the message to the terminating DGK. At this time, the DGK sends out only one LRQ message to one of the member gatekeepers in the terminating cluster because it does not need to send five LRQs. The reason is that each gatekeeper is aware of all the endpoints registered to all its member gatekeepers in the cluster. One of the gatekeepers in the cluster sends an LCF message or a location reject (LRJ) message, depending on the availability of the data.

Gatekeeper clustering uses a protocol called *Gateway Update Protocol (GUP)*, which was introduced in IOS 12.2(2)T. GUP is a lightweight protocol that exchanges announcement messages every 30 seconds or a configurable amount of time between gatekeepers, which enables the gatekeepers in the cluster to collect vital information from each other. This resource information includes CPU use, call capacity, and memory use.

NOTE   Each gatekeeper must be configured in a similar manner.

Each gatekeeper in a cluster is aware of each other's zone prefix responsibilities. The gatekeepers use these resource statistics to notify the gateways to reregister with other less loaded gatekeepers in the cluster, which allows a heavily loaded gatekeeper to offload one or more gateways to another less busy gatekeeper.

A number of GUP messages are exchanged in the cluster. A gatekeeper issues a GUP message to all members of the cluster any time a gateway registers with it. The gatekeeper also issues a GUP message to update the other members about its call capacity level. If a gatekeeper fails in a cluster, the gateways have a list of all the alternate gatekeepers in the cluster received at registration time; the gateways register with the gatekeeper with the highest priority. If the failed gatekeeper returns to an operational state, it receives GUP messages that identify the resource status of the other members.

Different thresholds are configured to set up load balancing. For example, load balancing in a gatekeeper cluster can begin when one of the following four events occur:

- Call volume reaches 10,000
- CPU use exceeds 90 percent
- More than 100 gateways register with a gatekeeper
- Memory use exceeds 90 percent

The following command specifies when a gatekeeper should begin load balancing:

```
Router(config-gk)#load-balance calls 10000 cpu 90 endpoints 100 memory 90
```

Example 7-6 shows an example of a gatekeeper configuration that supports GUP.

Example 7-6   *Gatekeeper GUP Configuration*

```
Gatekeeper
 zone local Zone1 cisco.com 10.10.2.201
 zone cluster local atl Zone1
  element Zone2 10.10.2.202 1719
  element Zone3 10.10.2.203 1719

Gatekeeper
 zone local Zone2 cisco.com 10.10.2.202
 zone cluster local atl Zone2
  element Zone1 10.10.2.201 1719
  element Zone3 10.10.2.203 1719

Gatekeeper
 zone local Zone3 cisco.com 10.10.2.203
 zone cluster local atl Zone3
  element Zone1 10.10.2.201 1719
  element Zone2 10.10.2.202 1719
```

DGK High Availability

In addition to clustering DGKs, two mechanisms support DGK high availability:

- HSRP-backup DGK
- Alternate DGK

HSRP-Backup DGK

HSRP-backup can be configured for a directory gatekeeper to provide high availability in a VoIP network. Example 7-7 shows an example of configuring HSRP-backup for a directory gatekeeper.

Example 7-7 *Directory Gatekeeper HSRP-Backup*

```
!
    int ethernet 0
        ip address 172.21.127.12 255.255.255.0
        ip standby 20 172.21.127.55
        ip standby 20 timers 5 15
    !
    Gatekeeper
      zone local directory-gk cisco.com 172.21.127.55
      zone remote atl-gk cisco.com 172.69.10.21
      zone prefix atl-gk 678.......
      zone prefix atl-gk 770.......
      zone prefix atl-gk 404.......
      lrq forward-queries
      no shut
```

Alternate DGK

In a service provider VoIP network, it is not sufficient to support only redundant DGKs. The DGK might take some time during the HSRP failure time from primary to backup. During that time, no new calls can be processed. Consequently, a new mechanism must be found to maintain the high call completion ratio that is expected in a service provider network. This new mechanism is an alternate DGK.

In the case of the JIT network, where the Atlanta gateway wants to call Frankfurt, the Atlanta gateway issues an ARQ to the Atlanta gatekeeper. The Atlanta gatekeeper sends the first LRQ to the DGK in New York. Using an alternate DGK in the JIT network, the Atlanta gatekeeper sends a second LRQ to the alternate DGK by using sequential LRQs (supported in Cisco IOS Software Release 12.2). The Atlanta gatekeeper recognizes a failure state when it does not receive any response back from the primary DGK. Because the alternate DGK is configured exactly the same as the primary DGK, the alternate DGK recognizes that the particular prefix matches the Frankfurt gatekeeper. The alternate DGK transmits a new LRQ onto the DGK and alternate DGK in the eastern zone. The DGK and alternate DGK issue multiple LRQs to the gatekeepers that are managing the eastern zone. At this time, the eastern zone gatekeeper issues an LCF or LRJ message to the originating gatekeeper (western zone).

Troubleshooting Gateways and Gatekeepers

Some examples of useful IOS troubleshooting commands to use when encountering H.323 signaling related problems are as follows:

- **debug voip ccapi inout**
- **debug ras**
- **debug h225 asn1**
- **debug vpm all**
- **debug dialpeer**
- **debug cch 323 h225**
- **show dialplan number**

These commands provide a view into the H.225 and H.245 level protocols. Also, RAS messages on the gatekeeper can be debugged to facilitate troubleshooting.

Summary

This chapter introduced the basic elements to consider when designing a VoIP network using H.323 gateways and gatekeepers. The process of calculating the gateways and gate-keepers required in a VoIP network is not complex. Similar to most solid designs, the key phase of this design process is planning.

Traffic engineering and capacity planning must be accomplished to properly size the gateways and gatekeepers. Items such as local dialing rules and number translations are also impor-tant elements of designing a VoIP network. Furthermore, a high-availability VoIP network must be supported in a service provider environment. Different mechanisms support a high-availability VoIP network, including the use of gateway clustering and alternate gatekeepers.

More components are required in a VoIP network. These components include signaling gateways, OSP servers, authentication, authorization, and accounting (AAA)/ Remote Authentication Dial-In User Service (RADIUS) Servers, and billing servers. Therefore, further design guidelines must be understood. Further gateway and gatekeeper design requirements can be found in a Cisco Press book, *Deploying Cisco Voice over IP Solutions*.

CHAPTER 8

Security Considerations for VoIP Networks

This chapter discusses security considerations as part of designing and implementing a VoIP network. Unquestionably, security is an important element during the design and implementation of a service provider's VoIP network. This chapter focuses on the three security measures that need to be implemented in a VoIP network:

- H.323 Registration, Admission, and Status Protocol (RAS) Authentication
- Network Access Security
- Device Security

These three security measures help prevent outside attackers and fraudulent users from accessing a service provider's network. However, a service provider will likely choose additional security mechanisms to implement. For example, physical site security and security management are required to prevent inside corporate users from misusing the VoIP infrastructure. Furthermore, service providers will likely implement audit trails, security log reports, and alarms to help track and prevent this misuse. Access to the VoIP network components is logged in an audit trail, and alarms are set off in conditions where security is compromised. These security management mechanisms authenticate users and control access to the many devices within the VoIP network. These mechanisms are not addressed in this chapter, but are equally important for a comprehensive security design.

H.323 RAS Authentication

The service provider must understand the network environment when implementing security measures in an H.323 VoIP network. For example, if the VoIP network traverses only the service provider's equipment in the end-to-end network (an intradomain network), passwords can be shared among devices.

If the VoIP network traverses another service provider's network (an interdomain network), certain security measures and policies must be addressed. For example, an interdomain network might require the service provider to share a database that contains gateway information with its peering partners. Therefore, a trusting relationship must exist between a service provider and its peering partner, or you can use an Open Settlement Protocol (OSP) architecture. Another security mechanism to consider is Inter-Zone Clear Token (IZCT), which is a new security feature in Cisco IOS Software that provides additional security for VoIP network security by authenticating and authorizing H.323 calls between administrative domains.

NOTE An OSP architecture offers an Internet telephony service provider (ITSP) lower cost alternatives to off-net destinations that are not served directly by a service provider's points of presence (POPs). An OSP architecture can also consolidate billing records for interdomain voice calls.

RAS authentication is an important aspect of a VoIP network because it has been defined as part of the H.323 standards within the International Telecommunication Union Telecommunication Standardization Sector (ITU-T) Recommendation H.235, which defines the protocol to exchange digital certificates or access tokens between the gateway and the gatekeeper to ensure secure communication on the RAS channel. H.235 enables gateways to include an authentication key in each RAS message that the gatekeeper uses to authenticate the gateway. In other words, H.235-based security enables VoIP calls to be authenticated, authorized, and routed by a gatekeeper, which is considered to be a known and trusted device.

Cisco gateways and gatekeepers support a level of security that is called *hashing-with-password authentication* by using a Challenge Handshake Authentication Protocol (CHAP)-like procedure.

NOTE CHAP is defined in RFC 1994. CHAP prevents clear-text passwords from being exchanged between a client (gateway) and a server (gatekeeper). CHAP uses MD5, which is a one-way hashing algorithm. This algorithm determines a hash value that is sent across a connection.

A Cisco access token (either clear or crypto) provides authentication for both registration and call admission. A Cisco access token contains timing information and a hash; therefore, it is important that a Network Time Protocol (NTP) server is one of the components of the VoIP network. The H.323 ID with the gateway's password generates a hash that the Remote Authentication Dial-In User Service (RADIUS) Server uses. The RADIUS Server rejects or grants authentication to the gateway based on this hash, as shown in Figure 8-1.

Figure 8-1   *Registration Security Call Flow*

Before sending the registration request (RRQ) message, the gateway generates a Cisco access token that contains the hash. The gateway sends the RRQ along with the token to the gatekeeper. The gatekeeper issues a formal challenge to the RADIUS Server after receiving this token. The RADIUS Server calculates the hash (commonly referred to as the CHAP secret) from its own database, which contains the gateway's password and H.323 ID. The RADIUS Server compares this calculated hash value with the hash received from the gate-keeper. If the two values are the same, the gatekeeper accepts the RRQ from the gateway and issues a Registration Confirmation (RCF) back to the gateway.

Figure 8-2 shows the flow of standard H.323 RAS messages along with H.235 messages.

Figure 8-2   *Example of Authentication for an H.225 Setup Request*

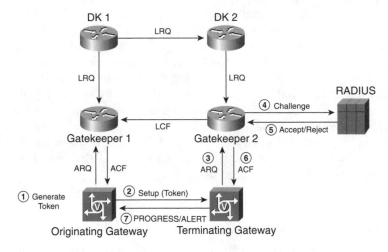

The grayed out messages and arrows indicate the sequence of address resolution messages that occur before gateway 1 issues the H.225 setup message:

1   The security process begins after the Admission Confirm Function (ACF) is received by the originating gateway. The gateway generates a token.

2   A setup message along with a token is sent to the terminating gateway.

3   After the token is received, the terminating gateway sends the token and the Admission Request request (ARQ) message to gatekeeper 2.

   4 Gatekeeper 2 then checks this token against a list of gateway H.323 IDs and
      passwords that are stored on a RADIUS Server.

   5 As with the previous example, the gatekeeper either accepts or rejects the setup
      request from the originating gateway.

   6 If accepted, the gatekeeper issues an ACF to the gateway.

   7 The terminating gateway establishes the call and then issues a PROGRESS/ALERT
      message to the originating gateway.

NOTE   Consider the latency tagged on to the total Post Dial Delay (PDD) of the voice call because
of the time required to authenticate the call from within the RADIUS Server. Use access
lists rather than H.235 security on a per-call basis when PDD is an issue.

An OSP server uses an OSP access token in a similar manner to the Cisco H.235 access
token method to validate call setups. The OSP server includes this OSP access token along
with the terminating gateway IP address in response to a route request from the originating
gateway. This procedure verifies that an incoming VoIP call is from a valid OSP peering
partner. As the next step, the originating gateway includes the OSP access token in the
H.225 SETUP message to the terminating gateway. If the token is valid, the terminating
gateway accepts the call. OSP access tokens and Cisco access tokens can be supported
on a POP gateway. In this scenario, the terminating gateway needs to identify if the call
originated from an OSP server or from a gateway using Cisco access tokens. The terminating gateway accomplishes this task by separating the VoIP dial peers that are associated
with the OSP and RAS targets. Thus, the terminating gateway uses Cisco access tokens for
calls arriving on the RAS dial peer and uses OSP access tokens for all other calls. However,
dedicated terminating gateways are required when the ITSP cannot distinguish between
OSP and RAS-based calls in their dial plans.

Network Access Security

Network access security prevents and detects unauthorized use of the VoIP network and
applications from either operational IP or PSTN interfaces. Security mechanisms such as
firewalls, access lists, virtual local-area networks (VLANs), Network Address Translation
(NAT), and RADIUS Servers perform these tasks:

- **VLANs** can separate voice traffic, voice signaling, and data traffic.

- **Access lists** and secure authentication can control telnet access to devices such as
  routers, Ethernet switches, and gateways.

- **Intrusion detection** can monitor network traffic for suspicious behavior.

Gateways in a VoIP network can be provisioned with access lists to accept calls from other known gateways; a TFTP server can be used as the central repository for storing and uploading gateway access configurations.

A firewall inspects packets and keeps track of connections. A connection is a source and destination address that is associated with a port. To enable connections to traverse a firewall, a hole in the firewall must be opened. Unfortunately, the available range of ports in VoIP networks can be very large, thereby creating a weak link in the overall security architecture. Allowing the firewall to inspect the signaling traffic for the particular session protocol, such as H.323v2, solves this problem. Therefore, the firewall can open the ports for the VoIP traffic. In a VoIP environment, both UDP and TCP ports must be opened for bearer and control traffic.

NOTE	PIX Firewall 5.2(1) supports this capability for H.323v2. PIX Firewall can support H.323v2 Fast Connect and H.245 Tunneling to reduce the call setup.

Firewalls can also prevent malicious behavior such as denial of service attacks. A denial of service attack is an attempt to disrupt the use of a network or host by consuming resources or by crashing network devices, which is commonly accomplished by generating illegal sized packets and by a ping attack. Generating illegal sized packets can cause some devices to reboot. A ping attack is a broadcast ping with a targeted IP address that is defined as the source address. Therefore, all receivers of the ping respond to the target IP address, which causes this device to use all its processing cycles to respond to these incoming packets.

Device Security

Because firewalls can be breached, device security needs to be implemented by the service provider. Implementing device security includes applying different types of account permissions for each type of user, such as an administrator who needs access to the various devices within a VoIP infrastructure. Also, a RADIUS Server can perform per-user authentication, authorization, and accounting (AAA) functions. This mechanism is crucial to ensure strong security and accountability for VoIP infrastructure devices.

Besides applying passwords, several other security measures need to be configured on Cisco devices to ensure a strong security implementation. The following are some of the key security measures to consider; however, this is not an exhaustive list:

- **Restrict virtual console access**—Limiting virtual console access to the IP address range(s) of operations staff and network management hosts is a useful way of preventing unauthorized users from accessing network devices.

- **Restrict Simple Network Management Protocol (SNMP) access**—Nearly all the information that is viewable or configurable through a virtual console can also be accessed through SNMP. Because an SNMP community is essentially a password that does not require a username, it is essential that you restrict this method of access as completely as possible. Only those hosts with a verified need to perform SNMP writes should have full access.

- **Disable key UNIX services**—Disable all nonessential services on UNIX worksta-tions and servers, such as sendmail, finger, and Domain Name System (DNS). Also, ensure that the root cannot telnet to the device.

- **Enable session timeouts**—Sometimes, operations staff can become distracted or be called away from their systems while logged on to network devices. Automatically disconnecting idle users helps prevent accidental access by unauthorized users.

- **Enable appropriate security on Ethernet switches**—This should include setting a password on Virtual Terminal Protocol (VTP) servers and applying port security.

- **Encrypt configured passwords**—Some passwords, such as those for dialup links or local users, must be stored in the device's configuration file. Encrypting the passwords that are stored in the configuration file makes it difficult for a casual observer to determine or remember these passwords if they come into possession of the configuration file.

- **Disable or restrict the Hypertext Transfer Protocol (HTTP) server**—Web config-uration is disabled on most platforms; however, novice network administrators often enable it. If HTTP configuration is not necessary, disable it entirely. If disabling the service is not feasible, restrict HTTP access to management addresses.

- **Disable forwarding of directed broadcasts**—Directed broadcasts are unicast packets that are addressed to another subnet's broadcast address. Although forwarding these packets has a limited diagnostic value, there is a significant risk in becoming an amplifier in various types of denial-of-service attacks. IOS versions 12.0 and later disable directed broadcasts by default, but they should be manually disabled on all prior versions.

- **Disable remote copy protocol (rcp) and remote shell protocol (rsh) services**—Use the Berkeley **rcp** command to copy files to a device and the **rsh** command to execute commands without logging in. However, these services have extremely weak authen-tication and should not be enabled unless no other option (such as Secure Shell Pro-tocol (SSH) support in IOS version 12.1T) is available.

- **Enable neighbor authentication**—Most common networking protocols provide a means for neighbors to authenticate each other to ensure that unauthorized devices are not allowed to affect the stability or security of the network.

- **Hot Standby Router Protocol (HSRP)**—Enable authentication for HSRP.

- **Routing protocols**—Enable authentication for Enhanced Interior Gateway Routing Protocol (EIGRP), Open Shortest Path First (OSPF), Intermediate System-to-Intermediate System (IS-IS), and Border Gateway Protocol (BGP).

- **Point-to-Point Protocol (PPP)**—PPP CHAP authentication requires neighboring routers to verify each others' identity over a link before the link can be used for traffic.

- **Configure accurate time stamping**—Many troubleshooting tasks, such as determining the nature of a DoS attack or tracing attempts to pass through firewalls, involve correlating logs from several devices. Unless the clocks of these devices are synchronized, it is much more difficult to correlate different logs.

- **Syslog server**—Logging all system notices and error messages often provides valuable insight into the operational status of network devices. If access list violations are logged, the logs can also be correlated between devices to determine that the network is being probed or that a device has been compromised.

Using IPSec for Additional Security

IP Security (IPSec) is a standards-based method of providing privacy, integrity, and authenticity to information that is transferred across IP networks. IPSec defines an additional set of headers to IP datagrams. These headers are placed after the IP header and before the Transmission Control Protocol (TCP) or User Datagram Protocol (UDP) layer. IPSec sessions can be used between gateways and the gatekeeper to protect H.323 signaling. An IPSec security association must be set up before any traffic is passed in or out of the interface.

Using IPSec in a voice and data network has some limitations:

- IPSec adds delay to the total PDD. This additional delay is introduced by IPSec's computational process and the required setup time for the IPSec security association.

- IPSec requires using a hardware crypto to achieve good voice quality.

- IPSec has a profound effect on voice bandwidth requirements. IPSec adds significant overhead bytes to the headers and payload of the packet. As a result, bandwidth engineering quality of service (QoS) and connection admission control (CAC) need to be re-evaluated when deploying IPSec in the network.

- IPSec requires the low latency queuing (LLQ) to be placed before the crypto engine in some situations to support voice services.

NOTE   Secure Real-Time Transport Protocol (sRTP) is another security mechanism that is being considered to secure VoIP networks. sRTP encrypts the payload of VoIP packets but does not encrypt the header or the voice signaling packets. sRTP uses an additional 4 bytes to encrypt the VoIP payload. sRTP is compatible with the following VoIP elements:

- QoS mechanisms

- RTP header compression

- Firewalls

Summary

This chapter provided an overview of RAS authentication, network access security, and device security, which are three important security mechanisms needed in a VoIP network. RAS authentication has been defined in the ITU-T Recommendation H.235 and defines how to exchange digital certificates or access tokens between the gateway and gatekeeper to ensure secure communications. Network access security can prevent and detect malicious use of the VoIP network resources. Network access security mechanisms include firewalls, access lists, NAT, and RADIUS Servers. Device security must also be implemented. This area of security encompasses setting up account permissions for users of the VoIP network. You can also use RADIUS and Terminal Access Controller Access Control System Plus (TACACS+) servers to implement this security function.

This chapter also highlighted new security mechanisms that are being considered for VoIP networks. These mechanisms include interdomain H.323 security using IZCT, IPSec, and sRTP.

CHAPTER 9

Network Management: Maintaining an SLA

This chapter discusses the procedures and mechanisms necessary to sustain the appropriate level of service in a VoIP network. Network management is an important aspect of this process. Network Management performs multiple functions that are categorized as follows:

- Fault management
- Configuration management
- Accounting management
- Performance management
- Security management

These different management functions are collectively called *FCAPS* and are normally present at all layers of the TMN framework (discussed in the next section).

Performance management and fault management functions are important in supporting an SLA. Performance management has the task of determining how the network performs, and fault management has the task of providing detection, diagnostics, and resolution of network faults. Essential information collected by the performance management and fault management functions are given to higher layers of management systems that support and maintain a Service Level Agreement (SLA) for a customer. Supporting and maintaining an SLA is called *SLA management*. Analyzing and reporting metrics defined in the SLA are part of SLA management. An SLA establishes a set of metrics that describes the level of service sold by a service provider to a customer. These metrics normally include latency, packet loss, and jitter. The metrics associated with a customer's VoIP service need to be closely monitored and might be offered to the customer using a customer network management (CNM) application; CNM enables service provider customers to view the status of their network services.The customer uses the SLA as a contract to ensure that the service provided by the service provider is maintained at the quality defined in the SLA contract.

This chapter addresses several areas that are essential in supporting and maintaining an SLA for a customer:

- VoIP SLA Management Architecture
- Collecting the VoIP Performance and Fault Data
- Identifying the Data to Calculate the VoIP SLA Indicators
- Filtering and Correlating the Collected Data
- Presenting and Reporting the Data

Overview of Management Layers

It is important to understand network management concepts. The Telecommunication Management Network (TMN) framework defines how management is logically separated in supporting a communications network. The TMN framework, developed within the International Telecommunication Union (ITU), breaks down the management functions into different layers that represent a hierarchical structure, as shown in Figure 9-1.

Figure 9-1   *TMN Framework*

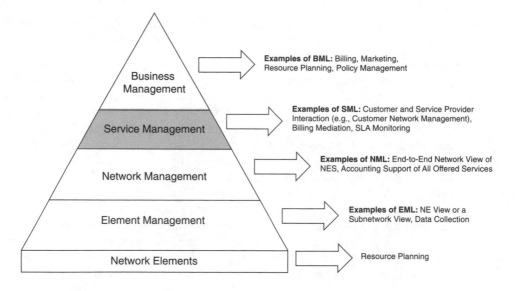

The TMN framework has four distinct layers:

- **Element Management Layer (EML)** — The bottom of the pyramid, referred to as the EML, is responsible for managing each individual element of the network. The EML communicates management data (such as error rates and alarms) collected from the individual network elements to the next higher layer: Network Management.

- **Network Management Level (NML)** — The NML includes the responsibility for ensuring end-to-end connectivity, network reliability, and capacity planning. These responsibilities can be carried out only by having access to the management data presented from the EML.

  The NML has complete visibility of the entire network and a technology independent view. The NML also is responsible for the technical performance of the actual network. This includes the NML collecting any failures or performance degradations in the network that will violate an SLA or will help to provide advance warning of an SLA violation. Failures can be measured in various forms such as error rates, alarms, and performance levels.

  In many cases, the network management function for a service provider includes traditional public switched telephone network (PSTN) network management software, and network management software for IP-based networks. In either case, the NML has the responsibility to report service-affecting problems to the layer above it: Service Management, where the SLA application exists. Therefore, the appropriate performance and fault management functions must be supported at the NML in order to provide the information required by the SLA application.

- **Service Management Layer (SML)** — The SML is responsible for managing the services VoIP in the case of an Internet telephony service provider (ITSP) to the customer. The SML includes the contractual aspects of services that are provided to customers. The SLA is supported at this layer, as shown in Figure 9-1.

- **Business Management Layer (BML)** — The BML's responsibilities include billing, marketing, resource planning, and defining company policies.

NOTE   The management data might not be passed from one layer to the layer directly above it in all cases. Management data has the potential to pass from one layer to any layer above it, or to another system within the same layer, if required. For example, the EML passes VoIP Call Detail Records data to a billing mediation system in the SML layer.

An SLA establishes realistic expectations for consistent service delivery for a service provider customer, such as a peering partner or a large enterprise. In fact, a service provider can be asked by their peering partner to have procedures in place for compensation in case of service delivery failure. Therefore, an SLA must be accurate and traceable. In other words, an SLA must be auditable to be of any use because an SLA is a contractual guarantee that defines a specified minimum level of VoIP service that a customer receives. A service provider must accomplish three main steps to support and maintain an SLA for its customers:

Step 1　Collect the VoIP performance and fault data.

Step 2　Filter, aggregate, and correlate the collected data.

Step 3　Present and report the data.

Later sections in the chapter will discuss these three steps.

VoIP SLA Management Architecture

The following list is a common set of requirements typically included as part of a VoIP SLA management architecture:

- Provide a scalable management architecture that can be integrated into an existing network operations center (NOC).
- Monitor threshold events for critical VoIP service levels.
- Provide intelligent polling for both Simple Network Management Protocol (SNMP) and non-SNMP devices.
- Provide a database or databases for all network events.
- Provide a filter and correlation engine for polled data and events.
- Provide the ability to generate reports and graphs through the web.
- Provide e-mail and paging notifications for selected VoIP service-affecting events.
- Provide a trouble ticket interface.

Figure 9-2 is a possible architecture for supporting these requirements.

Figure 9-2   *Example of a VoIP SLA Management Architecture*

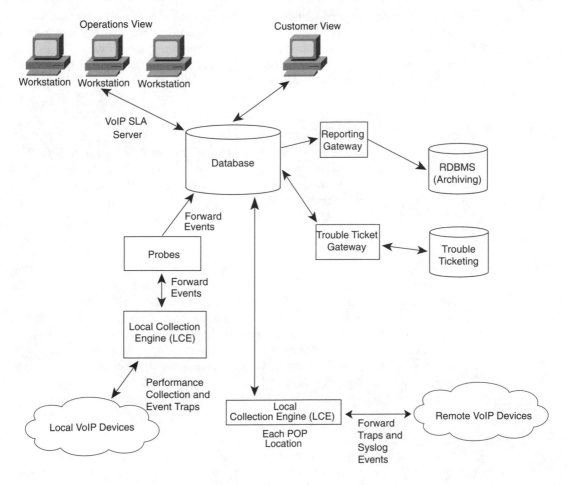

A service-level monitoring and diagnostics tool that supports built-in mediation and correlation mechanisms is required. Various software components are typically needed to satisfy many of the management requirements previously listed.

This architecture has four main components:

- Database
- Probes and Local Collection Engine
- Archive and Reporting Database
- Trouble Ticket Application

Database

The database stores performance and fault VoIP data. The database receives management information from the VoIP network through various mechanisms and transmits management information to outside systems, such as a performance reporting system or a trouble ticketing system. Multiple databases normally exist to support different applications. For example, a trouble ticket application will have its own database.

Probes and Local Collection Engine

This VoIP management architecture must be capable of processing events from SNMP sources, non-SNMP sources, proprietary or legacy systems, private branch exchanges (PBXs), enterprise applications, or any other source that can produce some type of an event stream. The probe provides this capability. The probe collects VoIP fault and performance data from the network.

NOTE   A *syslog* is a mechanism supported in operating systems (initially defined in UNIX) to log messages generated by a device. These syslog messages provide finer granularity of device information than SNMP traps because traps are partially standardized. A standardized syslog protocol exists to send messages to a centralized repository where a syslog daemon manages the syslog files. The syslog is an important aspect of VoIP service-level management because devices are likely in the VoIP network that provide important syslog messages that describe some aspect of the status or performance level of the VoIP network. For example, Cisco routers and gateways provide syslog messages that can provide a wealth of information in formulating performance trends or a snapshot of the network status.

The element layer filter and correlation engine, referred to here as the *local collection engine (LCE),* is another important component in this architecture. The LCE is a local probe that can be present at each VoIP networking POP. The LCE has the responsibility of collecting and processing VoIP performance and fault information from the VoIP devices. The value of supporting an LCE is twofold:

- The LCE eliminates unnecessary traffic that traverses expensive regional and international WAN circuits. In other words, polling and sending extraneous or redundant information is unnecessary.

- The LCE can scale with the addition of devices at the point of presence (POP) location. After filtering and correlating the information at the local POP, the LCE might forward the VoIP performance data within an SNMP trap to the centralized NOC. Alternatively, events can be forwarded by using a reliable mechanism, such as reliable traps, or XML messages.

Cisco Systems provides a tool to aid in supporting the probe and LCE functionality. This tool, called the Cisco Network Services (CNS) Performance Engineer (PerfE), collects selected network data from various data sources. These data sources include Management Information Bases (MIBs), flat files, call history detail records, and the Cisco Service Assurance Agent (SA Agent). CNS-PerfE can provide capabilities that include the following:

- Collecting and correlating VoIP performance data from multiple sources.
- Providing temporary data storage.
- Exporting data.
- Issuing notifications for threshold violations.
- Supporting an XML control interface that enables interfacing to other management systems, such as converting syslog messages to reliable SNMP traps, deduplicating repeat events, fault correlation and filtering, and clearing alarms. These capabilities need to exist as part of an SLA management architecture.

Archive and Reporting Database

As shown in Figure 9-2, an interface to an Oracle Relational Database Management System (RDBMS) is a common requirement to archive VoIP service-level information. This is important because reports and graphs are required to support different views of SLA information by internal service provider personnel or by the service provider's peering partners. Today's reporting software, such as Concord eHealth, can automatically generate web-based reports and graphs. Defining a data schema is an important aspect of using a relational database. For example, database tables and keys must be created and grouped accordingly before you can use the database. This task should not be underestimated. A significant amount of time must be dedicated to this task.

The design of the database dictates which type of graphs and reports can be generated. One of the advantages to using a relational database is that complex Structured Query Language (SQL) queries can be generated from a reporting application on-the-fly. These applications generate scheduled reports and Web-based graphs without user intervention. However, at certain times, unique one-time reports or graphs will likely be needed for a manager or executive within the service provider. For example, you might want to use an RDBMS to locate all VoIP gateways with less than 20 percent port use during the last 60 days.

Trouble Ticket Application

A trouble ticket application is a required component to help maintian an SLA for a service provider customer. A trouble ticket system, which falls under Fault Management, has the responsibility of assigning device events with asset, contact, customer, contract, circuit information, and so on as part of the issued trouble ticket. For example, a service provider might issue a trouble ticket when a circuit fault lasts longer than five minutes. Typically, the NOC opens a trouble ticket and informs its peering partner of the following information:

- Circuit identification
- Trouble ticket number
- Start time of fault
- Type of fault
- Detailed fault description

Collecting the VoIP Management Data

In accordance with the TMN framework, element management software must exist to extract the necessary data from the devices in the VoIP network to assist in sustaining the SLA. The data that is collected must be able to compute four fundamental indicators of an SLA:

- **Round trip delay (RTD) and packet jitter**—Round-trip delay (RTD) is defined as the maximum round-trip time between the originating and terminating VoIP endpoints. Depending upon the desired voice quality, the RTD for VoIP should not exceed 300 ms. Packet jitter is the variation of packet arrival intervals. Packet jitter is also called the amount of swing or change in packet latency. Depending upon the SLA, packet jitter is typically defined not to exceed 100 ms. RTD and packet jitter are critical parameters in sustaining VoIP quality. It is crucial that the round-trip response is at an appropriate level and that this value does not drift outside, which is also known as the *latency swing*. Each end-to-end VoIP link can support a different set of values, especially if the service provider has international presence. Many SLAs identify the RTD with a percentile, as follows:

  - < 300 ms in 100 percent of the time
  - < 250 ms in 95 percent of the time

- **Packet loss**—Packet loss is defined as ((total number packets received) / (total number packets sent)) × 100. A packet loss less than 0.1 percent should be achieved.

- **Post Dial Delay (PDD)**— PDD is defined as the period between the last number being dialed and the distant telephone ringing. Most domestic calls have a PDD of less than two seconds. International calls can have up to four or more seconds of PPD.

- **Answer Seizure Ratio (ASR)**— ASR is defined as ((total number calls seizing a circuit / total number of answered calls)) × 100. SLAs use ASR data to indicate call level reliabilities. ASRs identify possible changes in performance of a service. These changes might provide clues of where to look for possible problems in the network.

NOTE   In addition to these four indicators, other parameters might be defined in the SLA contract. Examples include guaranteed bandwidth, maximum number of simultaneous calls, and policing and marking polices that determine how voice traffic that exceeds certain thresholds defined in the SLA contract is handled.

These four SLA indicators cannot simply be polled from the network devices in one shot but must be filtered and correlated from various pieces of network data. The service provider faces three challenges in determining these four SLA indicators:

1 The service provider must determine which pieces of data are necessary to calculate these indicators.

2 The service provider must determine where to find this information.

3 The service provider must determine how to filter and correlate the exacted data.

The first two steps are discussed in the next section and the third step is discussed in the "Filtering and Correlating the Collected Data" section.

Identifying the Data to Calculate the VoIP SLA Indicators

Unfortunately, in today's heterogeneous networks, identifying the data to compute the VoIP SLA indicators can be a daunting task. Each service provider network has a unique set of management data sources as part of the VoIP network; therefore, each service provider must design its own data schema to define the SLA indicators. For example, the gatekeeper can generate call records in the form of a syslog or as records within a relational database. Using the management architecture defined in the preceding section, a syslog or oracle probe can collect this data.

This section provides you with an example of identifying the data required from a VoIP network composed of Cisco platforms and traditional PSTN voice switches. Figure 9-3 shows the five management data sources that can exist in a VoIP network:

- SNMP MIBs and Traps
- Syslog and ASCII Messages
- Relational Database and Triggers
- SA Agent
- NetFlow
- Call Detail Records (CDRs)

Figure 9-3 *Examples of VoIP Management Data Sources*

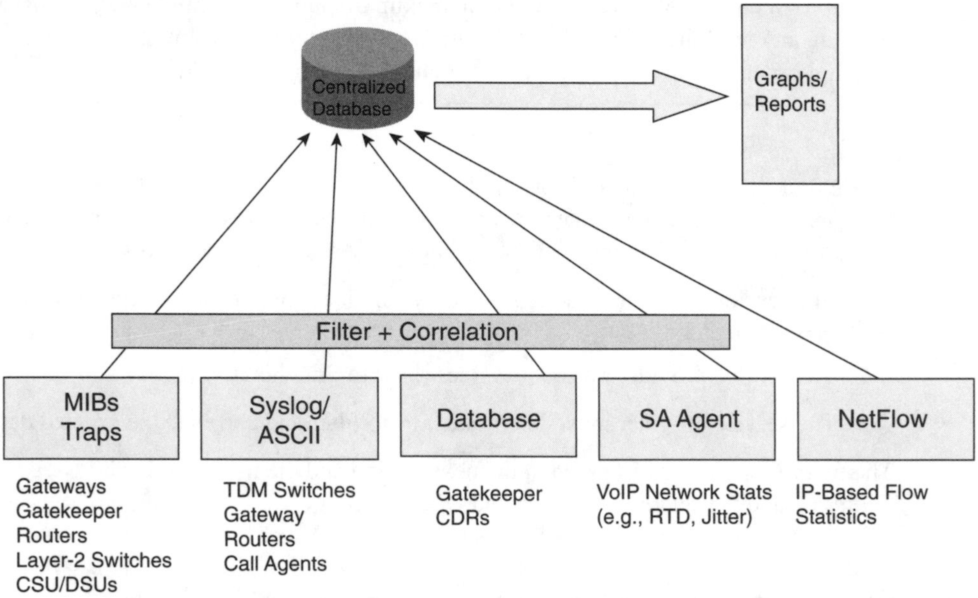

These data sources are further described in the following paragraphs.

VoIP Management Data Sources: SNMP MIBs and Traps

SNMP MIBs can be overwhelming because of the large number of objects supported by Cisco platforms. Obviously, not all MIB objects need to be collected; Cisco MIBs can be accessed through the web at www.cisco.com/public/mibs. MIB objects supported by Cisco IOS-based platforms that facilitate SLA monitoring include the following:

- Call history
- Interface layer
- Physical interface layer
- Resource Management layer

Call History MIB Variables

The CISCO-VOICE-DIAL-CONTROL-MIB provides historical record information regarding VoIP call detail records (CDRs). The cCallHistory Table that follows identifies the available parameters; the definition is not provided because of the descriptive variable names.

cCallHistory Table
cCallHistorySetupTime
cCallHistoryPeerAddress
cCallHistoryPeerSubAddress
cCallHistoryPeerId
cCallHistoryPeerIfIndex
cCallHistoryLogicalIfIndex
cCallHistoryDisconnectCause
cCallHistoryDisconnectText
cCallHistoryConnectTime
cCallHistoryDisconnectTime
cCallHistoryCallOrigin
cCallHistoryChargedUnits
cCallHistoryInfoType
cCallHistoryTransmitPackets
cCallHistoryTransmitBytes
cCallHistoryReceivePackets
cCallHistoryReceiveBytes

Besides this call history MIB, similar information can be stored as CDRs in a centralized RADIUS server. Collecting this information from the RADIUS server rather than from the MIB maximizes the gateway performance. The RADIUS server tracks VoIP calls by the connect time record generated at each leg of the call. These records, containing both successful and abnormally completed calls, are passed from the Gatekeeper to the Radius server. The RADIUS server typically interfaces to an outside billing system that has the responsibility of consolidating the multiple legs of the call into a single record. Complete and accurate VoIP CDRs are critical because service providers must exchange settlement payments with their peering partners (discussed further in Chapter 3, "Offering Wholesale VoIP Services").

Interface Layer MIB Variables

The interface layer MIBs provide status and configuration information with the interface layer such as a bearer channel (B channel), a channel associated signaling (CAS) channel, or a cable modem interface. The interface layer status and fault information can be collected from the interface MIBs that are located in the CISCO-ISDN-LINE-MIB, the CISCO-DS3-MIB, IF-MIB, and the CISCO-CAS-IF-MIB. The CISCO-VOICE-IF-MIB manages voice-specific information such as echo cancellation values. This MIB also supports dual tone multifrequency (DTMF) timing values that play an important role in configuring and troubleshooting DTMF timing problems in international peering relationships. These MIB parameters are as follows:

- **cvIfCfgInitialDigitTimeOut**—The initial digit timeout parameter indicates the amount of time the managed system waits for an initial input digit from the caller. The timer is activated when the call is accepted and is deactivated upon digit input. If the timer expires, the caller is signalled through the appropriate tone and the call is abandoned. The value of 0 disables the timer. The default value of this object is ten seconds.

- **cvIfCfgInterDigitTimeOut**—This parameter is the interdigit timeout that indicates the amount of time the managed system waits for a subsequent input digit from the caller. The timer is started upon receipt of an input digit and restarted as each digit is received until the destination address is identified. If the timer expires and no destination address is identified, the caller is signalled through the appropriate tone and the call is abandoned. The value of 0 disables the timer. The default value of this object is ten seconds.

Physical Interface Layer MIB

Physical interface status and faults can be collected from RFC1406-MIB (T1/E1 Trunk MIB), and the CISCO-VOICE-ANALOG-IF-MIB (Analog voice interface data—e.g, FXO/FXS/E&M). The CISCO-VOICE-ANALOG-IF-MIB is used on Cisco platforms that support analog ear and mouth/Foreign Exchange Office/Foreign Exchange Station (E&M/FXO/FXS) interfaces. RFC 1406 is used on Cisco platforms that support T1/E1.

Resource Management Layer MIB

The VoIP management application must always be aware of resource exhaustion on all VoIP-supported devices. The CISCO-DSP-MGMT-MIB manages DSP resources on Cisco gateways. The RSVP-MIB&INT-SERV-MIB is used for Resource Reservation Protocol (RSVP) management. RSVP-supporting VoIP services are discussed in Chapter 5, "QoS Considerations in VoIP Network Design." The Cisco Class Based QoS MIB (CCBQOS-MIB) monitors packet drops on high-priority queues that carry voice traffic. Bandwidth usage and QoS validation information can be obtained from this MIB.

VoIP Management Data Sources: Syslog and ASCII Message Collection

Service provider networks can contain regional time-division multiplexing (TDM) circuit switches that provide local voice termination. These TDM circuit switches typically do not support SNMP MIBs, but they do support syslog messages from their element management system or ASCII serial messages from a local management serial interface. In either case, a probe or LCE is capable of collecting this data, as shown in Figure 9-4.

Figure 9-4   *Local Collection Architecture*

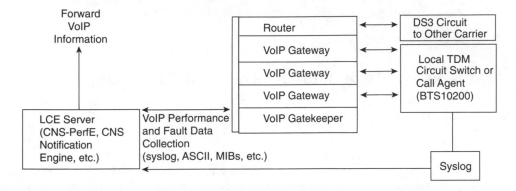

Figure 9-4 shows the CNS-PerfE and CNS Notification Engine collecting VoIP performance data from various sources. It is important to have the machine local to the router or switch rather than located over a WAN; the reason is twofold:

- Data is User Datagram Protocol (UDP) (not guaranteed).

- WAN links are costly.

CNS-PerfE and CNS Collection Engine collect VoIP performance information. CNS-PerfE also filters out any unnecessary data and then generates an event that indicates the status or performance information of the device, such as a Call Agent or TDM circuit switch.

VoIP Management Data Sources: Relational Database and Trigger Collection

Relational databases are used extensively in a service provider environment. Databases store performance and status information either polled or received through an SNMP trap. The architecture shown in Figure 9-2 should automatically update collected VoIP performance data to an archive and reporting database. As described earlier, a database schema must be created. The *data schema*, also known as the *entity relationship diagram (ERD)*, is the standard method of selecting and grouping the data to be stored within a database. This process takes a significant amount of time because it takes multiple people within a service provider to define ERD. In other words, a single person typically does not have all the knowledge of the service provider network to formulate all the rules for filtering and correlating the VoIP network data.

A database trigger is another mechanism to detect performance. A *database trigger* is associated with a single table in the database and is configured to perform an action at a certain point when data is modified. Database triggers can signal that certain events have occurred. For example, the daily bandwidth use of the VoIP gateway's T1 circuits can be inserted as a row within a database table, which is called a gateways_table. This row can have columns such as circuit ID, circuit type, peak rate, and minimum rate. A trigger can create another row in a separate database table that identifies when the peak rate is greater than 30 Mbps.

VoIP Management Data Sources: SA Agent Collection

Cisco SA Agent exists on most Cisco IOS platforms, which enables users to monitor network performance between a Cisco router and another remote device.

NOTE   SA Agent was previously known as Response Time Reporter (RTR), which historically provided response time measurements. The SA Agent provides a much richer set of measurements.

Various performance metrics are measured such as RTD, packet loss, and jitter. Many service providers use the SA Agent as the core technology to measure service assurance. For example, the SA Agent can guarantee the SLA that was agreed upon between the service provider and its peering partner. The SA Agent provides a better assessment of quality of voice than traditional methods such as ping measurements. Figure 9-5 shows the SA Agent architecture.

Figure 9-5   *SA Agent Architecture*

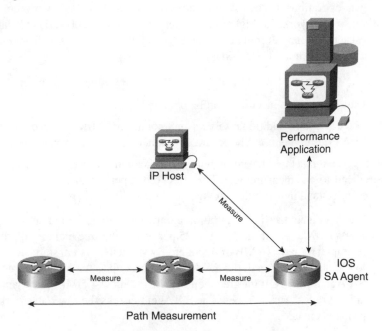

The SA Agent is useful in a service provider network because it provides the capability to collect performance metrics that are relevant to VoIP service, including the following:

- Measure packet loss
- Measure a ping response time on a specific path
- Measure VoIP traffic response by using UDP packets
- Measure the inter-packet delay variance (jitter) of SA Agent-generated UDP packets
- Measure response time between end points for a specific quality of service (QoS) level
- Define threshold definitions
- Generate SNMP Traps when a threshold is violated
- Trigger another operation for more detailed analysis
- Schedule an operation in the future
- Support MPLS network topologies

NOTE   A ping is typically not a good mechanism to measure the response time of a voice packet path as it does not follow the LLQ/QoS path. Using SA Agent probes is a better approach.

It is common to use a dedicated router, often referred to as a *shadow router*, to perform the SA Agent operations. Cisco recommends 2600 or 3600 as shadow routers for small to medium size networks, or higher end routers such as the 7200 series for large networks. These shadow routers eliminate the need for taking measurements from channel service unit/data service units (CSU/DSUs).

The following are two advantages to performing these functions inside the router in IOS:

- Data that is more accurate can be obtained.

- The expense of additional servers and monitoring software can be eliminated, and the SLA measurements can be accurately audited for service provider peering relationships.

The SA Agent must be present on both the target and source IOS platforms to identify the desired end-to-end measurement. The affect of the performance of the router also is important to understand in using the SA Agent. Some guidelines are as follows:

- The SA Agent has a configuration parameter to limit the memory. This parameter, lowWaterMark, is initially set to 25 percent of the free memory on the router. For example, if there is 6 MB of free memory when the system starts up, and if the default lowWaterMark is used, the SA Agent can use up to 4.5 MB of memory for creating SA Agent probes. If the free memory drops below 1.5 MB, SA Agent cannot create any more SA Agent probes. The SA Agent checks the lowWaterMark before a new probe is created.

- The SA Agent provides a MIB variable called rttMonApplProbeCapacity to track how many probes can be created with the available memory.

SA Agent can detect performance problems, such as cases where IP traffic might be interfering with the VoIP traffic. For example, there might be a congested link in the VoIP path, which results in latency jitter outside the defined SLA levels.

VoIP Management Data Sources: NetFlow

Besides data sources such as SNMP MIBs and traps, you can use real-time data technology called NetFlow. As shown in Figure 9-6, NetFlow captures the network flow within a router or gateway.

Figure 9-6   *NetFlow Scenario*

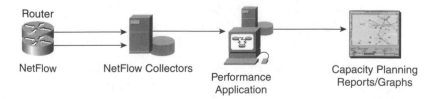

Router

NetFlow   NetFlow Collectors   Performance   Capacity Planning
                                           Application   Reports/Graphs

A network flow is defined as a unidirectional sequence of packets between given source and destination endpoints. Network flows are highly granular; flow endpoints are identified both by IP address and transport layer application port numbers. NetFlow can determine where certain traffic is originating and help determine if the agreement is being met. Net-Flow is useful in capacity planning, as well as accounting and billing. NetFlow works on all Cisco VoIP-capable routers with a miminum of 12.0 IOS.

Netflow supports the identification of packet priority and allows further granularity of VoIP management data. This is ideal for charging based on QoS for billing purposes. NetFlow characterizes traffic patterns by matching up the following seven keys:

- Source Address
- Destination Address
- Source Port
- Destination Port
- Layer-3 Protocol
- Type of Service (ToS) byte (DSCP)
- Input Interface

NetFlow provides the start and end time of the flow. The NetFlow collector stage provides data collection, data filtering, data aggregation, and data storage. The NetFlow collector should be local and dedicated. Aggregating the data on the router is done in much the same way as it is on the collector, except that it is done before it leaves the router. For example, a service provider might only require UDP-based traffic to determine VoIP link use and to filter out unwanted traffic. The NetFlow collector can export the aggregate data to the VoIP management system.

A NetFlow Collector, on either a Sun or HP rack mountable chassis, can collect data from the devices. Another feature in NetFlow is dual export. This provides two duplicate data streams that are pushed out two separate ports on two different cards. As a result, two collectors can be running simultaneously, which allows the collection of this data in two separate locations, in case of failure.

Filtering and Correlating the Collected Data

Filtering and correlating the data is the second step that a service provider must accomplish to support and maintain an SLA. The process of filtering and correlating is required after the VoIP management data is gathered from the various sources that are described in the previous sections. The results of filtering and correlating the data provide different levels of data abstraction. Data abstraction provides meaningful information to both the service provider and the customer. For example, a large number of errored seconds can be detected on a T1 trunk that connects a VoIP gateway to a voice switch. This information is sufficient to enable a NOC technician to detect and correct the problem. The errored seconds can also notify that a VoIP route is insufficient for terminating any calls into a certain area of the world. This end-to-end VoIP path might be displayed as down to the NOC team. Thus, the errored seconds are abstracted to a higher level. Most likely, the abstracted data triggered an automatic reroute to another carrier to continue to terminate the calls to the destined country, but most likely at a higher termination rate.

NOTE   The SLA parameters and other operational needs help determine the required data abstraction, which helps produce the appropriate graphs to support and maintain the SLA.

Data abstraction determines the set of rules that must be applied to determine how to filter and correlate the data. These rules are sometimes called a behavior model. A behavior model defines how to detect, interpret, and respond in different ways to network conditions. The behavior model provides the ability to program automated actions based on the specific events that caused a device to enter the state it resides at any given instant in time.

An LCE is one mechanism that filters and correlates element data. Filtering and correlating also can be accomplished inside a Cisco platform. An IOS feature called the Expression MIB can filter and correlate MIB variables. The Expression MIB, which is available in 12.0(3)T, enables a set of complex expressions of MIB variables to be configured within the Cisco platform. Another IOS feature called the Event MIB provides the capability to create thresholds on MIB parameters. Furthermore, the Expression MIB can compare the results of the MIB thresholds instantiated by the Event MIB, along with the results of a complex expression to determine if an SNMP trap needs to be issued. For example, an expression can be created by using the cCallHistoryConnectTime, cCallHistoryDisconnectTime, and cCallHistoryDisconnectCause variables from the CISCO-VOICE-DIAL-CONTROL-MIB. This expression can notify the VoIP management system of abnormal call terminations that exceed a threshold by triggering an SNMP trap.

These two MIB types provide an event-driven model inside the Cisco platform. This results in more intelligence at the network element, which results in less SNMP polling activity across the VoIP network. This has two benefits:

- Less management traffic exists in the network.
- Faster response times can be achieved in calculating network performance levels.

One example of a benefit gained from the fast response times is in rerouting. An important aspect of sustaining an SLA is being able to reroute to another service provider such as a PSTN provider; for example, service providers must occasionally reroute to the PSTN to sustain SLAs even if the termination rate is higher. Although various traditional TDM mechanisms can reroute in a service provider network, rerouting at the IP level can be achieved by using the SA Agent. By creating a reroute decision expression by using the Expression MIB, the SA Agent can use the results of this expression to determine when to generate a new route to a partnering service provider or to the PSTN.

Final Product: SLA Data

One purpose of filtering and correlating data is to obtain meaningful performance information to track SLAs. This information can answer important questions such as "Is the SLA being met with my customers and partners?" and "Can additional bandwidth capacity be added quickly?" To answer questions such as these, multiple views of the filtered and correlated data need to be readily accessible. These views are normally grouped into three categories to accommodate different organizational levels and service provider customers:

- Executive
- Operational
- Customer

Views are also based on geographical region. The executive level view can include summarized information as the usage trend of voice minutes on a daily, weekly, monthly, or yearly basis. The operational level needs to include near real-time fault and performance information on the VoIP network. Various different levels of information must be quickly accessible to the operational staff. Table 9-7 groups the possible information that might be available to an operations person.

Table 9-1   *Operational Level Fault and Performance Information*

Type of Fault and Performance Information	What It Includes
General Network and System Faults	Number of critical network alarms
	Number of minor network alarms
	Number of network alarms per alarm cause code
	CPU utilization, memory and disk space use on routers, switches, and gateways
Physical Port Level	Total number of active ports per gateway or domain
	Total number of disabled ports per gateway or domain
	Total number of ports in use per gateway or domain
	Average packet received and transmitted by port gateway or domain
	Maximum port use per gateway or domain
	Minimum port use per gateway or domain
Trunk Level	Trunk bandwidth use
	Frame synchronization state
	Number of errored seconds
	Number of failed seconds
	Number of code violations
	Number of slips

Table 9-1 *Operational Level Fault and Performance Information (Continued)*

Type of Fault and Performance Information	What It Includes
IP Level	End-to-end voice call latency
	End-to-end voice call jitter
	End-to-end voice call packet loss
	Average packet loss per call per trunk
Call Control Level	Response time for call setup request from the call agent
	Number of gateway authentication failures
	Number of ISDN User Part (ISUP) failures or timer expiration
	Number of Signaling System 7 (SS7) link failures
	Number of SS7 link restorations
	Number of ISDN link failures
	Number of ISDN link restorations
Call (Voice, Fax, Data) Level	Graph usage of voice minutes per gateway or domain on a daily, weekly, monthly, or yearly basis
	Average call duration
	Number of calls attempted per gateway or domain
	Number of calls successfully completed per gateway or domain
	Number of calls abnormally completed per cause code per gateway or domain
	Number of calls rejected per cause code per gateway or domain
	Number of terminations by originating carrier
	Number of terminations by terminating carrier
	Number of terminations by country code
	PDD per gateway Port
	PDD average per gateway trunk
	ASR per gateway trunk or gateway
	Total ingress and egress minutes passed per gateway or domain
	VoIP rating and routing failures per gateway or domain
	Perceptual Speech Quality Measurement (PSQM)

Service provider customers expect to view relevant SLA statistics through the Internet. The availability of these SLA statistics dramatically increases the level of service that a service provider provides its customers. The service provider can provide its customer SLA information on specific components of the VoIP network that it uses. The availability of this information dramatically increases the confidence level of service that the service provider provides for its carrier partners. This information should be available to the service provider customer through a web page. The information viewed by the customer might include the following:

- Number of calls (fax, data, and voice) attempted and completed
- Total ingress and egress minutes passed through a VoIP gateway
- Latency trend
- Jitter
- Packet loss trend
- ASR trend
- Bandwidth use

Presenting and Reporting the Data

Creating meaningful reports and graphs can significantly decrease the time required to resolve problems within a VoIP network. Selecting the correct performance view can provide clear visibility into the network. This can help to quickly identify the root of a performance problem, which results in faster repair and improved network uptime. Besides sustaining the SLA, reporting and graphing performance data can help capacity planning. For example, adding additional bandwidth capacity or upgrading network devices can be planned accurately by using these reports and graphs in identifying traffic patterns. Typically, an alarm is generated when a capacity threshold is exceeded in the VoIP network. Typically, the capacity threshold is set somewhere in the range of 60 percent to 80 percent capacity use. Ultimately, capacity planning results in increased network reliability to a service provider. Poor capacity planning can disrupt an SLA, which results in compensatory procedures and an increased likelihood of dissatisfied customers.

Multiple tools can display the SLA information such as graphs or reports on the web. One example is the Multi Router Traffic Grapher (MRTG), shown below, which can monitor certain SLA parameters on network-links.

NOTE	MRTG is available under the GNU General Public License.

MRTG generates HTML pages automatically, which contains GIF images of a particular SLA parameter. The underlying intelligence of MRTG is a Perl script, which uses SNMP to read any SNMP MIB value, which is supported by a router, switch, or VoIP gateway. MRTG logs the traffic data that enables a daily, weekly, monthly, and yearly time perio be viewed. Figure 9-7 shows an example of the daily usage of a digital signal level 3 (D link that is transporting VoIP traffic.

Figure 9-7   *MRTG Daily Graph of DS-3 Link*

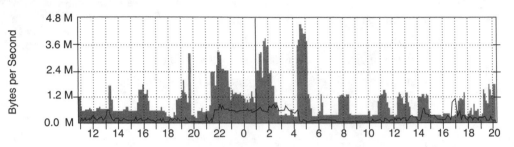

Max In: 4611.4 kbps (36.9%)   Average In: 1037.4 kbps (8.3%)   Current In: 542.5 kbps (4.3%)
Max Out: 1174.8 kbps (9.4%)   Average Out: 257.0 kbps (2.1%)   Current Out: 122.9 kbps (1.0%)

One of the reports that can be provided to a service provider customer is bandwidth use. This report might summarize the bandwidth usage for a certain time period at five-minute samples. The bandwidth usage is commonly represented as average usage, busy hour usage, and peak usage. Average usage simply defines the average value of all five-minute samples over a designated period of time. Busy period usage defines that 90 percent of the five-minute samples fell below the bandwidth usage, and 10 percent were above, during a designated period of time. The busy period value can represent the busy hour usage for the circuit that connects the service provider to its partner. This information is useful for capacity planning. For example, if this value is a large percentage of the line rate of the circuit (e.g., T1), additional bandwidth should be provisioned. Another important statistic is "deviation from normal," which can help to detect unusual behavior in the network.

Figure 9-8 shows a web-based report of bandwidth usage from a DS3 circuit during a two-week period. This graph can be used to allow a service provider customer, such as a peering partner, to view their bandwidth use.

Figure 9-8   *Web-Based Report of Bandwidth Usage During a Two-Week Period*

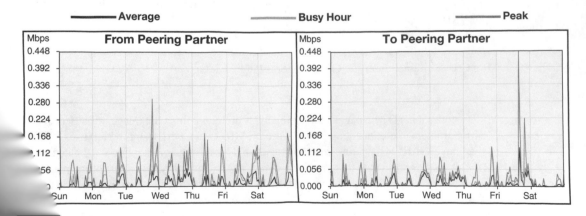

Summary

This chapter focused on key components required to support and maintain an SLA for a service provider offering VoIP services, such as an ITSP. The three main steps that a service provider must accomplish to support and maintain an SLA for its customers are as follows:

1 Collect the VoIP management data.

2 Filter, aggregate, and correlate the collected data.

3 Present and report the data.

Software products such as CNS-PerfE and CNS Notification Engine from Cisco can carry out these three steps. However, you should understand that CIC, DAS, and any other software products require upfront planning and designing of appropriate filtering and correlating rules. These rules must be designed to support the meaningful information required for an SLA. Supporting and maintaining an SLA requires various reports and graphs.

Symbols

^ (caret), translation rule syntax, 26

A

AAL2 (ATM Abstraction Layer 2)
    CPS, 77
    managed voice and data services, 75–77
    profiles, 79
    SSCS, 77
access rules, 144–145
ACLs (access control lists), traffic classification, 90–91
aggregation routers, call agent architecture, 58
A-links, SS7 interconnection, 67
AMA (Automatic Message Accounting), 67
Amphenol connectors, 113
application servers, H.232 VoIP networks, 35–36
architecture, managed voice and data service, 73–74
    AAL2, 75–77
    DS1/T1 access, 74–75
archiving and reporting database, VoIP management architecture, 173
ASCII messages, harvesting VoIP management data, 179
ASR (Answer Seizure Ratio), 140
    extracting from VoIP network data, 174
assigning
    alternate DGKs, 154
    alternate gatekeepers, 151–152
associated signaling, 67
authentication
    CHAP, 158
    H.323 RAS, 157–160
AVBO (Advanced Voice Busyout), 102
avoiding congestion, 100–101

B

B channels, 121
bandwidth, overprovisioning, 86
bearer channels, 33

best effort, 87
billing systems, 67–68
    reconciliation, 68–69
bit stuffing, C-bit parity method, 116
BML (Business Management Layer), TMN framework, 169
busy hour, estimating, 139

C

CAC (call admission control), 101
    local CAC, 102
    network CAC, 103
    RSVP CAC, 103
call agent architectures, 19
    aggregation routers, 58
    call agent signaling, 54–55
    edge routers, 58
    feature servers, 59
    gateways, 57–58
    interworking, 56
    local access services, 52–53
    MGCP, 52
    solutions, 73
    voice services, 49, 51
    VoIP services, 49
call centers, screen pop applications, 61
call legs, 23
call settlement, 9
calling card services, 9–10
carrier IDs, 27
carrier sensitive routing, 65
carrier systems, 109–110
CAS (channel associated signaling), T1 trunks, 117–119
case studies, VoIP network direct IP interconnect, 111–113
categories of service providers, 62
C-bits, 116
cCallHistory MIB as SLA indictor source, 177
CDRs (call detail records), 68
    example, 69–70
    reconciling billing data, 69
    related MIBs, 177

central database, VoIP management architecture,
172–173
CHAP (Challenge Handshake Authentication
Protocol), 158
characteristics
of call legs, 23
of DS3, 117
CIC mapping, SS7, 130
CID (channel ID) field (CPS packets), 79
circuit types, 109–110
Cisco access tokens, 158
Cisco IOS Software
gateways, enhanced number translation, 27
rotary calling pattern feature, 150
Class 4 switches, 63
Class 5 switches, 75
classification, 89
CB-marking, 95
QPPB, 96–97
clear channel connections, 116
clearinghouse peering arrangements, 63
CLECs (competitive local exchange carriers), direct
IP interconnect with DS3, 115–117
clients, SIP, 39
clipping, 85–86
clustering SIP servers, 42
coloring, 90
congestion avoidance in VoIP networks, 100–101
congestion management, LLQ, 98–100
control plane architecture, IntServ, 87
correlating harvested VoIP management data,
183–184
CPS (common part sublayer), 77
CSRs (Campus Switch Routers), 35
CSUs (channel service units), 114–115

D

D channel, 121
NFAS, 124–125
data plane architecture, DiffServ, 87
databases, harvesting VoIP management data, 180
delay variance, effect on voice quality, 85

deploying

QoS, DiffServe, 90–92
VoIP networks, 13
designing VoIP networks, 20
DGK sizing, 147
dial peers, 141–143
dial plan administration, 146
gateway and gatekeeper, 135–138
high availability, 148–154
normalization rules, 143–145
GKTMP, 146
requirements, 19
traffic engineering, grade of service
requirements, 139
zones, 141
devices
Class 5 switches, 75
security, 161–162
Tandem Switches, 75
DGKs (directory gatekeepers)
call routing, 65
dial plan administration, 146
high availability, 153–154
peering, 63
sizing, 147
dial peers, 22–23, 141–143
dial plans, 22
administration, 146
normalization rules, 143–145
GKTMP, 146
translation rules, 26
DiffServ, 87–88
DSCP, traffic classes, 88
EF PHB, 92
implementing, 90–95
services, 89
direct IP interconnect
carrier systems, 109–110
signaling types
in-band, 110
out-of-band, 111
with DS3, 115–117
with E1, 115
with PRI trunks, 121
digit sending method, 125
incoming digit format, 126
NFAS, 124–125
Q.921 protocol, 121–122

Q.931 protocol, 122–123
with SS7 trunks, 127
CIC mapping, 130
FAS, 128
link speeds, 129
point codes, 129–130
with T1s, 113–114
line termination, 114–115
punchdown blocks, 113
direct mode gatekeepers, H.323, 31
direct peering, 63
directory gatekeepers
H.232 VoIP networks, 32–33
peering, 33
dropping packets, 91
DS1 architecture, managed voice and data services,
74–75
DS3 architecture
characteristics, 117
interconnecting to CLECs, 115–117
unframed connections, 116
DSCP (Diffserv Codepoint), 87
PHBs, EF, 92–95
traffic classes, 88
DSUs (data service units), 115
DSX-3 interfaces, 117

E

E&M signaling on T1 lines, 118
E1 lines
interconnecting to PTT, 115
multiframe, 115
edge routers, call agent architecture, 58
EML (element management layer), TMN
framework, 169
end-to-end delay, effect on voice quality, 84
enterprise services
H.323 VoIP networks, 20
managed voice and data service architecture,
customers, 74
ERD (entity relationship diagram), 179
Erlangs, calculating VoIP trunking requirements,
140
ESF (Extended Super Frame) format, 120
estimating busy hour, 139

executive level views, correlated SLA data, 185
extracting SLA indicators from VoIP network
data, 174

F

FAS (Facility Associated Signaling), 111
FEAC (far end alarm and control), 116
feature servers, call agent architecture, 59
fields
of CDRs, 68
of CPS packets, 78–79
FIFO (first in first out) queuing, 91
filtering harvested VoIP data, 183–184
firewalls, 161
fixed delay, effect on voice quality, 84
F-links, SS7 interconnection, 67
fragmentation, 92
framing mode, T1, 120
FRR (Fast Re-Route), 106
fully associated signaling, SS7, 128
functionality of gatekeepers, 28

G

G.704 framing methods, 120
gatekeepers, 13, 154
clustering, 29
dial peers, 141–143
dial plan administration, 146
H.232 VoIP networks, 28–29
high availability, 151–153
load balancing, 152–153
normalization rules, 143–145
GKTMP, 146
signaling, 29
sizing, 147
troubleshooting, 155
VoIP network design, 135–137
bandwidth requirements, 137–138
zones, 141
gateways, 11
call agent architecture, 57–58
Cisco IOS Software supported features, 27–28
dial peers, 141–143

dial plan administration, 146
direct mode, 31
H.232 VoIP networks, 22–25
    Cisco IOS Software supported features,
       27–28
    interconnecting to PSTN, 33–34
    translation rules, 26
high availability, 148–151
normalization rules, 143–145
    GKTMP, 146
OGW, call establishment, 24
signaling, 29
SIP network architecture, 40–41
translation rules, 26
troubleshooting, 155
VoIP network design, 135–137
    bandwidth requirements, 137–138
zones, 141
GKTMP (Gatekeeper Transaction Message
  Protocol), 28, 146
    call routing, 65
grade of service, traffic engineering
  requirements, 139

H

H.225 protocol in H.232 VoIP networks, 30–31
H.245 protocol in H.232 VoIP networks, 31
H.323 VoIP network architecture, 17, 20
    application servers, 35–36
    directory gatekeepers, 32–33
    enterprise services, 20
    gatekeepers, 28–29
    gateways, 22–25
        Cisco IOS Software supported features,
           27–28
        translation rules, 26
    H.225, 30–31
    H.245, 31
    RAS, 30
        authentication, 157–160
    retail services, 21
    RTP, 31
    signaling, 29
    SIP interworking, 47–48

SS7, 33–34
    wholesale services, 20
hairpin, 143
harvesting VoIP management data, 174
HEC (Header Error Control) field (CPS packets), 79
hierarchical structure of international call routing,
  32
high availability, 148
    DGKs, 153–154
    gatekeepers, 151–153
    gateways, 148–151
hop-off zone, 142
hunt groups, 150

I

identifying SLA indicator data sources, 175
    MIBs, 176–183
idle channel suppression, 77
ILECs (incumbent local exchange carriers), 11
    call agent architecture, 19
    direct IP interconnect with T1s, 113–115
    migration to TDM-based architecture, 62–63
impetus for IP/voice convergence, 4–5
implementing
    device security, 161–162
    DiffServe, requirements, 90–92
    EF behavior, 93–95
    VoIP networks, 13
IMTs (Inter-Machine Trunks), 33, 67
in-band signaling, 110
indication bit, 116
integrated access architecture, AAL2, 75
interface layer MIBs as SLA indictor source, 178
interLATA toll calls, 113
international call routing, hierarchical structure, 32
interworking, call agent architecture, 56
intraLATA calls, 75
IntServ architecture, 87
INVITE messages, 45
IP packets, precedence bits (ToS field), 89
IPSec (IP Security), 163

ISDN (Integrated Services Digital Network)
    PRI signaling, 121
        digit sending method, 125
        incoming digit format, 126
        NFAS, 124–125
        Q.921 protocol, 121–122
        Q.931 protocol, 122–123
        variants, 124
ISPs (Internet service providers), 62
ITSPs (Internet telephony service providers), 62
ITU-T (International Telecommunications Union
    Telecommunication Standardization Sector),
    G.704 framing standards, 120
IVR (interactive voice response) applications, 12, 36
IZCT (Inter-Zone Clear Token), 157

J

JIT (Jim's International Traffic), VoIP network case
    study, 111–113
jitter
    effect on voice quality, 85
    latency swing, 174

L

LATAs (interlocal access and transport areas), 113
latency, effect of end-to-end delay on voice
    quality, 84
latency swing, 174
layers of TMN framework, 168–169
LBO (long-range build out), 117
LCR (Least Cost Routing), 8, 64–65
LI (Length Indicator) field (CPS packets), 79
limitations of IPSec security, 163
line coding, T1, 119
link speeds, SS7, 129
LLQ (Low Latency Queuing), congestion
    management, 98–100
load balancing, gatekeepers, 152–153
local access services, call agent architecture, 52–53
local CAC, 102
loopback testing on T1 lines, 132

M

managed voice and data service architecture, 73–74
    AAL2 architecture, 75–77
        CPS, 77
        SSCS, 77
    T1/DS1 access architecture, 74–75
management architecture (VoIP)
    harvesting data, 174
    SLAs, identifying data sources of, 175–183
marking, 90
    CB-marking, 95
    QPPB, 96–97
messages
    RAI, 148–150
    syslog, 172
        harvesting VoIP management data, 179
MGCP (Media Gateway Control Protocol), call
    agent architecture, 52
MIBs (management information bases) as SLA
    indicator source, 176–177
    cCallHistory MIB, 177
    interface layer MIB, 178
    physical layer MIB, 178
    resource management layer MIB, 178
migrating from TDM to VoIP architecture, 61–63
    billing systems, 67–68
        reconciliation, 68–69
    LCR, 64–65
    SS7 support, 65–67
motivation for IP/voice convergence, 4–5
MPLS TE (Multi-Protocol Layer Switching Traffic
    Engineering), 104–105
    FRR, 106
MQC (modular QOS CLI), 95
MSN Messenger PC-to-Phone, 17
multiframe, 115

N

NAM (Network Applications Manager), 35
NANP (North American Numbering Plan), 126
NetFlow, harvesting VoIP management data,
    182–183

network access security, 160–161
network CAC, 103
network management
    H.323 VoIP networks, 36
    SLAs, requirements for VoIP networks,
       170–171
    TMN framework, 168–169
    VoIP management architecture
       archiving and reporting database, 173
       central database, 172–173
       trouble ticket application, 173
NFAS (Non-Facility Associated Signaling), 111,
    124–125
NML (network management level), TMN
    framework, 169
Non-Facility Associated Signaling (NFAS), 111,
    124–125
normalization rules, 143–145
    GKTMP, 146

O

OGW (originating gateway), call establishment, 24
one-stage dialing, 24
one-way hashing algorithms, 158
OOS (out-of-service) conditions, local CAC, 102
operational level views of correlated SLA data, 185
OPT (Open Packet Telephony), 10
OSP (Open Settlement Protocol), 9, 63, 157
    access tokens, 160
    server functions, 63
out-of-band signaling, 111
outpulsing (ISDN), 125
overprovisioning, 86

P

packet loss
    effect on voice quality, 85–86
    extracting from VoIP network data, 174
packets, marking, 90
PDD (post dial delay), 84
    extracting from VoIP network data, 174

peering arrangements
    directory gatekeepers, 33
    wholesale VoIP, 63
peering partner views of correlated SLA data,
    186–187
PGW 2200 servers, interconnecting H.323 gateways
    to PSTN, 34
PHBs (per-hop behaviors), EF, 92
    implementing, 93–95
physical layer MIBs as SLA indicator source, 178
point codes, SS7, 129–130
policing, 90
POPs (points of presence), 11, 63, 75
    traffic engineering, grade of service
       requirements, 139
POTS (plain-old telephone service) dial peers, 22
precedence bits, 89
prefixes, 141
    hop-off zone, 142
presenting correlated SLA data, 187–188
proxy servers in SIP network architecture, 41
PSTN (public switched telephone network),
    connecting with SS7, 66–67
PTT (Post, Telephone, and Telegraph), direct IP
    interconnect with E1s, 115
punchdown blocks, 113

Q

Q.921 protocol, 121–122
Q.931 protocol, 122–123
QoS (quality of service)
    best effort, 87
    CAC, 101
       local CAC, 102
       network CAC, 103
       RSVP CAC, 103
    DiffServ, 87–88
       EF PHB, 92–95
       requirements for implementing, 90–92
       services, 89
    IntServ, 87
    MQC, 95
    QPPB, 96–97
    selecting mechanism of, 86

SLAs, 170
traffic classes, 88
QPPB (QoS Policy Propagation through BGP),
96–97
quasi-associated signaling, SS7, 128
queuing mechanisms, 91
LLQ congestion management, 98–100

R

RADIUS (Remote Authentication Dial-In User
Service), 12
billing records, 35
RAI (Resource Availability Indicator) messages, 28,
148–150
RAS (registration, admission, and status)
authentication, 158
H.232 VoIP networks, 30
RCFs (registration confirms), 29
real-time data collectors, harvesting VoIP
management data with NetFlow, 182–183
reconciling billing data, 68–69
redirect servers, SIP network architecture, 42
REGISTER messages, 45
registrar servers, SIP network architecture, 42
relational databases, harvesting VoIP management
data, 180
Remote Zone Priority, 65
reporting correlated SLA data, 187–188
requirements
for DiffServe deployment, 90–92
for SLA support on VoIP networks, 170–171
VoIP network design, 135–137
bandwidth, 137–138
high availability, 148–154
resource management layer MIBs as SLA indictor
source, 178
retail VoIP services
H.323 networks, 21
OPT, 10
OSP, 9–10
RJ-48C interface, 113
rotary calling pattern feature (Cisco IOS Software),
150
rotary dial peers, 25
route servers, 35
RRQs (registration requests), 29

RSVP (Resource Reservation Protocol), CAC, 103
RTD (round trip delay), extracting from VoIP
network data, 174
RTP (Real-Time Transport Protocol), H.232 VoIP
networks, 31
RUDP (Reliable User Datagram Protocol), 67

S

SA Agents, harvesting VoIP management data,
180–182
screen pop applications, 61
security
devices, 161–162
firewalls, 161
H.323 RAS authentication, 157–160
IPSec, 163
network access, 160
selecting QoS mechanisms, 86
best effort, 87
DiffServ, 87–88
IntServ, 87
servers
OSP, functions of, 63
SIP network architecture, 41
proxy servers, 41
redirect servers, 42
registrar servers, 42
service providers
categories of, 62
migration to VoIP architecture, 62–63
billing systems, 67–69
LCR, 64–65
SS7 support, 65–67
services (QoS), 89
SF (Super Frame) format, 120
shaping traffic, 92
signaling
call agent architecture, 54–55
E&M on T1 lines, 118
H.232 VoIP networks, 29
ISDN PRI, 121
digit sending method, 125
incoming digit format, 126
NFAS, 124–125
Q.921 protocol, 121–122

Q.931 protocol, 122–123
variants, 124
SIP
H.323 interworking, 47–48
messages, 45
services, 46–47
SS7, 127
CIC mapping, 130
FAS, 128
link speeds, 129
point codes, 129–130
T1 CAS schemes, 117–119
single-stage dialing, 13
SIP (Session Initiation Protocol) network
architecture, 37
clients, 39
gateways, 40–41
H.323 interworking, 47–48
servers, 41
proxy servers, 41
redirect servers, 42
registrar servers, 42
services, 46–47
signaling messages
INVITE, 45
REGISTER, 45
third-party registration, 45
UAs, 38
wholesale services, 38
sizing
gatekeepers, 147
trunks, 140
dial peers, 141–143
dial plan administration, 146
GKTMP, 146
normalization rules, 143–145
zones, 141
SLAs (Service Level Agreements), 170
correlated data
executive-level views, 185
operational-level views, 185
peering partner views, 186–187
presenting, 187–188
reporting, 187–188

data sources of
correlating harvested data, 183–184
filtering harvested data, 183–184
identifying, 175–183
extracting from VoIP network data, 174
smart jacks, line termination, 114
SMBs (server message blocks), managed voice and
data services, 73–75
AAL2, 75–77
T1/DS1 architecture, 74–75
SML (Service Management Layer), TMN
framework, 169
SNMP (Simple Network Management Protocol),
MIBs as SLA indicator source, 176–178
softswitches, call agent architecture
aggregation routers, 58
call agent signaling, 54–55
edge routers, 58
feature servers, 59
gateways, 57–58
interworking, 56
local access services, 52–53
MGCP, 52
voice services, 49, 51
VoIP services, 49
sRTP (Secure Real-Time Transport Protocol), 163
SS7 (Signaling System 7)
H.232 VoIP networks, interconnecting
gateways to PSTN, 33–34
wholesale VoIP implementations, 65–67
SSCS (service-specific convergence sublayer), 77
Start field (CPS packets), 78
statistical gains, 5
STPs (signal transfer points), 111
syslog messages, 172
harvesting VoIP management data, 179

T

T1 architecture
CAS schemes, 117–119
direct IP interconnect, 113–114
line termination, 114–115
punchdown blocks, 113
E&M signaling, 118

framing mode, 120
line coding, 119
loopback testing, 132
managed voice and data services, 74–75
Tandem Switches, 63, 75
tandem voice services, 20
TDM-based architecture, migration to VoIP, 61–63
 billing systems, 67–69
 LCR, 64–65
 SS7 support, 65–67
terminating T1 circuits, 113–114
TMN (Telecommunication Management Network)
 framework, layers of, 168–169
toll calls, LATA, 113
ToS field (IP packets), precedence bits, 89
traffic
 CAC, 101
  local CAC, 102
  network CAC, 103
  RSVP CAC, 103
 classification, 88–89
  CB-marking, 95
 congestion avoidance in VoIP networks,
  100–101
 congestion management, LLQ, 98–100
 fragmentation, 92
 marking, 90
 policing, 90
 queuing, 91
 shaping, 92
 SLAs, 170
traffic engineering
 grade of service requirements, 139
 MPLS, 104–105
  FRR, 106
transit voice services, 20
translation rules, 26, 144–145
triggers (database), harvesting VoIP management
 data, 180
trouble ticket applications, 173
troubleshooting
 gateways and gatekeepers, 155
 trunks, 131–133
trunk groups, 27
trunks, 110
 conditioning, local CAC, 102
 DS3s, 115–117

E1, 115
in-band signaling, 110
ISDN PRI
 digit sending method, 125
 incoming digit format, 126
 NFAS, 124–125
 Q.931, 122–123
out-of-band signaling, 111
sizing, 140
SS7, direct IP interconnect, 127–130
T1, 113–115
 CAS, 117, 119
 E&M signaling, 118
 framing mode, 120
 line coding, 119
 line termination, 114–115
 punchdown blocks, 113
troubleshooting, 131–133
tunnels, MPLS-TE, 105
two-stage dialing, 12, 24

U

UAs (User-Agents), 38
unframed connections, DS3, 116
unified messaging, 10
UUI (User-to-User Indication) field (CPS
 packets), 79

V

voice services, impetus for, 4–5
VoIP (Voice over IP)
 benefit to service providers, 5
 gatekeepers, 13
 gateways, 11
 H.323, 20
  application servers, 35–36
  directory gatekeepers, 32–33
  enterprise services, 20
  gatekeepers, 28–29
  gateways, 22, 24–28
  H.225, 30–31
  H.245, 31
  interworking, 47–48

RAS, 30
retail services, 21
RTP, 31
signaling, 29
SS7, 33–34
wholesale services, 20
management architecture
archiving and reporting database, 173
central database, 172–173
harvesting data, 174
SLA indicators, identifying data sources
of, 176–183
trouble ticket application, 173
network deployment, 13
peers, 22
retail services
OPT, 10
OSP, 9–10
services, 46–47
signaling messages
INVITE, 45
REGISTER, 45
SIP, 37
clients, 39
gateways, 40–41
servers, 41–42
UAs, 38
wholesale services, 38
SLA support, 170–171
wholesale services, 6, 61–63
billing systems, 67–69
call settlement, 9
LCR, 8, 64–65
OSP, 9
peering arrangements, 63
peering partner selection, 8
SS7 support, 65–67

peering arrangements, 63
peering partner selection, 8
SS7 support, 65–67
SIP network architecture, 38

X-Y-Z

XP operating system (Windows), MSN Messenger
PC-to-Phone, 17

zones, 141
hop-off zone, 142

W

wholesale VoIP services, 6, 61–63
H.323 networks, 17, 20
billing systems, 67–69
call settlement, 9
LCR, 8, 64–65
OSP, 9

Train with authorized Cisco Learning Partners.

Discover all that's possible on the Internet.

One of the biggest challenges facing networking professionals is how to stay current with today's ever-changing technologies in the global Internet economy. Nobody understands this better than Cisco Learning Partners, the only companies that deliver training developed by Cisco Systems.

Just go to **www.cisco.com/go/training_ad**. You'll find more than 120 Cisco Learning Partners in over 90 countries worldwide.* Only Cisco Learning Partners have instructors that are certified by Cisco to provide recommended training on Cisco networks and to prepare you for certifications.

To get ahead in this world, you first have to be able to keep up. Insist on training that is developed and authorized by Cisco, as indicated by the Cisco Learning Partner or Cisco Learning Solutions Partner logo.

Visit **www.cisco.com/go/training_ad** today.

CISCO SYSTEMS

EMPOWERING THE
INTERNET GENERATION™

Cisco Press

Learning is serious business.

Invest wisely.

Networking Technology:
Convergence/Voice/IP Telephony

Telecommunications Technologies Reference
Brad Dunsmore, Toby Skandier
1-58705-036-6 • **September 2002**

This book is a comprehensive guide to North American and International
Communications Standards. The scope of this book far surpasses other similar
titles, as most cover only NADH and do not provide historical background.
Tables and comparison charts provide a quick and effective comparison of
advantages and costs of the various standards. The "Expert Whiteboard"
sections provide practical applications from well-known, experienced industry
professionals.

Telecommunications Technologies Reference offers a complete reference for
technologies key to the telecommunications industry. Although many published
references address physical medium such as DDS, ISDN, and T1, far fewer
explain how their international counterparts work. Rare is the book that covers
both North American and international telecommunications technologies.
Simply and logically organized and easy to reference, this handy guide is an
invaluable reference to telecommunications standards. In addition to thorough
explanations of the practical applications of the technologies covered, there is
also a historical review on how and why each was designed. This comprehensive
approach to the material imparts a full understanding of a given technology's
background.

Deploying Cisco® Voice over IP Solutions
Jonathon Davidson
1-58705-030-7 • **Available Now**

Learn real-world voice over IP deployment solutions and strategies from the
Cisco experts. This book was written by Cisco CCIEs™, technical marketing
engineers, and systems engineers who have real-life experience with Cisco VoIP
networks. Deploying Cisco Voice over IP includes Virtual Private Networks
(VPNs), admission control, security, fax and modem traffic, and unified
messaging and offers real-world scenarios.

Deploying Cisco Voice over IP Solutions provides networking professionals the
knowledge, advice, and insight necessary to design and deploy VoIP networks
that meet customers' needs for scalability, service, and security. Compiled by
Jonathan Davidson, co-author of the Cisco Press title Voice over IP Fundamentals,
Deploying Cisco Voice over IP Solutions picks up where his first book left off
by demonstrating how to design these next-generation networks. Voice over IP
Fundamentals customers will look to this book as their next step in building
VoIP networks, and network engineers and architects will look to this book for
the second-to-none insight and solutions coming from the authorities at Cisco
Systems®.

Networking Technology: Convergence/Voice/IP Telephony

Integrating Voice and Data Networks
Scott Keagy
1-57870-196-1 • **Available Now**

Voice/Data Integration on Cisco Networks is both a conceptual reference and a practical how-to book that bridges the gap between existing telephony networks and the new world of packetized voice over data networks. Technologies are explained in a context that gives the reader a holistic understanding of voice/data integration. Reader can then follow a complete process to design and implement a variety of network scenarios, leveraging the author's experience with real voice/data networks. The audio accompaniment on CD-ROM is an excellent companion to demonstrate the expected voice quality using different voice/data networking scenarios. This allows professionals in the field to demonstrate different sound quality levels to customers.

Developing Cisco IP Phone Services: A Cisco® AVVID Solution
Darrick Deel, Mark Nelson, Anne Smith
1-58705-060-9 • **February 2002**

Get the most out of your IP phone systems with strategies and solutions direct from the Cisco CallManager team.

- Learn information and techniques vital to building services for Cisco IP phone systems.

- Companion CD-ROM includes an exclusiveCallManager Simulator, which until now was used only internally at Cisco Systems,that supports an IP phone for development purposes.

- Learn how to integrate services with the Cisco IP phones.

Cisco Call Manager Fundamentals, A Cisco AVVID Solution

Anne Smith, John Alexander, Chris Pierce, Delon Whetten

1-58705-008-0 • **July 2001**

This book specifically addresses Cisco CallManager, Cisco AVVID software, and its architecture. The configuration examples, configuration guidelines, troubleshooting tips, and case studies included in this book are features that have proven to be of great value to readers in helping them to acquire a true understanding of the technology.

Cisco Interactive Mentors: Voice Internetworking

CIM Voice Internetworking, Basic Voice over IP

Cisco Systems, Inc.

1-58720-023-6 • **October 2000**

With *CIM Voice Internetworking, Basic Voice over IP*, you can master the telephony and voice internetworking knowledge you need to enhance the versatility and value of your communications infrastructure. Offering self-paced instruction and practice, this robust learning tool gives you a quick and cost-effective way to acquire Cisco knowledge and expertise. From an overview of traditional telephony and voice transmission concepts to the basics of routing voice and fax packets over a data network, you learn how to configure typical software features of a VoIP network and perform operational application tasks with interactive voice response (IVR). Using techniques developed by Cisco Technical Assistance Center engineers, you can practice configuring and troubleshooting both analog and digital voice calls over IP networks. This book is an excellent preparation tool for the Cisco Certified Network Professionals (CCNP™) Voice Access Specialization and Cisco Certified Internetwork Expert (CCIE™) exam.

CIM Voice Internetworking, VoIP Quality of Service

Cisco Systems, Inc.

1-58720-050-3 • **December 2001**

CIM Voice Internetworking, VoIP Quality of Service is a computer-based learning tool that combines detailed tutorials with network simulation exercises to teach users how to apply fundamental QoS concepts in Voice over IP Networks. This interactive learning product includes an overview of QoS concepts, Cisco IOS® QoS and VoIP routing commands, and configuration and challenge labs that put the user in the role of a network administrator implementing QoS for VoIP networks.

For the latest on Cisco Press resources and Certification and Training guides, or for information on publishing opportunities, **visit www.ciscopress.com.**

CCIE Professional Development Series

Troubleshooting IP Routing Protocols

Zaheer Aziz CCIE, Johnson Liu CCIE, Abe Martey CCIE, Faraz Shamim CCIE

1-58705-019-6 • May 2002

As the Internet continues to grow exponentially, the need for network engineers to build, maintain, and troubleshoot the growing number of component networks has also increased significantly. Because network troubleshooting is a practical skill that requires on-the-job experience, it has become critical that the learning curve to gain expertise in internetworking technologies be reduced to quickly fill the void of skilled network engineers needed to support the fast growing internet.

Cisco BGP-4 Command and Configuration Handbook

William R. Parkhurst, Ph.D., CCIE

1-58705-017-X • April 2001

Cisco BGP Command and Configuration Handbook *features* over 100 configuration examples that enable readers to gain practical, hands-on knowledge of BGP-4 commands for Cisco IOS Software.